How a Nation Lost
the World Cup

GRAHAM McCOLL

headline

First published in 2006
by HEADLINE BOOK PUBLISHING

1

ISBN 0 7553 1409 3

Cataloguing in Publication Data
is available from the British Library

Typeset by Palimpsest Book Production Limited,
Polmont, Stirlingshire
Printed and bound in Great Britain
by Mackays of Chatham plc, Chatham, Kent

Headline's policy is to use papers that are natural,
renewable and recyclable products and made from wood
grown in sustainable forests. The logging and manufacturing
processes are expected to conform to the environmental
regulations of the country of origin.

HEADLINE BOOK PUBLISHING
A division of Hodder Headline
338 Euston Road
London NW1 3BH

www.headline.co.uk
www.hodderheadline.com

Thanks to the following for their invaluable help in the creation of this book:

Hugh Allan, Rodger Baillie, Jan Bekema, Queen of the South historian Ian Black, Andrea Brownlie at Scottish Television, Robert Connor, Bryan Cooney, Clare Cowan at Heart of Midlothian Football Club, Ronald de Haas at the Dutch Football Association, Jim Delahunt at Scottish Television, Peter Donald, Gillian Donaldson at Greenock Morton Football Club, Helene Fors at UEFA, Tommy Gemmell, John Hagart, Joe Harper, Willie Henderson, Sandy Jardine, Willie Johnston, Linda MacDonald at Aberdeen Football Club, Margo MacDonald, Faye MacLeod, Andy McArthur, Danny McGrain, John McKenzie, Gordon McQueen, John Mann, Andy Melvin at Sky Sports, Willie Miller, Arthur Montford, Sophie Nicholson at Scotsport, Johnny Rep, Bruce Rioch, Alan Rough, Andy Roxburgh, Alex Salmond MP, Jim Todd, Ernie Walker, Bill Wilson.

Thanks also to my agent Stan, my editor David Wilson, and to Bob McDevitt of Headline in Scotland.

Prologue

There did not appear to be a lot in common between Ally MacLeod and Prince Charles during the late 1970s. MacLeod, the Scotland manager, was a refined rabble-rouser whose infectious enthusiasm led thousands of people to follow in his wake; Charles, the heir to the British throne, had an uncertain, hesitant presence in public. Here was a privileged being desperate to find the common touch in the egalitarian, barrier-breaking seventies, but a young man seemingly without a clue how or where to start.

As part of Charles's doomed attempt to seem more at ease with the masses, he had perfected the mannerism when meeting commoners of placing one hand half in and half out of a blazer pocket. It was a gesture towards informality employed by the prince when dropped into a throng of strangers during public engagements, but this attempt to appear casual only served to make the young Charles – smartly tailored and buffed to a pristine shine – look even more stuffy and stiff, and like just one more eccentric aristocrat in the age of the common man. It was not the type of gesture to be expected of Ally MacLeod, Scotland manager in 1978, a man of the people, loquacious focus of roused Scots everywhere. Yet here was Ally, crown prince of populist pronouncements, just days away from what he had stated would be his finest hour, the Argentina World Cup, with not just one but both hands stuffed awkwardly in his blazer pockets and looking as uncomfortable as Prince Charles when confronted by a throng of northern factory workers.

The occasion was the staged send-off of the Scotland squad to the finals of that 1978 World Cup. The venue was Hampden Park. Thirty thousand people had assembled on the stadium's ashen slopes that sun-blessed May evening to send off, in style, Ally and his team. It seemed as though it should have been all that Ally desired: the climax to months and months in which he had rallied the people of Scotland to get behind his cause. Yet those hands thrust in pockets betrayed a certain nervousness on the part of MacLeod as he ambled uncertainly along the red carpet laid out between serried ranks of pipers and majorettes. His smile appeared half fixed, half forced as he strolled bashfully forward from touchline to halfway line. He looked like a schoolboy summoned to the headmaster's office with bravado fighting a losing battle with apprehension all over his face.

Perhaps Ally was beginning to think he had gone too far in promising the nation that his team would capture the World Cup. Perhaps he was looking one month into the future, attempting to envisage himself and his players parading the trophy back there at Hampden – with West Germany, Brazil, Argentina, Holland, France, Italy and Spain lying vanquished in their challenges for the prize – and finding that his imagination was failing him. Perhaps he was beginning to realise, in the face of this emotional show of support, how so many had truly taken his lightly-spun words to heart and the void that would result if he was unable to fulfil his pronouncements by scooping the ultimate prize in football.

That send-off was unprecedented; never before had thousands turned up at Hampden Park, without a ball in sight, simply to cheer footballers as they paraded in their suits. It had not been, contrary to popular belief, Ally MacLeod's idea but the public embraced this ritual, which was a brainchild of the Scottish Football Association. MacLeod himself found it an emotional but embarrassing evening. 'Ally didn't want it,' says John Hagart, the manager's assistant, 'because he thought it was too over the top, too much like show biz.'

The players had spent the afternoon relaxing at the North British hotel on George Square in Glasgow and the event at Hampden was to be the final staging post for the squad prior to their departure for Prestwick airport and embarkation on the flight to Argentina. Feelings were mixed among the footballers as to whether the send-off was a good idea. One or two thought it a magnificent prospect; others were neutral, a number were embarrassed by it and a few were contemplating whether to opt out of it altogether. On the night, they all participated but some of the waving to the crowd was forced.

At half past six that evening of 25 May, proceedings had begun with ten massed pipe bands taking to the field and the skirl of their pipes was accompanied by a swirl of majorettes. The dancing girls were followed, twenty minutes later, by Andy Cameron, the Glasgow comedian who had enjoyed a 1978 UK top ten hit with *Ally's Tartan Army*; then at seven o'clock each of the twenty-two players, plus members of the backroom staff and management, were presented individually to the supporters before stepping on to an open-topped bus to lap the track twice, with the players engulfed in a twenty-feet-long flag of Argentina. All of this was broadcast live on Scottish Television. The fans, whose vocal muscle had done so much to guarantee the trip to Argentina, would see no football but that did not deter the SFA from charging them fifty pence for entry to the stand and thirty pence for the ground; this during an era when Scottish Premier Division football could be watched for eighty pence. The willingness of 30,000 Scots to pay these sums and roll up en masse at a time when no Scottish club side could regularly generate attendances of that size, was a sign that the natural order of things had been turned on its head.

It did not end there. The route from Hampden down through Ayrshire to Prestwick, just a quick run up the coast from MacLeod's adopted home town of Ayr, was lined with thousands of well-wishers. One man was seen running from his bath, dripping wet, to watch the Scottish team bus as it passed. Fenwick Moor, normally deserted and desolate, was suddenly populated by cheering, waving individuals. Women swept to their back doors to wave tea towels. Every bridge had flags draped over it and was lined with people. Every field of every farm contained well-wishers speeding the squad on its way. The populaces of towns and villages a mile away from the dual carriageway that careers down through Ayrshire could be seen hanging out of their house windows, some even dangling babies in the air. 'It was like D-Day,' says Andy Roxburgh, then director of coaching at the SFA. There were an estimated 30,000 out on the streets in the environs of the small towns of Troon and Prestwick alone. Gordon McQueen, the Scotland centre-back, describes the scenes at Prestwick airport as reminiscent of Beatlemania.

Even as their plane took off the runway and into the air, there was no escaping the fervour. The beach at Prestwick was crammed with people waving to the aircraft as it began its ascent over the Firth of Clyde and into the atmosphere high above the Atlantic. Finally, the rugged Scottish coastline receded into the distance, those well-wishers became black dots on the beach, then faded out of sight and Argentina loomed ahead. Few of those on board that long night-flight to South America would return without deep scarring on their souls.

1

Pally Ally

Herr Helmut Schoen was one of the great sophisticates of world football and a man imbued with natural modesty, despite being the manager of the reigning world champions. Schoen, who had won the World Cup with West Germany in 1974, was the son of an antiques dealer and a keen theatre-goer. This tall, stately, diffident gentleman had overcome great grief at witnessing his native Dresden being razed to the ground by Allied bombers during the Second World War. He had, in the fifties, defected, at severe danger to himself and his family, from the newly created communist East Germany to the western sector of his divided country. This was a man who had known the harshest vagaries of life and whose experiences allowed him to maintain perspective on most things, including the sporting successes that he had achieved. Schoen had led his West German side to victory, in sublime style, in the 1972 European Nations Cup and then captured the World Cup on home soil in July 1974 by defeating Holland 2-1 in the final, played at Munich's architecturally magnificent Olympic stadium. He was, in early 1978, on the verge of guiding the West German national team through a fourth World Cup; a unique managerial achievement.

Even the statesmanlike Schoen, though, may have found his natural equilibrium knocked out of kilter, briefly at least, on encountering Ally MacLeod only a few weeks prior to the 1978 finals. MacLeod wasted little time in breezing up to Schoen and informing his German counterpart that, as Scotland manager, his major concern was not whether the Scots would win the 1978 World Cup – that, said MacLeod, was already a certainty. Instead, Ally told Schoen, he was already thinking ahead to the next great challenge. 'There can be few things more important in life to us than winning this World Cup,' chirped MacLeod on emerging from his meeting with the urbane German, 'unless it is, as I told Helmut Schoen, winning it again.'

Shortly before the World Cup in 1974, Schoen, charitable individual that he was, had offered the following considered comment to the Scots: 'You really will be among the favourites. We have known that for some time. It puzzles me that the Scots do not regard themselves in the same way as the rest of the world sees them.' It was clear to Schoen, four years later, that there was no need to offer such encouragement this time around. In the face of Ally's full-frontal verbal assault on the assured destiny of the Scottish team in Argentina, Schoen simply proffered the stately reply, 'It's possible.'

Ally MacLeod was a starfish in a net full of herring; a man the likes of whom Scottish football had never seen before and has never seen since. A tall, energetic individual, and very quick in his movements and in his speech; a smile always seemed to be playing around MacLeod's mouth, his elongated features always about to stretch into any one of a thousand different expressions, most of them sunny. The effect was topped off by a thatch of untamed, straw-coloured hair that often appeared to have made only the most casual acquaintance with brush or comb. The short-back-and-sides of MacLeod's youth had been allowed to grow into a longer, stragglier version of his original style, but now more in keeping with the fashionably hirsute seventies.

'Ally was a very kind person, very happy-go-lucky. I was sixteen when I first met him,' says Faye MacLeod, who would become Ally's wife soon after that initial meeting at 'the dancing' on the south side of Glasgow. 'I hadn't long lost my father and he was kind to me and my two sisters. He used to buy us a pound of dolly mixtures but by the time he arrived at our house it was about half-a-pound because he would have been eating them. He wouldn't do anyone any harm; if he could do them a kindness, he did.'

The flexible, cheerful, outgoing approach employed by MacLeod the manager made him look less like a stern, all-seeing football manager and more like a feckless but friendly uncle sailing smilingly, unworriedly, into middle-age. Dour managers had for years strutted around Scotland's football grounds, barking out orders to their players from deep within belted overcoats. Ally, in contrast, offered the shock of the new during his dozen years as a club manager, bouncing, like Tigger in a tracksuit, around football boardrooms, dispensing cheer and instilling in others his infectiously bright outlook on life. For more formal occasions he favoured the safari suit, something of a fashion statement in the seventies, popular with those – maverick politicians and individualistic school teachers, for example – whose professional dress codes constrained them to wear collar and tie but who wanted to display just a smidgen of rebellion. The safari suit, half way between smart and casual, with its rectangular, buttoned-down pockets at the chest was perfect for them – being much more Maoist egalitarian worker than staid, besuited bore.

Ally MacLeod was a gentleman; the type of man who could not go to bed at night until the cat was indoors, or who would gather up snails infesting his garden and carefully take the time and trouble to place them gently elsewhere. As his wife Faye puts it, Ally was the only man who could be manager of Ayr United and still get away with running, very successfully, a pub in Kilmarnock. A charming man, he always made time to speak to everyone, from the smallest to the biggest name, and by pushing himself forward for interviews and taking the spotlight MacLeod deflected attention and pressure away from his players. His arrival on the scene as Scotland manager in 1977 had been like dropping an effervescent tablet into a glass of still water.

'MacLeod was so honest and very straight,' says Arthur Montford, anchor man and commentator during the seventies on Scottish Television's *Scotsport*. 'He wasn't ever devious, like some other managers. He'd be up front over matters like team selection. If Ally told you the team in advance of the match, that's what the team would be.

'He was a perfect media man. He took all the pressure away from the SFA. He was also very good with us. He never turned us down for an interview and never asked our television people for money or did one-to-one exclusives, like some managers.'

It would be incorrect to look at his gentility and see Ally MacLeod as a lightweight manager: during his two years of national service with the Royal Scots he made the rank of corporal and was then asked to join the officer corps, an offer he turned down having decided that he certainly did not want a career in the army. Strong willed and passionate, he was one of the first managers to bob in and out of his dugout yelling orders at his men yet simultaneously looking as though he was undergoing psychological torture.

At one stage, when manager of Ayr, he had taken up smoking a pipe to try and calm himself down, but after popping out of the dugout to yell at a player or two he would sit back down in the dugout, on the pipe, and break it. One of Ally's friends used to pay entrance money at Ayr not to watch the game but solely to observe the manager's antics in the dugout. MacLeod's style, though, was not only entertaining but also highly effective.

The impact that Ally made as a manager meant it was often overlooked that he had enjoyed a highly successful playing career. He started in the fifties as a smiling winger at Third Lanark, the club that had been closest to his heart when he was a pupil at Queen's Park school and growing up in Mount Florida – the tenement-heavy area on the south side of Glasgow that for the past century has housed Hampden Park, Scotland's national stadium.

Thirds, who had been Scottish champions in 1904 were, in the post-war years during which Ally joined them, holding their own in mid-table in Scotland's top division. During his time at Third Lanark, Ally made such an impression that Glasgow Rangers attempted to secure his transfer. Third Lanark, on learning of that interest, quickly raised their requested transfer fee to a level they thought their rich Glasgow neighbours might afford, but raised it so high that they put off the Ibrox club.

Ally, a popular player at all his clubs, eventually moved on to St Mirren in 1955, a transfer that kept Third Lanark temporarily solvent. Within eight weeks the Paisley side had made a quick buck by selling him on to Blackburn Rovers where he was well loved for being a hard working, entertaining player. He was among the club's top goal scorers in each of his five seasons at Ewood Park, and it was here that he collected the nickname Noddy, because of the way his head bobbed up and down when he was on the ball.

MacLeod was a success in England and the outstanding player at Wembley in the 1960 FA Cup final between

Blackburn and Wolverhampton Wanderers. Even though Blackburn, reduced to ten men early in the match, lost 3-0, that match proved to be the high point of Ally's playing career. He recalled having been selected for several Scotland squads but he stated that he had had to withdraw each time because of club commitments or injury.

The 1960s forced Ally to confront the same crossroads confronted by every footballer in that era. Having enjoyed a good standard of living from the game, but one nowhere good enough to enable him to retire once his playing days were over, he had to decide what he was going to do with his future. As Ally approached the mid-sixties, and reached his mid-thirties, he began to wind down his career with Hibernian, whom he had joined from Blackburn in 1961 following a disagreement over pay. One sentimental year back at Third Lanark followed his stint at Easter Road, leaving Ally entirely ready to sever his connections with football in order to concentrate on a new career. Having qualified as an industrial chemist after leaving school in the late forties Ally was set to become a sales representative for a pharmaceutical company.

Just as Scottish football teetered on the verge of losing Ally MacLeod for ever, Bobby Flavell, the manager of Ayr United, intervened and persuaded him to play on in the game for a short while longer. 'Six months more won't hurt you,' Flavell said, unwittingly changing utterly the course of Scottish football in much the same way as a butterfly fluttering its wings in the Amazonian rainforest is said to be able to set off a chain of seismic, cataclysmic, natural events. Ally's contract at Ayr was to be on a part-time basis only, so that he could also focus on his new career as a salesman. But when Flavell parted company with Ayr, Ally was offered the post of team manager combined, significantly, with the role of commercial manager. The natural ebullience that had made him a perfect sales rep he would now channel into his new, dual role; selling his football club and making his team one worth selling.

Ayr had survived on meagre attendances of a few hundred prior to Ally's arrival but he transformed the club into one of those provincial sides who could, on the right day, defeat the largest clubs in the land and who, by the mid-seventies, after a decade of Ally's management, were accepted as a seriously good top-six club in Scotland. George McLean and Alex Ferguson, former Rangers strikers, were among those whom Ally attracted to Somerset Park to add colour and style to the club during the years in which he made his part-time outfit sparkle more brightly than ever before among the more finely cut diamonds of the Scottish game.

'I never, ever heard him swear,' says Faye MacLeod. 'Although one Ayr United player did say to me that if Ally hadn't sworn at him whenever they were talking then he wouldn't have understood what he was saying. So I think Ally was a different person when he was at the football.

'I heard he was very strict on timekeeping and when we were going to any function we would be rushing out of the door so that we would be the first to arrive. He was also said to be keen on tidiness in the dressing room but at home he wasn't the tidiest of people.'

Ally's departure from Ayr for Aberdeen in November 1975 signalled the start of a period of decline for the Somerset Park club but one of resurgence for Aberdeen. Shortly after his arrival at Pittodrie, while Ally was having lunch with Jim Rust, the club secretary, a woman approached their table and said to Rust, 'I hear you've got a new manager and I hear he's a right nutter.' As she turned to leave, Rust asked her, 'Would you like to meet him?' The club had recruited MacLeod in an attempt to evade the first relegation in its history but it was only in the final hours of the 1975-76 season that MacLeod's team avoided the drop – and then only by the narrowest of margins, on goal difference from Dundee.

Moving from homely, small-town Ayr to Aberdeen, a city in the throes of rapid economic growth since the discovery of oil in the North Sea, was a cosmic leap in terms of football management. At Ayr, for example, Ally had once presided over an auction in which sheep from local farms featured among the items for sale to help raise funds for a set of floodlights. And there was the occasion when an Ayr player, having fallen out with his wife, arrived for training with their children in tow – and Ally had to ring his wife Faye and ask her to look after the young ones.

Aberdeen was a considerably bigger club. Unlike Ayr, the Dons had won the top prizes in Scottish football and had featured in European competition. But Ayr and Aberdeen, in addition to being fellow seaside resorts, did share similarities. In common with Ayr United, Aberdeen was the only professional football club in town and here, too, the locals were not exactly fanatical about football – they would have to be coaxed into enthusiasm for their club. If anyone was fit for coaxing them, it was Ally. A quick way to get his thoughts and ambitions across to supporters and players was by using the local press with enthusiasm and that made MacLeod a media-friendly manager.

'At Aberdeen he was very approachable,' says John Mann, football writer for the *Scottish Daily Express* in the seventies. 'I could phone him from Dundee and know I was going to get a story, unlike so many other managers who, when you phoned, would be "in the bath". Managers in those days had more baths than anybody; they spent hours in the bath so they couldn't come to the phone for the press.

'I never found him a braggart. He was never cruel; whenever he talked of other teams and managers he always did it in a friendly way. At Aberdeen, he would say some outrageous things and then he would say, "For goodness sake, don't write that." When you got him going, he didn't hold much back. He had a puckish sense of humour and a very fertile imagination.

'It had occurred to him that the rugby kick-off was quite good, where they kick from the halfway line and everybody moves down one wing. At Aberdeen he had half his team lined up on the left and then they kicked off. I remember asking him, "What was the point of that?" and he said, "Did you see the state of the opposition for the first five minutes?" He used that several times in that season at Aberdeen; it was about the element of surprise. I thought that showed a lot of imagination.

'I'd also say he was a hard-headed football man. His insights into players and other teams and games from the past were very interesting; he could draw pictures of this team, that player and what this player needed to do to add to his game.'

Within six months of suffering near-relegation with Aberdeen, Ally had cajoled his new players into winning the League Cup by beating Celtic 2-1 in the 1976 final, a year to the day from when he had become manager at Pittodrie. Aberdeen had also whipped Rangers 5-1 in the semi-final. At the end of the final, watched by a 70,000-strong crowd, an overjoyed MacLeod – in tomato-red shirt and blue safari suit – looked as though he was going to burst out of his body as he gambolled about on the Hampden pitch, limbs flying this way and that, head lolling joyfully from side to side, clapping and clasping his hands in uncontainable glee. As he returned to the dressing room area, Jock Stein, the defeated manager, proffered a hand and as the lively MacLeod took it, Stein – eight years MacLeod's senior – who had been master manager in the Scottish game for the previous decade, suddenly looked tired and jaded.

For a long stretch of that season Ally's Aberdeen pushed Celtic hard for the title, the Dons drawing a mammoth crowd of 47,000 to Celtic Park on Boxing Day 1976 – an unexpectedly large attendance for a domestic League match in those roll up, pay-at-the-gate days, and at a time when Scottish club football was in a trough. Much of the interest in that match had been due to a combination of Aberdeen's stunning form during MacLeod's first full season and a series of ebullient interviews Ally had given prior to the match, almost like a commission-hungry boxing promoter.

He wasn't all talk, though: his team played a key part in a rollicking 2-2 draw. Ally had revitalised the Pittodrie side in style and at speed and his showmanship had become more noticeable now that he was on a larger stage – at Celtic Park that Boxing Day, the home supporters directed at the Aberdeen dugout the chant, 'Ally, Ally, shut your mouth; Ally, shut your mouth'. He had in a single year transformed the Pittodrie club from one that had been struggling against relegation into one that would finish third in the Scottish Premier Division at the end of the 1976-77 season.

'He had a personality that the Aberdeen people warmed to and he stimulated their interest,' says Dons player Willie Miller, who was aged twenty-one when MacLeod became manager at Pittodrie. 'I think that was his main quality; his personality and the way he went about his job. The things he said in the newspapers were outrageous – that was Ally's style. He would say that we were going to win the treble and I think the idea was that if you aim high enough and you miss a little, then there is still success there to be had.

'He was never the type of guy to play anything down; he was always the type to try to play everything he possibly could up, to raise expectations in the hope that he could deliver. He was, I think, trying to get people's mindsets attuned to thinking of lifting trophies; that's a good, positive aspect to have. I suppose the downside of that is, do you raise expectations so high that if it does fail then you're left in kind of no man's land?

'He was outrageous and I would say that he wasn't everybody's cup of tea in terms of what he was saying and what he did on the training field. For instance, you would be playing five-a-sides and winning five-nil and he would make the next goal count as four goals and he would always make sure that that would happen until the opposition got a little closer to you. You would also be playing the five-a-sides and leading and just about to put the ball in the net when he would shout that you were now shooting the other way so you would have to start all over again. That kind of thing, I must admit, for myself and people like Bobby Clark, got a little bit annoying, so for us, what Bobby used to do was to keep the correct score.

'One of his big strengths was to try to instil self belief in you, to make you believe that anything was possible; he would do that by every means he had, whether it was through individual chats, group chats. He liked getting his message across through the newspapers, in the assumption that players always read newspapers.

'He would make statements in the press about what the team was going to achieve and it worked. The more thoughtful players may have had reservations; I think there would be some who sat down and thought all about it but as a group he brought you together with a focus. When you are sitting in third place, and Ally's giving it his all, then, as a group, you think, "Well, why not?" We all wanted to achieve success anyway and you've got to have that belief, otherwise it never happens; and it did happen during the five years after Ally went, when we won the championship under Fergie. We needed that same belief then, as well; it was just that Fergie went about it in a different way to the way Ally went about it.'

An all-round sportsman ever since boyhood, Ally had enjoyed playing football, rugby, and hockey in his early years, as well as golf and tennis which he continued with in adulthood. On court, instead of playing a right-handed backhand shot he would switch the racket to his left hand to play the ball forehand, infuriating his opponents. For MacLeod, a former schoolboy tennis champion, this was little more than routine unorthodoxy.

His methods as a manager were equally surprising, eccentric, disarming and unusual enough to demand attention from players who will happily accept anything that helps them win or spices up the day-to-day slog of keeping in trim for match day. When he was manager of Ayr, the team bus became stuck in traffic on the way to a match in Edinburgh and, with time ticking away before kick-off, MacLeod had Henry Templeton running up and down Princes Street as a pre-match fitness test. Early in his time as manager at Pittodrie, he ordered some players back to the ground one evening to lap the track because of a misdemeanour on their part but, being new to the stadium, did not know how to switch on the floodlights. He still made the players run the laps, but had to follow their progress by torch light to ensure they were carrying out their punishment properly. He would also make players play head tennis in three feet of snow or five-a-sides on the beach in two inches of water.

Eleven days after MacLeod's League Cup triumph with Aberdeen at Hampden in November 1976, Scotland, managed by Willie Ormond, took to the field at the same venue and defeated Wales 1-0 in a World Cup qualifying tie – the Scots' second outing in their three-nation quali-fying group for the 1978 finals. It was an impressively constructed victory – Scotland played very well and domi-nated the game – with the winner coming courtesy of a fifteenth-minute back-heel flick from Kenny Dalglish that the Welsh centre-back, Ian Evans, touched before it went into the net and which, to Dalglish's chagrin, was later recorded as an own goal. It left Scotland with two points from a possible four with half of their fixtures completed; they had lost 2-0 to Czechoslovakia in Prague in their opening tie five weeks earlier. It meant they were balanced uncomfortably half way between qualification and elim-ination.

Willie Ormond was subsequently allowed, with no great resistance from the Scottish Football Association, to leave the post of Scotland manager to take up the job of manager at Heart of Midlothian. Ormond's departure in May 1977 had been on the agenda since mid-1975, when the SFA had offered Jock Stein the position of Scotland boss only for him to turn it down just when it had seemed that he was about to accept. Two years later, when Ormond did quit, a similar scenario developed. Stein was again offered the job and again, after appearing to those at the SFA to be on the verge of accepting the challenge, he decided to remain at Celtic. Celtic had just won the Scottish Cup and League double and Stein was nurturing a good, young team. Equally importantly, perhaps, there was not a great deal of difference between the salary on offer from the SFA –

£14,000 – and the amount he could pick up in terms of the various bonuses and other monies available to him through being manager of Celtic, on top of his £10,000 basic annual salary.

By turning down the post Stein had left the SFA in something of a pickle. They had the three-game 1977 Home International series on the immediate horizon, followed swiftly by another prestigious three-game series: a tour of South America. There, Scotland would face Chile, Argentina – the hosts of the 1978 World Cup finals – and Brazil, three times world champions. It would have been fine in the fifties to go into those games without a manager in place; not so in the seventies, by which time the media had turned up the heat on those involved in football.

So the SFA turned to the man who had been the last before Stein to win a domestic trophy in Scottish football: Ally MacLeod. He was, he recalled, interviewed on 18 May 1977 by three SFA executives – Rankin Grimshaw, Tom Clark and Tom Lauchlan. Ally also recalled Ernie Walker, the assistant secretary, being present and that he was offered the job at the conclusion of the interview, on the salary of £14,000 per year.

MacLeod asked for forty-eight hours to consider whether or not to accept but Clark swiftly interjected, asking him why he required any more time to think things over when all his stipulations as to how he would run the team had already been answered positively. A more crafty, manipulative manager, such as Stein, might have insisted on taking the proposed forty-eight hours and then, with the SFA obviously under pressure to make an appointment, used the situation to squeeze even better working conditions and/or salary out of them. Ally, in contrast, was persuaded to accept the position then and there. Such was his self belief, he even insisted on working without a contract as this made him feel freer; able to decide when he wished to quit the job.

'I always felt the Scotland job came too soon,' says Faye MacLeod. 'We hadn't been up there in Aberdeen very long and we loved it but Ally felt that the opportunity was there and that he had to take it. He talked about it and thought about it but if your ambition in life is to get the top job . . . And he considered Scotland to be the top job. As he said, "If I turn it down now I might not get it again."'

MacLeod remembered Walker introducing him to the press the following day with the words, 'This is Ally MacLeod; he's not very good at talking'. MacLeod tapped the side of his nose and stated, 'Concorde has landed'. That quip was a mere light appetiser before Ally got down to discussing the serious business of exactly what he planned to do with Scotland in the future months and years.

'I want to prove that I am the best manager in the world,' he said, encapsulating matters neatly. 'People might laugh but I firmly believe I was born to be a success.' Andy Roxburgh recalls the initial hours of MacLeod's stint as Scotland manager at SFA headquarters: 'Ally was very focused and very enthusiastic. On the first day he was in the job he was making noises about what he would do. He was so full of expectation you had to admire him for that. It was so infectious.'

A frenzy of face-twisting alcohol helped rid the Aberdeen players of some of the disappointment they felt at the departure of the manager who had guided them so swiftly to a trophy win.

'It had been mooted that he was going to become Scotland manager,' says Willie Miller, 'so I wouldn't say it was a shock when we heard. He took us away on an end-of-season trip to Dubrovnik to say cheerio. That's when he told us, over there. Even his going away party was outrageous because we all had to drink this foreign fire-water that he had brought back from one of our trips abroad; that was mandatory. You didn't have any option on that, whether you fancied it or not. The pot plants in his house took a bit of a doing that night.

'He was enthusiastic, he was bubbly and he always had something to say,' is how Miller sums up Ally's brief span at Aberdeen. 'There was never a quiet or dull moment, whether it be in the changing rooms or out on the playing field. He was like a whirlwind. He came in, stirred everything up, won a trophy and then went away to Scotland.'

There were pronounced differences in character between MacLeod and Stein, his only rival for the Scotland post, but the two managers also shared certain similarities. Like Stein, MacLeod would stay up late at night in hotels on tour to talk quietly about football. He would discuss players, matches and various matters, such as whether he or anyone else could have done more to save his beloved Third Lanark from folding in 1967. The team from Cathkin had been Ally's first love and it was there that he had first been encouraged to show his individualism. The player whom he had looked up to most and was his mentor at the club, Jimmy Mason, a Scottish international inside-forward, would smoke a cigarette up until it was time to take the field, hand it to trainer Hughie Good, and then receive it, already re-lit, from Good immediately on re-entering the dressing room at half time. Cathkin Park shortly after the Second World War had been a haven of such eccentricity and MacLeod had thrived on that.

'There's a fine line between genius and madness and Ally walked that fine line,' says John Hagart, Ally's assistant manager with Scotland. 'Ally was a great storyteller but there would be a bit added on to the story every time he told it to someone different. At times you didn't know if Ally was telling you the truth or telling you a wee fib although there was nothing malicious about Ally as such. He was straight down the middle and he was a lovely guy but there were times when you would say, "Is that right?"

'His mind would jump away with him and he would think things and say things and think that they had actually taken place, sometimes. He was also a clever man, a very intelligent guy, a chemist; more intelligent than me.'

One of Ally's first actions as Scotland manager was a significant one and indicative of the direction in which his particular wind of change would blow: he reinstated Jimmy Steele, then the masseur for Celtic, to his former role as masseur with the Scotland squad. Steele, who had been removed by Willie Ormond for being 'too cheery', combined his work with that of all-round court jester, mime artist and song-and-dance-man. Few players failed to appreciate Steele's verve and wit and that fitted in with the type of relaxed atmosphere that MacLeod wished to establish around the Scotland team.

'Ally talked all the time,' recalls Hugh Allan, one of two physiotherapists attached to the Scottish national squad during the MacLeod era. 'He was steeped in football and he just held court generally.

'I can't recall him asking other people's opinions too much. I'm sure that he didn't even know if I had a family or anything – he would never, ever ask you personal questions. If you went out shopping you had to follow Ally because he would want to go to this shop and that shop. He would never ask, "What do you fancy doing?" Ally was, though, good to work for and he didn't bother me in any way, I'd have to say.'

The public persona of a man who believed in filling every hour with fun did not disappear once MacLeod was behind closed doors at his family's modest home in a cul-de-sac opposite the Abbotsford Hotel in Ayr.

'There was a lot of laughter with Ally,' says Faye MacLeod. 'He'd say, "If you can't have a laugh, life's not worth living." If you were going up the stairs, you would suddenly hear a barking noise and Ally would be like a dog at your heels. If you were going out, he would call you back and when you went back up to the door he would say, "Where would I have been if I hadn't called you back?"

'He used to get a carton of water and jam it above the door in such a way that it would fall on the person entering the room. You'd open this door and the water would pour down on to you. As our David says, he was twenty-five before he stopped looking up at the top of a door when he entered a room.'

Hugh Allan had worked as a physiotherapist at the 1974 World Cup and he was pleased when MacLeod was appointed. 'Ally was flamboyant, very positive,' says Allan, 'and I thought, "Good", because, you know, we'd had discipline problems with Willie [Ormond]. I thought Ally would tighten up on that and he did, to a certain extent, but probably not enough.

'I'd heard that he had a good record for discipline in terms of being a stickler for time and all that sort of thing. Again, that's maybe all right at club level but when you're dealing with the big-time boys it's a wee bit different. I think he probably did find it harder to handle the big names.'

A long, loose-limbed individual, MacLeod employed a gangly walk and Donnie McKinnon, the other physiotherapist attached to the Scotland squad, would mimic the way MacLeod's leg would swing out like a compass describing a semicircle as he strolled.

'Sometimes, when he was speaking, you'd wonder if he

wasn't quite the full shilling,' noted another member of the Scottish party that would travel to the World Cup in Argentina. That may seem harsh but if some of Ally's pronouncements were wildly outlandish, it is possible that it was not so much madness that inspired them as, most surprisingly, bashfulness. Joe Harper, a player for MacLeod with Aberdeen and Scotland, confirms that Ally was quite different to the public perception of him: 'He was a very quiet man although he was OK when he was among the players. Then he would tell jokes.'

Faye MacLeod, the person who knew him best, concurs. 'People are surprised when I say to them that Ally was basically a shy person. But it was because of that shyness that he would tend to go in and try to make things happen to cover it over. Going anywhere or meeting new people, it at first took him a wee while to adjust to it but then once he would start talking he would forget about his shyness. Once he got going on his subject of football he was all right.

'He still found some of the things that came with being a successful football manager quite embarrassing – when he went to dances and women would ask him to dance; that, for example, was something that he did not particularly like.'

The colour and spectacle that her husband brought to the nation during his time as Scotland manager was enjoyed greatly by Faye MacLeod. 'He was a very patriotic person and he felt he was doing his wee bit to lift the country, and he did do that. There's no doubt about it and I don't think anyone will ever manage to do it again to that extent. He was just beating the big drum to get people behind his team, which he seemed to manage, whether it was Scotland or Ayr. '

On his appointment as Scotland manager in May 1977, it was quickly clear that MacLeod was revitalising the post through his enthusiasm, energy and optimism. Privately, in those initial days and weeks, he was fully aware of how big a task he had taken on and was determined to approach it cautiously. No one, not even MacLeod himself, was aware of just how radical the new man would eventually prove to be. The fun had just begun.

2

It was easy to imagine Gordon McQueen wielding a claymore and wearing a plaid when he rose into the air to meet the challenge of connecting with the free kick. The gargantuan centre-back timed his climb exquisitely, used his strength to beat off the flimsy challenges of the English defenders and skelped the ball furiously with his forehead, low into the net. As the great Scottish warrior crashed to the turf – a flurry of despairing English bodies sprawled around him – with Lion Rampants waving crazily and furiously in the background, it could almost have been a scene from a 19th-century oil painting of some furiously fought military encounter.

This was no ordinary football match. This was England against Scotland, and this was Scotland dominating the Auld Enemy on their own turf in a manner rarely matched before. At Wembley stadium, on that hot June day in 1977 Scotland were clearly the superior side – their nimbler, neater, cleverer, more inventive play made the English look as cumbersome as blinkered warhorses. In this traditional 'hate' match, though, gory core values were prized as much as skilful football and McQueen's gritty goal had fitted the bill for those who liked to see the English pummelled, demonstrably.

McQueen's header put Scotland 1-0 ahead late in the first half of that annual encounter. The Scots' second goal, in the second half, again epitomised all that their supporters loved to see. Emlyn Hughes, the English centre-back and a man who loved riling the Scots, had gone head to head, off the ball, with Kenny Dalglish, the Scottish forward, who although a hardy competitor was no fighter. But he stood up to the bully Hughes, and once play resumed Dalglish extracted justice in the finest manner possible. Willie Johnston, the Scots' quickfire winger, pelted to the goal line and sent a superb cross slewing high into the English penalty area, even as the momentum of Johnston's run sent him careering side on into the phalanx of photographers behind the goal line.

As when McQueen scored, a battle scene quickly developed with a pile of players scrambling for a taste of the ball. It was Dalglish who got the vital, final touch, bravely beating off a battery of desperate English challenges before nudging the ball past Hughes and over the line to send wild a Wembley stadium in which the majority of the visiting supporters were, as always in the Scotland-England match, in the tartan. A late English penalty did nothing to dent the spirits of those supporters; they were unanimous and correct in feeling that their team's 2-1 victory was one of the most memorable Scotland had achieved in the 105 years over which this fixture with England had become an annual event.

Nothing, not even World Cups, induced greater emotion in fanatical Scottish football followers during the seventies than the match with England. Supporters would save steadily for two years to pay for the biennial trip to London and every game against the Auld Enemy was guaranteed to pack out Hampden or Wembley with Scottish supporters. It was a tradition as fixed and as seemingly unassailable in Scottish life as first-footing with coal and black bun at Hogmanay. More often than not, the trip south ended in bitter defeat but that only made the victories taste as sweet as fresh water after days in the desert – although few who followed Scotland on those occasions demanded fresh water to slake their thirsts in the minutes and hours after, or before, the match. It had been ten years since Scotland had beaten England at Wembley but the tempo and style of that thunderous 1977 victory obliterated the four successive defeats there since 1967.

It would soon become fashionable for Scots commentators, and even managers and players, to try to play down the importance of the Scotland-England match. It was, they would say, a huge, unwanted distraction, a parochial, small-minded occasion, irrelevant outside the British Isles and much less important to the English than to the Scots; a match that had become puffed-up and that had jumped well above its station. It also, they would argue, distracted attention from the much more important business of collecting points to qualify for the finals of World Cups. This, however, was to overlook the importance of the Scotland-England match in 1977 in imbuing a vitality and cohesion in the Scottish side that would energise them for their two vital World Cup qualifiers against Czechoslovakia and Wales later that year. The lasting effects of defeating England at Wembley ensured that spirits would be high for those later matches.

The pummelling of the Auld Enemy had been Ally MacLeod's third match since his appointment as Scotland manager just seventeen days earlier. His first had been against Wales on 28 May and, two days before that encounter, he had introduced himself to the players at the Mercury Hotel in Chester with the words, 'My name is Ally MacLeod and I am a winner.' He was happy enough not to win but to draw his first game, 0-0, at the Racecourse Ground in Wrexham, then to follow up with a 3-0 victory over Northern Ireland at Hampden Park. But it was at Wembley that MacLeod really came into his own, greeting Dalglish's goal with unrestrained joy and punching both arms in the air in flamboyant celebration. This was a sight the Scots supporters had never seen before: fan as manager.

MacLeod's predecessor, the undemonstrative Willie Ormond, had sat like stone on the bench, through good times and bad, but in MacLeod the Scots seemed to have a man who was as wrapped up in the emotions of the event as those on the terraces. It was easy for most supporters to share his enthusiasm: Scotland had a strong defence and intelligent, creative midfield players plus dynamic forwards. MacLeod received boundless praise for the victory at Wembley but he played it down saying, 'Much tougher battles are to be faced. We still have a lot to do but we do have a magnificent squad.'

Ten days after slapping down England the Scots were in Chile for the first match on their tour of South America. The game's Santiago venue attracted controversy: four years earlier, after a US-backed military coup led by General Augusto Pinochet had booted out Salvador Allende's left-wing government, the national stadium had served for two months as an open-air prison. Thousands of political prisoners had been tortured and a number had been executed inside the stadium.

During their stay in Santiago some officials from the Scottish party met, unwittingly, with political dissidents; the Scottish officials had been under the impression that they were simply attending another innocent, if informal, reception. The meeting, however, brought the heavy hand of Pinochet's junta into action with armed security men descending on the team's hotel and refusing to allow groups of more than four Scots to leave together.

The match itself resulted in a 4-2 victory for Scotland,

with Lou Macari scoring twice. There was a nice, settled look about this Scotland side and experience ran through it as seamlessly as the lettering through a stick of seaside rock. Don Masson was the only player whose cap tally did not extend into double figures but the midfielder seemed a mature player, with years of experience in the top tier of English football. Masson was nudging thirty years of age when he played his first international in 1976; his appearance against the Chileans had won him his ninth international cap.

The encounter with Chile had been marred by the issues surrounding the venue but in Argentina, three days later, all intensity was reserved for the match itself. A Masson penalty gave Scotland a 1-1 draw in Buenos Aires, in a match during which Willie Johnston was dismissed, in tears, after being spat on and punched by Vicente Pernia. Pernia, the opposing full-back, had lost his composure and discipline in hysterical fashion after being outmanoeuvred and outclassed by Johnston.

'They were a dirty team,' says Johnston of the Argentinians – who had a player named Daniel Killer as their left-back. 'They would kick, bite, spit, anything. I got dragged off. The boy marking me got sent off – he did me – but what they do is just level it up. I got sent off, for absolutely nothing, and that was the first time I'd ever been sent off while playing for Scotland.

'Ally MacLeod said, "If that had been your fault, you would never have played again." It wasn't my fault. I didn't get banned or anything.'

Five days later, on 23 June, Johnston was seen to be vindicated when he was selected for the final match in the tour, which ended in a 2-0 defeat by Brazil. On the pitch afterwards, Scottish Television commentator Arthur Montford was larking about with Bobby Clark, a goalkeeper in the squad, and netted a penalty in the cavernous Maracana stadium just before the floodlights were switched off. It was a cheerful coda to a tour that had been harmonious for players, management and press.

The tour was judged to have been a great success: Scotland had attained highly respectable results against the South American sides on their opponents' home turf; MacLeod had engendered a good team spirit and had been well supported by the then president of the SFA, Queen of the South's Willie Harkness. The squad's bond had been strengthened. The seriousness with which the Scots had prepared for the tour was underlined in that the team was barely altered for each match. The 4-2 victory in Santiago had been especially impressive and in the other two matches the Scots had played reasonably well, if a little defensively. Ally MacLeod did later admit to Montford that he could have been a bit more adventurous in the way he set out his side.

'We had a good team,' reflects Willie Johnston. 'But after being away for a couple of weeks we'd had one game too many; when we played Brazil we were all knackered. We just wanted to come home. We played well against Argentina and although we drew with them we should have beaten them. It was good.'

While flamboyancy matching that of a Paisley-patterned kipper tie often characterised MacLeod's actions as a club manager, it was caution rather than experimentation that was proving to be his forte as Scotland manager during those early days as he eased himself into the job. In his opening six matches with the national team MacLeod had handed out only one debut cap, and that had been to Jim Stewart, the Kilmarnock goalkeeper, who had been on the bench in Scotland squads for years. Even then, Stewart appeared only as a half-time substitute for Alan Rough during the Chile match when the score was already 3-0 in Scotland's favour.

All MacLeod's other selected players were fully familiar to those who had followed Scotland throughout the Ormond era, and with good reason; as his final duty prior to resigning on 6 May, it was Ormond who had named the squad for the Home Internationals and the tour of South America. MacLeod did not even go so far as to experiment with the players Ormond had chosen. Davie Cooper, for example, a twenty-one-year-old winger who had weeks earlier won promotion to the Scottish Premier Division with tiny Clydebank was an exciting, up-and-coming talent. Cooper was on the bench for all three South American matches but MacLeod didn't play him at any stage, despite the fact that Willie Johnston – an outside-left, like Cooper – was assessed by MacLeod in his private notes as having had a 'quiet game' against Chile after a 'brilliant opening twenty minutes' and a 'poor game' in which he 'really did nothing' against Brazil.

Those personal notes of MacLeod's from this time, compiled privately after every international, sketch a picture of a man feeling his way into football at international level with extreme caution. Following the match against Wales MacLeod wrote, 'As this was my first international, played very safe and side selected achieved the aim required . . . nil-nil was most satisfactory.' A week later, his remarks on the match with England read slightly more expansively, 'Contained England for first fifteen minutes. Opened out and won quite convincingly. Score does not reflect play.' After the South American tour MacLeod reflected, 'Following on from the Home International series, this tour helped strengthen the view that the squad selected was not far from the best available.'

On arriving back from South America in late June 1977,

even as Ally stepped off the plane in Scotland his thoughts would have been turning to the rapidly advancing fixtures planned for the autumn when the Scots would play Czechoslovakia at Hampden Park and Wales away; matches that would hold the key to qualification for the 1978 World Cup.

The Czechs were as formidable a set of opponents as it was possible for Scotland to face. Fifteen months earlier they had become champions of Europe and six of the side that had won that title lined up at Hampden on 21 September 1977. It was, though, a wan Czech team that took to the turf and one that really did not want to be playing at all that Wednesday evening. The Czechoslovakian Football Association had requested, unsuccessfully, a postponement of the match after a problem-ridden journey to Scotland that had left their players in less than peak condition. The team's flight from Prague to London the previous day had been delayed for three hours so that they missed the connecting flight to Glasgow, which forced them to travel north by overnight train, consigned to upright seats because the sleeper accommodation was fully booked, and they had arrived in Glasgow only shortly before dawn. So it was an understandably weary string of Czech players who found their ears pounded by the noise from the 85,000-strong Hampden crowd as the teams lined up for the national anthems.

Hampden, in the seventies, provided a great tumult of emotion on evenings and afternoons that were vital to the Scottish side. The south stand, where the well-heeled watched statically from their seats, was engulfed by three huge terraces cloaked by a jumping, jostling mass of supporters – swaying shoulder to shoulder, crammed together in support of their team. Only the most phlegmatic could fail to be carried away by such a crowd giving rein to the most voluminous, vociferous, frenetic, febrile roars of support for any national team in Europe. The Scottish side contained skilful, intelligent players, but in such an atmosphere the team became crowd-driven, urged to force play forward incessantly. The din was so loud and unrelenting that the players could not hear advice or a shout from a team mate five yards away, all they could hear were the constant demands of the crowd to take the game to their opponents. The evening of the Czechoslovakian match was one on which the crowd wrote an impromptu score for those on the park. They, in turn, responded by conjuring up all the right notes.

Willie Johnston was on Scotland's left wing that evening, 'Ally was brilliant; he was of the old school,' says Johnston. 'His best one was when we were playing Czechoslovakia at Hampden and we had a team talk on the Tuesday night and he said, "What we're going to do is have Willie Johnston, Joe Jordan and Gordon McQueen all line up at outside-left. Don Masson and Bruce Rioch, if we get the kick-off, will fire the ball towards the corner flag. Big Gordon will go up, nod it down and Bud will have a shot at goal."

'Well, we did win the kick-off, the ball was fired forward but the Czechs' big centre-half went up, nodded it down and they went up the park and hit the post. So, tactically, Ally wasn't great but he made you want to play for the jersey and play for your country.'

It was Johnston who played a pivotal role in the opening goal. With eighteen minutes gone, blue jerseys flooded the Czech penalty area as Johnston teed up a corner. The winger crossed from right to left and as the ball sailed to the edge of the six-yard box, Joe Jordan leapt to smack a header into the Czech net. Ten minutes before half time, Johnston, on fire, swayed down the flank and teased the ball into the air inside the penalty area. Jordan piled into the Czech goalkeeper and centre-half, the ball fell free and Asa Hartford shuffled his feet to slip the ball tidily into the unguarded goal. Nine minutes after half time, Scotland sealed the win. Masson's corner was punched clear by the Czech goalkeeper but headed back goalwards by Sandy Jardine, who twisted like a salmon in mid air to send the ball on to Dalglish – whose natty header shot into the net.

The Czechs managed to score close to the conclusion of the match to leave it at 3-1 to Scotland but as the fans poured out of Hampden to spread out across the south side of Glasgow, or join the train queues snaking round towering tenements, they were convinced that Scotland were irresistible and that, even though the Welsh might still stand in their way, it would be the Scots who would be going to Argentina and the 1978 World Cup finals. The Hampden crowd had seen a display of skill and high speed precision in all aspects of the game; the consummate committed Scottish performance. In fact, their display had been so exceptional that West Germany's manager Helmut Schoen obtained a film of the match to show to his players, the world champions.

'They were unbelievably competitive, those matches, because of the desire. We were absolutely desperate to get to the World Cup,' says Gordon McQueen of the encounters with Czechoslovakia and Wales in the autumn of 1977. 'I don't think the Czechs knew what had hit them but at international level you can't just bully teams to win games, and with players like Danny McGrain, Willie Johnston and Kenny Dalglish in the side there was plenty of skill. It wasn't just about it being a battle.'

The sense of euphoria that now swept the country was played down by MacLeod, who had refused to allow his players to return to the field after the Czechoslovakia match for the lap of honour that the supporters, rooted to their spots on the terraces, demanded loud and long. The manager was aware that there were a mere three weeks before Scotland would face Wales in a match they had to win to be sure of reaching the World Cup finals.

A defeat for Scotland would open up the group again for the Czechs and the Welsh while a draw would eliminate the Czechs but leave the Welsh requiring a win in Prague to qualify. Such a thought was not even worth contemplating. Neither did anyone consider how much of a role the Czechs' fatigue had played in the Scottish victory, nor what the result might have been if Jordan's hefty, mid-air challenge at the second goal had been penalised by the referee. These were not even afterthoughts in the wake of victory; to the Scottish supporters such considerations were of as little importance as detritus in the gutter to a driver of a high performance sports car. The Scots now sped on to meet Wales.

The Welsh faced a major problem over where they should stage the game. Ninian Park in Cardiff, their major venue, was out of bounds to them. A pitch invasion after their match with Yugoslavia in May 1976 had led to that ground being banned as a venue for internationals for two years by UEFA. If Wales were to compete on home soil, that left the option of staging the match at either the Racecourse Ground in Wrexham or Vetch Field in Swansea, third and fourth division venues respectively. A horde of Scots was anticipated and with their own supporters clamouring for tickets the Welsh FA opted to maximise the attendance, not to mention the revenue, and settled on Liverpool's Anfield ground. Although just across the Welsh border, for Scotland, this was as good as, if not better than, a neutral venue. On the night of the match, 12 October 1977, a conservative estimate placed 30,000 Scots in a crowd of slightly more than 50,000. In reality there appeared to be more like five or six Scotsmen for every Welshman at Anfield.

Wales fielded the usual jumble of players from major clubs such as Liverpool, Everton and Aston Villa, along-side others from clubs such as Wrexham, Burnley and Coventry City. It was a Welsh side that, of necessity, played within certain limits and on the night they successfully bottled up the Scots' exuberant skills without creating too many chances themselves until, on the hour, the Welsh got the opportunity for which they had been waiting patiently. Suddenly, John Toshack, their striker, found freedom on the edge of the Scottish penalty area, loped on to the ball and extended a leg to lob it towards goal. It was a well-judged shot that rose in an arc then swiftly plummeted down, clearly on target. Scotland goalkeeper Alan Rough was well off his line, but he stretched back lithely and extended a hand to scoop the ball safely over the crossbar. Argentina was still in view.

The match meandered on and a 0-0 draw, that would take qualification out of Scotland's hands, was on the horizon. Then, in seventy-eight minutes, Joe Jordan and Dave Jones, the Welsh centre-back, both jumped simulta-neously to try to meet Willie Johnston's throw-in. As the ball reached the duelling players, Jordan's right hand shot up directly from alongside his body towards the ball. Robert Wurtz, the French referee, immediately pointed to the penalty spot for handball against Jones. Don Masson, ice cubes coursing through his veins, stepped up to hook the ball past Dai Davies in the Welsh goal. Nine minutes later, with the Welsh pounding forward in search of an equaliser, Martin Buchan swept into space that had been opened up invitingly on the right wing and angled a neat cross into the Welsh penalty area where Kenny Dalglish, with characteristic deftness, nicked a clever header over Davies and into the net to make it 2-0 for Scotland. It was a magnificent way for Dalglish to celebrate his fiftieth cap.

There would be one lingering afterthought from the match. Television pictures suggested that it might just have been Jordan's hand, rather than Jones's, that had made connection with the ball when the penalty was awarded to Scotland. MacLeod stated that he had not seen any dubious involvement on the part of Jordan but looking at replays on television after the game, he saw what everyone else had by now noticed.

'It looked as if the offending hand belonged to Joe Jordan,' said MacLeod, looking back months later. 'I went back into the dressing room and asked him about it. He denied handling and we never talked about the incident again. This was one of the examples of the breaks in this game of ours. It may seem unfair that we went to the World Cup partly because of one controversial refereeing decision but I believe that these things balance out at the end of a season – and perhaps if we had got some of the decisions that should have gone for us in earlier games, then this one would not have mattered.'

A bonus of £2,000 was duly delivered to MacLeod by the SFA for qualifying for Argentina. When he queried how the sum had been calculated the SFA told him that it would have been £4,000 if he had been in charge for all four World Cup qualifying games rather than only two. The money came in handy in the MacLeod household, but one key member of his family was one of the few in Scotland not totally delighted that the national team had managed to progress to the finals. 'I was a bit sorry he had qualified,' says Faye MacLeod who, as the Scotland manager's wife, was about to experience the slippery helter-skelter of celebrity after spending the bulk of her life in relative privacy.

'He'd been thrown in at the deep end,' continues Faye. 'And I thought that if he hadn't got there [to Argentina], nothing would have been said because of that. Then he would have had four years to build up a team for the next one, in Spain – and that wasn't away on the other side of the world.

'Ally just took it all in his stride when he got those successes so quickly – beating England, winning the Home International championship and qualifying for the World Cup. The trouble is, the bit more success you have, the more pressure there is on you but I don't think Ally was surprised at how well things had gone for him at the start of his management of Scotland. He always had faith in his own ability.'

Following that October qualifier with Wales, MacLeod was quietly convinced that Scotland had a side good enough to win the World Cup itself. Arthur Montford remembers watching MacLeod standing in the Scotland dressing room after the match with Wales. 'I never saw a manager looking so chuffed as he was that night,' recalls Montford. 'He had won the match to get through to the World Cup finals and no matter what else happened, he knew he would be remembered for that.'

The confidence that was coursing through the side was exemplified by the thoughts expressed immediately after the game by its opening goal-scorer Don Masson. 'We want to show the world just how well we can play,' he said. 'The draw will be important. If it favours us at all then we can go on to do what we all want to do – win the World Cup.' Such soundbites suggest that Scotland may have been brimming with over-confidence prior to Argentina but – and it was one of the many paradoxes of the time

– that over-confidence was, in fact, built on firm foundations. The vim and vigour, blended with no little skill, that had won Scotland so many matches in style during 1977 had created that expectation to win in Argentina. There had never previously been a more uniformly successful year for the Scottish national team, who ended it as Home International champions and as the first European qualifiers for the 1978 World Cup.

At that point, MacLeod reckoned that only four matches in his entire managerial career had gone exactly to plan; matches in which everything had worked to perfection. One of those games had been with Ayr United, one with Aberdeen and two with Scotland – the recent victories over Chile and Czechoslovakia. This meant that, in his own mind, half of his greatest successes as a manager had arrived within his first six months as national manager. Ally MacLeod felt he was on a roll and he had no reason to believe that it would come to a halt any time soon.

3

Prime Time

Technology and timing had seen the World Cup tournament soar to its zenith during the seventies and secure a new-found status as the greatest show on earth. The finals had never been quite as magical before the dawn of that decade, when they exploded on to the world's television screens in a glorious sunburst. Since its inception in 1930, the 1970 tournament was the first World Cup to be beamed on to televisions around the globe by satellite, and that breakthrough was matched by the quality of the football when a Brazilian team dripping with talent took the game to a level never previously witnessed in any corner of the planet. It had taken four decades for the World Cup to set the globe spinning and as if by clever design, Scotland had finally begun to produce national teams with the right to feel that they, alongside teams such as Brazil, should be centre stage at the tournament.

That 1970 World Cup in Mexico had seen Brazil become the greatest team to take the trophy up to that point. Spearheaded by Pele, the team's greatest star, and ably supported by arch-creators such as Tostao, Gerson, Rivelino and Jairzinho, the Brazilians won over the world with daring and imaginative football. Defeating Italy 4-1, they had won the trophy with football of verve and skill: swerving 'banana kicks' round defensive walls; trying to score from the halfway line; bending themselves round defenders so lithely and pliably that it seemed their limbs must be made of rubber. The vibrant gold and blue of the Brazil strip matched the vivacity of their players' style; this was football as performance art on a world stage.

Forty years after it had been initiated, the small but perfectly formed World Cup tournament, confined exclusively to sixteen nations in the finals and contested over only three weeks every four years, drew in the people of the world. Television coverage attracted not only football aficionados but also men, women and children who would rarely, if ever, venture forth to watch their local club. The spectacle of great and small nations colliding was irresistible. The World Cup had won a place in the world's heart.

The second tournament of the seventies had also seared the imagination. The four-year time interval between each World Cup allowed fresh new teams and individuals to come to the fore and give each tournament a special, distinctive character. After Mexico in 1970, played at high altitude and in high humidity, came West Germany in 1974. The character of the tournament in 1970 had been distinctly Latin. Four years later, the northern Europeans showed that they could be equally spectacular, albeit in a more understated, less flamboyant manner. Holland – absent from the finals since 1938 – took the game to a new and different level in 1974, with a style of football that looked less instinctive and more cerebral than that of the Brazilians, but that was just as prized by all who saw it.

The Dutch played a geometrically excellent form of the game described as 'total football' that demanded complete mastery of the ball from every player in every position in the team – other than goalkeeper. All Dutch defenders were expected to be composed and controlled and to have the brainpower to spur attacking movements and every player was expected to have the capability to fill in in any position on the field – attackers were expected to defend and vice versa. At any given point in a game a centre-half, in the Dutch system, had to be able to metamorphose into a winger, a full-back into a centre-forward. Players in every position had to know how to switch roles with their team mates, instantaneously. Total football proved effective and charismatic; players such as Johan Cruyff and Johan Neeskens, with a colourful array of skills, put flesh on the bones of the tactics. Few outside the host nation were anything other than distraught when the Dutch streaked all the way to the final in sumptuous style, only to lose 2-1 to the ever-efficient Germans.

The momentum built up in Mexico and Germany ensured that the third World Cup tournament of the decade was anticipated with enormous eagerness around the world, nowhere more so than in Scotland, whose national team would feature in the finals for a fourth time and who appeared to have a better chance than ever before of making a serious impact on the festival of world football.

Prior to the seventies Scotland had had a less than genial relationship with the World Cup. It had been impossible for Scotland to feature in the finals during the thirties because the Scottish Football Association, along with the Football Association of England, had resigned in 1928 from the Fédération Internationale de Football Association (FIFA), the governing body of the world game, as a result of disagreements between both sides. The British nations, as the founders of the game, possessed a rather haughty attitude that made it hard for them to rub along with their continental counterparts – especially as the Frenchman Jules Rimet had upstaged the Brits in coming up with the idea of the World Cup.

The Scots rejoined FIFA in 1946 and the first World Cup for which they were eligible to qualify was the 1950 tournament in Brazil. FIFA, generously acknowledging the importance of the British game, were willing to allow the top two in the 1950 Home International championship – which comprised Scotland, England, Northern Ireland and Wales – to advance to the finals. Scotland finished second to England but the SFA had decided that Scotland would only travel to Brazil if they were Home International champions. English players pleaded with their Scottish counterparts to ask the SFA for a change of mind but that august body was not for turning.

Farce followed upon farce when Scotland did eventually reach the finals, held in Switzerland in 1954. Rangers questioned the legality of the SFA taking their players off for the several weeks required for them to compete in the World Cup and the club worried about 'indoctrination' in terms of the different training methods and tactics that their players would receive during their time with Scotland. Rangers deliberately timed a tour of Canada to clash with the World Cup, ensuring that the national team could not field any of the club's players.

The SFA then told Scotland manager Andy Beattie that he could select a squad of only thirteen, when other nations were taking along the full complement of twenty-two players. Even allowing for the fact that they did things differently in those days, it is deeply puzzling to ponder the SFA's thinking on this matter. If Scotland were travelling as serious competitors it meant that, if they were to reach the final, those thirteen players were expected to remain fully fit, fresh and uninjured for almost a month of football and half-a-dozen fixtures against some of the most accomplished nations in the world game; Uruguay, the world champions, were in Scotland's group in 1954.

The Scottish 'squad' contained only one goalkeeper and one player for each position plus Bobby Johnstone, a winger, and Bobby Evans, a midfield player, as cover. Pleas were made to the SFA to reconsider their decision but they responded that they had already had their final meeting of the 1953-54 season and could not have another one, even if there was a World Cup on the horizon.

It was perhaps just as well that few Scots would witness their team's efforts in the 1954 tournament, either in person or on television. The growth of television would go hand in hand with the growth in popularity of the World Cup but in the mid-fifties it was available only to the well heeled. At that time an Ekcovision receiver with a fifteen-inch screen and 'spot-the-wobble' picture-and-sound control cost around £80, a sum far beyond the reach of workers waged mostly at only a few pounds per week. In post-war Britain, even in the mid-fifties, basic items such as food remained rationed and money was tight. The few who did have access to the small screen were to find that coverage of Scotland's matches was limited in the extreme: anyone tuning in to the only available channel, the BBC, at six o'clock on the evening of 16 June 1954, hoping to watch Scotland's first ever World Cup finals fixture – against Austria – was presented with France versus Yugoslavia, one of four World Cup fixtures that kicked off simultaneously that night. Radio – much more accessible to people in the fifties – also failed to broadcast any live commentary on that first fixture.

Those back in Scotland awaiting the occasional bulletin on the progress of their side could seek 'reassurance' in the words of Tam Reid, chairman of the Scottish selection committee, the group of SFA men who picked the team and then presented it to the manager. As the Scottish team prepared to face an Austrian side that was among those favoured to win the World Cup, Reid explained, 'Our forwards have been instructed to go all out for an early goal, knowing from experience that the continentals don't like to have to fight back. Special emphasis has been laid on the necessity of hard, but always fair tackling. This should knock some of the funny notions out of the heads of the Austrians.' It did not take a university professor to interpret exactly what he meant.

The match resulted in a 1-0 victory for Austria but Scotland did play exceptionally well, leading Andy Beattie to state how proud he was with 'the spirit of the whole eleven'. Two days later, on the eve of the team's second group match with Uruguay, a less happy Beattie – troubled by repeated interference in his work from SFA officials, and now having fallen out with his players – announced that he would be resigning as manager. Beattie remained in place for the Uruguay match and on a blisteringly hot afternoon in Basle the Scottish national team promptly suffered the worst defeat in its history to date: a 7-0 thrashing at the hands of the reigning world champions.

Such a series of events might have been expected to chasten a nation but when Scotland qualified for the 1958 finals in Sweden Willie Allan, the SFA secretary, was moved to say: 'I don't think the final itself is beyond us.' Matt Busby, manager of Manchester United, had been, in mid-January, appointed Scotland manager for that year's tournament but sadly, only three weeks later, Busby was so severely injured in the tragic Munich Disaster which befell his club on 5 February 1958, that he would be unable to make the journey to Sweden in June.

The SFA did not appoint another manager in his place; instead of the great Busby, Dawson Walker, the squad's trainer, was put in charge of World Cup preparation in the weeks prior to the tournament. Once in Sweden, he cobbled together matchday plans with team captain Tommy Younger, while squad members such as Archie Robertson and Johnny Coyle were despatched to watch the forth-coming opposition. The Scots opened with a 1-1 draw against Yugoslavia but that would be their only World Cup finals point of the fifties. They lost their subsequent group fixtures, to Paraguay and then France.

Again, the Scots had limped from the tournament largely out of sight of the nation. On the night of Scotland's second fixture, a 3-2 defeat by the Paraguayans, the live match broadcast for television viewers in Scotland was England's 0-0 draw with Brazil. The concluding match in Scotland's group had been an exciting encounter with France that the Scots had to win if they were to progress and in which they fought hard before succumbing to a 2-1 defeat. It was a match made for engaging television viewing; except that that Sunday afternoon Scottish viewers were instead treated to the 0-0 draw between Sweden and Wales. Two days after the Scotland-France match, early evening viewers were treated to just twenty minutes of highlights from it.

The overall lack of television coverage and the prohib-itive cost of travel to countries such as Sweden and Switzerland meant that the impact of those results in the fifties was greatly diminished. The Home Internationals and, especially, the annual clash with England were of much greater significance to those who made up the great swaying masses at important Scotland matches at Hampden. The fans could actually see those games.

A marvellous crop of Scottish players was to strut the world stage during the sixties – but not with Scotland. Players such as Jimmy Johnstone and Tommy Gemmell helped Celtic sweep to the European Cup in cavalier fashion; Willie Henderson and Jim Baxter helped Rangers reach European finals; Billy Bremner and Eddie Gray won European trophies and English titles with Leeds United, as did Dave Mackay with Tottenham Hotspur; Denis Law of Manchester United was named European Footballer of the Year. The Scottish national team, though, was still picked by SFA selectors and while that alone would have been enough to make the national side's progress a haphazard one, the very niggardly, petty and provincial nature of those in charge made it doubly hard for success to come Scotland's way.

Having travelled to watch players in action in England during the sixties, SFA selectors would put them forward for the national squad not on the basis of how they had played but on how good the hospitality had been at White Hart Lane, Anfield, Old Trafford or whichever other English club ground they had visited. A succession of anodyne managers aided and abetted them and when the SFA did persuade Jock Stein, the outstanding Scottish manager of the sixties, to take the post on a part-time basis while still manager of Celtic, he chafed against the actions of the selection committee during his six months in charge.

Stein was astonished, on away trips, to witness how much alcohol was downed by some members of the SFA and discipline was lax – players would book their friends into the team hotel on away trips. Stein recalled hearing one selector tell some players that he had been personally responsible for their selection, while another told the fine midfielder Bobby Murdoch that he was 'lucky to be in the party'. The World Cups of 1962, '66 and '70, unsurprisingly, evaded the Scots and their merry band of officials.

By the time Scotland next qualified, in 1974, the entire tournament was decidedly different to the one they had last experienced, and it would generate unprecedented interest in the national team. The nation was now firmly entrenched in the television age – the hazy, black-and-white sets that had seen service through the fifties and sixties were rapidly being replaced by bigger screens and, most importantly, colour transmission had been introduced in late 1967. The nation was hooked on the flirtatious flickerings. Many now felt that watching television coverage was almost as good as being at a match and, with this, the World Cup came into its own at a time when there were few live football games of any description on British television.

This sparse diet of football for the armchair viewer was broken in spectacular style with each World Cup, when an orgy of live football dominated the world's small screens leaving, by the end of the tournament, even the most fanatical devotee entirely satiated.

The Scottish team was no longer the spectre at the feast and in 1974 every minute of each of their matches was transmitted live and in colour, with key incidents replayed, analysed, highlighted and pored over by that new invention, 'the panel of experts'; a group of professional footballers and managers specially selected to sit in a television studio and say the first words that bounced into their heads before the match, at half time and afterwards. The band of Scottish footballers who had gathered just one point from five games in the more gracious fifties must have breathed a collective sigh of relief that they had not been victims of such cruel, unbending scrutiny.

The Scottish squad of 1974 went to Germany with great good wishes from those at home but the team had been absent from the top level for so long that no one knew quite what to expect from them once they got there. 'There was none of this, "Oh, we're going to bring the cup back," sort of stuff,' says Hugh Allan, physiotherapist with the 1974 squad. The Scots' first opponents, the

African representatives Zaire, were expected to be beaten easily but Scotland would then be plunged into an encounter with Brazil, the holders, and would conclude their group with a match against the 'Brazilians of Europe', Yugoslavia – ever-talented and inventive but who had made the finals only after a play-off against Spain. For the Scots, however, it was enough just to be there, at those finals. England had missed out but any temptation for the Scots to gloat, or to celebrate too much in advance of the tournament, was held back by the ominous presence in Scotland's group of world champions Brazil – and by the low-key attitude of Willie Ormond, the Scotland manager.

Matters did not proceed entirely smoothly. Denis Law, Billy Bremner and Jimmy Johnstone, senior professionals all, were difficult for the manager to control and Johnstone and Bremner both risked being sent home after incidents involving extreme drunkenness. 'These incidents were a bit unfortunate,' says Sandy Jardine, a fellow member of that squad, 'but one of the benefits that did come out of it was that it helped to form a bond and we got closer together; whether they helped the results or not is difficult to say.'

Disagreements over sponsorship affected the entire squad and saw players scraping the white stripes off their boots with breakfast knives because of a dispute over payments from kit manufacturers. Despite these drawbacks momentum grew during that World Cup. Scots supporters, engaged by what they saw from their team on television, abandoned jobs mid-tournament to high-tail it to West Germany and cheer on the players. The players, in turn, did well enough to become the first national team to be eliminated from a World Cup finals while still unbeaten, exiting on goal difference alone.

Scotland's 0-0 draw with Brazil proved to be the high

point of their 1974 World Cup experience. This was the most significant result the national team had ever achieved against non-British opposition – and they should have won, indeed could have won if they had been less tentative, shown less stand-offishness and respect for the world champions. The narrow margin of elimination left Scots despairing at the hard hand of fate.

If they had scored more than two goals against Zaire, rather than easing off and holding on to the lead, they might have taken care of the goal difference problem . . . If Billy Bremner's shot from inches out hadn't trickled just wide of the post against Brazil . . . If Zaire hadn't conceded a crucial, late, late, third goal to Brazil while the Scots were drawing 1-1 with the Yugoslavs . . . A feeling spread that Scotland had underestimated their ability and that by the time they realised they had the talent to hold their own at the World Cup the damage that would result in their early elimination had already been done.

'We were the better team against Brazil and drew 1-1 with Yugoslavia, who were a great team,' recalls Sandy Jardine, who had been at right-back for Scotland in all three of their matches. 'So, all in all, we were a wee bit unfortunate that we didn't progress in the tournament. In many ways, we came back from the World Cup glorious failures.'

That glorious failure was, though, enough to draw 10,000 people to Glasgow airport to welcome home the squad and it meant that when Scotland did qualify for the 1978 finals there was a sense that this time they could not be so unlucky. Having shown in 1974 that they could hold their own on the world stage, they were expected to progress further.

It was the English who laid down the rules of football in the late 19th century but it was the Scots who had added real heart and spirit and flesh to its bones for the best part of the subsequent one hundred years. English clubs sent scouts north to scour Scotland for talent and were rarely disappointed: they had taken Scots south in droves down the decades and the story remained the same throughout the seventies. No self-respecting English team could go about its business without several Scots to add flair and inventiveness to English craftsmanship.

Nottingham Forest, the Football League champions and League Cup winners in the season preceding the 1978 World Cup, relied heavily on the Scots Kenny Burns, Archie Gemmill, John Robertson, John O'Hare and John McGovern. European champions Liverpool had Alan Hansen, Graeme Souness and Kenny Dalglish. FA Cup winners Ipswich Town fielded George Burley and John Wark. With all this high-achieving talent at the top level there seemed no reason for Scotland to founder on lack of self belief, or to doubt that they could challenge for the World Cup itself. Several of those trophy-winners in England – Wark, Burley, Hansen, McGovern and O'Hare – would even be allowed to proceed unhindered on their 1978 summer holidays because so many layers of talent were available to Scotland.

In England, Scottish players were hugely prized for an almost fanatical will to win that was equalled only, and almost contrarily, by their great natural inventiveness in achieving that end. This combination of Caledonian imagination and aggression was something that the English could not match and it seemed, in 1978, as though the wider world might just be about to wake up in wonderment at the qualities of the Scottish footballer.

No other nation could field the finest striker in Europe – Kenny Dalglish – who had proven his status by scooping the ball over the flailing body of Birger Jensen, the Bruges goalkeeper, to score the winning goal in the 1978 European Cup final. Graeme Souness, a midfield player in the Scotland squad, had provided the pass for Dalglish to display his brilliance and Souness was not even guaranteed a place in the Scotland midfield.

The Scots also featured in their squad the most expensive of all British footballers, Gordon McQueen of Manchester United, who had been transferred from Leeds United to Manchester United for £450,000 in February 1978. One month earlier Joe Jordan, McQueen's Scotland team mate, had also moved from Leeds to Manchester United for a then record fee of £350,000, which had been broken days later when Souness switched from Middlesbrough to Liverpool for £352,000. Martin Buchan and Lou Macari were also at Manchester United, Europe's biggest and most popular club. Rangers, winners of the 'treble' in Scotland, provided Derek Johnstone, Sandy Jardine and Tom Forsyth. Nottingham Forest's Burns, Gemmill and Robertson also made the squad. Burns had been elected Footballer of the Year by football writers in England. It seemed a formidable group and one that in terms of its players' achievements could be rivalled only by the Dutch among the European nations heading for the 1978 finals. 'I thought we were capable of getting into the next stage of the tournament,' says Jardine. 'After '74 you were optimistic and excited by the possibilities.'

Bookmakers, the supposed barometers of sobriety, stability and sense in a fickle sporting world, certainly seemed to think Scotland could live up to the hype that was as inseparable from their 1978 tilt at the World Cup as the froth on a cappuccino. Those stone-visaged assessors of reality appeared to have been carried away on the tide of wild words issuing forth from the mouth of Ally MacLeod. Ladbrokes had the Scots at a mere 8-1 to lift the trophy on 25 June. Only Brazil, three times winners, Argentina, the hosts, and West Germany, twice winners and the holders, were rated as having a better chance.

There was some logic in this: there were no clear favourites for the 1978 World Cup and no team had shone extraordinarily brightly in the months and years preceding it. Argentina was a major footballing nation but their team's form in major competitions had been patchy: they had finished winless and bottom of their second-phase group at the 1974 finals. Brazil seemed still to be resting on their reputation from 1970 and, as in their approach to the game in '74, seemed to have traded, at a considerable loss, beauty for the boot. Germany, the holders, had lost from the 1974 side the two greatest players in their history: the magisterial captain, Franz Beckenbauer, and the chunky striker, Gerd Muller. The Dutch would be without Johan Cruyff, their matchless creator and captain, and Wim van Hanegem, their most inventive midfield player. France, Hungary and Spain were dipping their toes in World Cup waters for the first time since 1966; the Austrians had been absent since 1954. Poland and Sweden had done well in 1974 but neither could field an array of talented achievers to match those available to Scotland. Italy might creep under the radar but they had been ordinary at international and club level after reaching the 1970 final. It was a World Cup that looked open enough for a new team to come through and capture the imagination of onlookers around the world – the type of open field that the Dutch had swept into in 1974. Joao Havelange, president of FIFA, and a Brazilian, had, for one, believed that Argentina would face Scotland in the final.

That the 1978 World Cup would be staged in Argentina, a country often referred to by its own people as 'the end of the world', did little to deflect Ally MacLeod from his belief that the Scots could land the trophy. No European nation had ever won a World Cup held in the Americas but MacLeod believed that the breakthrough for the Europeans might just come in Argentina. And, compared to Mexico where in 1970 altitude and humidity had hampered the European sides, Argentina was much further south so it would be midwinter there in June.

In May, before leaving Scotland for Argentina, MacLeod had been sent, courtesy of a television station, a selection of tapes of teams involved in the World Cup. Ally had watched one tape repeatedly, that of the friendly international played in Hamburg between West Germany and Brazil, and had been deeply impressed, seeing something different in the game every time. 'Still,' he concluded, 'after all these hours of football-watching, studying the best the rest of the world has to offer, I've gone to bed in the small hours convinced that we are just as skilful, just as fast, just as sure in the tackle as any of them. I remain utterly certain that in possession we are much less predictable than any of them.'

It may have been this that helped prompt MacLeod, on the eve of the Home Internationals in May 1978, to say of the trio of matches with England, Northern Ireland and Wales, 'I will be looking upon the tournament in the same way as a world heavyweight champion warming up for a title fight, sparring against a few unknowns. You can mark down the twenty-fifth of June 1978 as the day Scottish football conquers the world. For on that Sunday I'm convinced the finest team this country has ever produced can play in the final of the World Cup in Buenos Aires and win.

'We have the talent. We have the temperament and the ambition and the courage. All that stands between us and the crown is the right kind of luck. I'm so sure we can do

it that I give my permission here and now for the big celebration on the twenty-fifth of June to be made a national
festival; a national Ally-day.'

The unorthodoxy that was so habitually employed by
MacLeod even extended to the manner in which he told
players that spring that they had been chosen to represent Scotland in the World Cup finals. Joe Harper recalls
the unusual circumstances in which he was told of his
selection. 'We were at a dinner in the Albany Hotel in
Glasgow,' says Harper, 'a black-tie do, and Ally was
speaking at it. He had just finished and I had gone to the
toilet. He came in behind me, there were a lot of people
there, and he said, "How are you doing?" I said to him
that his speech had been quite funny; because he was a
funny man.

'He said to me, "You can't tell the press but I want you
to go and phone your mum and dad." I said, "What do
you mean?" He said, "Phone them and tell them you're
going to Argentina." I was elated. I came out of there
bouncing although I wasn't allowed to say anything to
anybody. Needless to say, the next day it was all over the
paper.'

After the opening 1978 Home International, a 1-1 draw
with Northern Ireland in front of a crowd of almost 65,000,
MacLeod told his players that too many of them had been
lacking commitment; their minds seemed already to be on
Argentina. That game, in which he used the two large,
aerially dangerous players Derek Johnstone and Joe Jordan
as his pairing in attack, also convinced MacLeod that he
could not use such a partnership in the World Cup, even
though Johnstone had headed a neat goal. Scotland's slack
performance had not been received warmly by the crowd
at a packed Hampden but Ally remained upbeat in the
only way he knew how. 'I know the supporters want wins

and not experiments,' he had said, 'but if we come back from Argentina with that gold cup, everything will be forgotten.'

The next match, a Wednesday evening encounter with Wales at Hampden, attracted another attendance of more than 60,000 and an element of comedy was introduced to the proceedings. With seconds remaining and Scotland 1-0 ahead thanks to another fine headed goal from Johnstone, Jim Blyth – in goal for Scotland – could only watch helplessly as his left-back, Willie Donachie, swept the ball past him into his own goal in the final minute of the match. On top of that, Scotland lost Gordon McQueen after thirty-three minutes. Attempting to make a clearance close to his goal line, the defender stood on the ball and took a tumble that sent him crashing into one of the sturdy wooden goalposts at Hampden, injuring his knee in the process. Again, the lament was sounded for another patchy performance and again MacLeod remained confident. Once the Home Internationals were over he and his players would be spending a few days relaxing at home prior to heading off to Argentina and MacLeod would, he said, be using the time to carry out some necessary home improvements; 'I'm putting in a new corner unit to hold the World Cup.'

Three days after the draw with Wales, a crowd of 88,000 watched Scotland play England off the park in the final Home International but still lose 1-0 to a goal from winger Steve Coppell. MacLeod, with characteristic insouciance, immediately dubbed Coppell 'the invisible man' for his lack, in MacLeod's opinion, of a clear contribution to the match other than scoring his side's goal. The Scottish fans, long practised at identifying a moral victory when they saw one, remained behind for twenty-five minutes afterwards, stamping feet, singing, swaying like a field of wheat in the wind, waiting for the players to re-emerge from the dressing room to salute them. Eventually, the players and their manager did so – they could hardly disappoint such a persistent crowd.

Immediately after the Home Internationals MacLeod admitted that he was worried about the lack of goals from his team as he contemplated leaving for Argentina on the back of three matches that had been deeply disappointing; not least in that they had concluded with England seizing the British championship at Hampden Park. Yet his incorrigible optimism still surfaced unerringly, 'We go with this warning to England. Enjoy your reign as champions because we want our title back next year. We fancy the Home International trophy will look well at Park Gardens even if it could be dwarfed by the World Cup.'

The Scotland squad had been billeted at Dunblane Hydro, in central Scotland, during the Home Internationals and in preparation for the World Cup. While there an element of restlessness began to creep in that would not lift entirely from the squad over the forthcoming May and June weeks.

'I felt the mood among the players was very good when we first went to Dunblane,' says John Hagart, 'but I kind of felt that Ally was always leaving them to their own devices. I don't mean that they could go anywhere they wanted but I would maybe say, "What about going down to the fields today and having a wee head tennis tournament because it will take up a bit of time?"

'Football players are just like any other bunch of young lads. If they're not being occupied and they've not got things to occupy them, even things they're not awfully keen on, they get bored – get looking at the telly, get one Coca-Cola, another Coca-Cola, start eating too much – and I felt we didn't do enough on that. I would be wanting to get in among them and Ally would say, "No, just leave them to their own devices. They're all international players."'

MacLeod himself found plenty to do at Dunblane. When they were not with their players, other managers might retire to their room to read, or have a quiet chat with their staff, but that was not Ally's style. He would be found lingering, looking for company, under the chandeliers in the hotel's expansive public rooms, or hovering at the foot of the main staircase inside the hotel, ready to engage in small talk with anyone he might meet. A busload of douce wee women from a church women's guild in Glasgow or Edinburgh or Stirling would stop in at Dunblane Hydro for a fish tea or afternoon coffee, only to be met and greeted by none other than the towering figure of Ally MacLeod, the Scottish national team manager, standing inside the vestibule and welcoming them all as they entered the hotel. The manager of the hotel would muse that he ought really to employ Ally as his PR man. Hundreds of fans also descended on Dunblane every day and although the players gladly signed autographs, it helped create an atmosphere that was rarely restful.

Even those inside the SFA were swept away by the mood of the country – the euphoria, all the more exotic and irresistible for being so alien to the normally cautious Scottish character, had managed to seep into the Association's traditionally staid corridors of power. Ernie Walker, who had been appointed secretary of the SFA in July 1977, found himself trying to hold on to a firework of a manager as he settled into his new post, but he could do little to prevent MacLeod's declarations of intent with regard to bringing the World Cup to Scottish shores for the first time. 'He wouldn't say that sitting round the table with the international committee, naturally,' says

Walker, 'although maybe, at that time, we would all have said, "You're bloody right."'

'It's an absurd way to behave before anything has happened at a World Cup finals,' Walker continues. 'There was, though, a sort of general acceptance in the country that Ally was leading his Tartan Army and that the ball was rolling so much in our favour that the whole thing was permitted. I accept that I should have been intervening but it's easy looking back. You have to know the feeling of the time.'

No fewer than nineteen players had been used by MacLeod in the 1978 Home Internationals and in the light of such experimentation the draws with the Irish and Welsh did not look so bad. As evidenced by the reception for the side after the England match, the fans had been wholly convinced of the talents of their team and its manager and remained so as the squad dispersed for their few days at home before regrouping for the great Argentinian adventure.

'He [Ally] didn't value the Home Internationals because we were going to the World Cup,' says Joe Harper, one of the few members of the Scotland squad who did not feature in any of those three games. 'It was a case of he wanted to get his best team and he knew his best team.

'I was never going to be there rather than Kenny Dalglish; Kenny was a great player, a superb player. So Kenny was fine. He didn't need to try anybody out for Kenny, he just needed to have somebody who would be able to come in for Kenny, if necessary, and he took me for that. Whereas Joe Jordan and Derek he wasn't too sure about. What was the best formula? He knew very well that Derek and Joe together was not a formula because they were both going for virtually the same balls. So he then picked Joe as his main man.'

Hugh Allan – the physiotherapist worked with MacLeod throughout his tenure as Scotland manager – was quietly concerned by MacLeod's belligerent and repeated boasts that Scotland would return with the greatest football trophy on earth. 'That worried me a bit I've got to say, because I think, deep down, everybody had the feeling that he was talking a lot of rubbish, as it were.

'I don't, though, think it did any harm. I don't think it got through to the players that they were going to win the World Cup just because Ally had said so. I think they were well aware of the tough matches they had to play.'

Back in Aberdeen, where MacLeod had made such a meteoric impact – as much through his eloquent effusiveness as through his team's achievements on the field of play – Willie Miller, who had played for him there, was nonplussed to hear the things that Ally was promising the nation. Since MacLeod had become Scotland manager Miller had been monitoring with interest how Ally's gift for attracting publicity through provocative promises would unfold on the larger stage. Miller was unsurprised to hear Ally say Scotland would win the World Cup. 'That's Ally,' says Miller. 'I knew him and had worked with him. He was a nice guy, with a nice personality, but you obviously get concerned when he starts saying things like that.

'I was concerned that people would take it seriously. I think it was a case of him again aiming for the stars and if he falls short, then it depends how short he falls, and where the success comes in. If they [Scotland] had got qualification for the next round, then maybe that would be success. My concern was if people were going to believe him and then he didn't deliver.

'Dealing with stronger players might have been difficult for him, the man-management of these players. You've got to look at the strength of the characters that he had – players such as Derek Johnstone, Archie Gemmill, Kenny Burns, Bruce Rioch. I was in and out of Scotland squads at that time and I trained with them, I listened to them, I played with them, and they were all highly acclaimed individuals, playing with big clubs, and Ally hadn't had too much experience of dealing with that type.

'So with Ally saying some of the things that he said, you would just anticipate that there would be certain questions posed to him from these strong characters and I always assumed that it would be a test for Ally. I think it would be unusual for them to be working with a manager like him. We didn't have too many big names like them at Aberdeen; we were a young team with players in the early stages of their football careers.'

Intriguingly, shortly before the Scottish squad's departure for Argentina, and unbeknown to Scottish supporters primed for World Cup success, a tempting alternative job offer had been made to MacLeod. Rangers had parted company with Jock Wallace, their gruff sergeant-major-style manager, and wanted MacLeod as his replacement.

'He was offered a lot of jobs, including the Rangers job,' says Faye MacLeod, 'but because he had just taken on Scotland, he turned it down. That's the way the cookie crumbles. As Ally said, you make what you think is the right decision at the time. He toyed with it because he would have loved to have been the Rangers manager but he felt he would have been letting the country down if he had taken it – because of the euphoria and all the rest of it.'

Faye, more than most, was aware of the degree to which Ally's extreme outbursts had pushed him into an extreme situation. 'When he left to go to Argentina,' she recalls, 'his last words to me were, "I'll either come back a hero or a villain." The pressure was on.'

4 Song And Dance Men

Fantasists and freaks populated television's *Top of the Pops* throughout the seventies so it was inevitable that a representative of Scotland's 1978 World Cup effort would make it on to the show. That man was Andy Cameron, who in March that year generously shared a key part of his Scottish-working-man's-club act with a bemused British nation. Cameron's contribution to popular music involved him careering, in full Scotland strip, around a stage in a studio packed with baffled teenagers, yelling the ditty:

'Hey, we're on the march wi' Ally's Army/We're going to the Argentine/And we'll really shake them up/When we win the World Cup/For Scotland are the greatest football team . . .'

Later in the tune Cameron would taunt those same awkward English teenagers – who were having enough trouble trying to find a way to bop to his pop – with the line, 'And England cannae do it 'cos they didnae qualify'; which would have been great if his audience had, first, been paying any real attention to his lyrics and, second, had been able to decipher the cement-mixer, West of Scotland accent in which he battered out his relentlessly-paced marching song.

The audience's innate indifference to any rebellious or nationalistic Scottish message was underlined by the dutiful round of lukewarm applause from the teens as Cameron's tune drew to an end. To those youngsters craning their necks to see if Billy Idol could be spotted anywhere in the Manchester studio, Cameron was just the latest in a long line of novelty acts on the show; entertainers who emphasised the often-overlooked music hall roots of British popular music: his predecessors during the seventies included Clive Dunn of *Dad's Army* with his song *Grandad*, Benny Hill with *Ernie (The Fastest Milkman In The West)* and Rolf Harris with *Two Little Boys*.

If in the opening half of 1978 Ally MacLeod was presiding over a six-month-long festival of Scotch kitsch, Andy Cameron was its shaman, putting to music the message that MacLeod was drip drip dripping to the nation: Scotland were going to steamroller any opposition bold enough to face them in Argentina and fulfil their destiny of taking the trophy; P.S. don't worry about the detail. Cameron's song took the story beyond the black and white reportage of the sports pages, helped to illustrate the message colourfully and drew in the population as a whole, broadening the appeal of the venture beyond football: the message was that the great, upcoming sporting triumph, under Ally, would be fun all the way.

Sporadic brushes with show business had helped to prime Ally MacLeod for his limelight time. In the early sixties, he had visited the London Palladium with the Blackburn squad and participated in Bruce Forsyth's *Beat the Clock* show, which had achieved nationwide fame on television as a precursor to *The Generation Game*. Ally had been happy to be the Blackburn Rovers' player put forward, with his wife Faye, as one of the couples who would take the stage. The young Bruce Forsyth had plenty of opportunity during the MacLeods' stint to practise turning to the audience with his look of frozen mock-horror and disbelief.

The MacLeods' first challenge was for Ally to squeeze Faye into a telephone box to burst four balloons, each of which contained a one-pound note. In his enthusiasm at bundling Faye into the box Ally became so exuberant that he pushed the telephone box, with Faye in it, over on to its side. The balloons duly burst but Ally could locate only three one-pound notes and when he tried to add a note from his own pocket to make up the quartet he was caught by Forsyth who, again, feigned shock at the craziness he was witnessing. Husband and wife then had to play for a thousand-pound jackpot by manipulating a snooker table surface to manoeuvre balls into side pockets, with a thirty-second countdown ringing in their ears. Frustrated at their lack of success and inability to beat the clock Ally eventually slammed the plaything hard on to the stage floor, for which he received enormous applause from the audience; but also what now appeared to be genuinely disapproving looks from Forsyth.

Neither was Ally unfamiliar with the showbiz-tinged eccentricity of promoters by then intruding on the game of football itself. When he was on tour with Hibernian in Czechoslovakia during the early sixties an oversized model clock was wheeled into the centre circle during a match – the clock was being used to promote a cycle race planned to end at the same time as the football match. The players were told simply to get on with the game and play around the clock; it is not recorded whether additional time was added on for stoppages. On the same tour, a parachutist – part of the ongoing entertainment programme – landed in the centre circle during a match and again the players were told to continue with the game.

On accepting the Scotland job on a relatively modest salary for such a prestigious post, MacLeod had been told by SFA officials that he should use his status as manager to earn himself some extra cash. 'I'm sure those words came back to haunt a few people in high football places in the exciting months ahead,' reflected Ally, when the dust had settled and he was looking back on those days. In early 1978, though, he was on a magic carpet ride.

Carpets had already featured in Ally's career when, as a player at Blackburn, he had suffered a knee injury – he used cabbage poultices to help heal it – after helping a friend lay one. This time, though, he was using his popularity as Scotland manager to advertise carpets, and reaping a larger and more enjoyable financial reward by doing so. Ally's promotional work found him sitting cross legged on a rug, doing his best to look like an Argentinian gaucho. He was wearing a poncho and a sombrero, holding a pistol in his right hand and showing a smile that looked slightly more sheepish than usual. 'Any man that can sell five million carpets to the nation can get a football team playing for him,' jokes Willie Johnston.

The Scotland manager also appeared on Radio Clyde as a disc jockey. This diversion came naturally to the chirpy MacLeod who, again while he was at Blackburn, had been approached by a woman who wanted to train him as a stand-up comedian – she had thought his mannerisms and way of putting things over ideal for the job. Now, twenty years down the line, Radio Clyde listeners were being treated to the raw talent that woman had spotted. During his stint with the radio station MacLeod was asked on air if he hated the English. 'Hate them?' he had responded. 'I detest them.'

Gravitas was clearly not Ally's bag; not for him the image of football manager as chess grandmaster, spending hours poring over tactical formations. That anti-English outburst on radio prompted the Scottish press to question whether it was suitable for a World Cup manager to be donning headphones on a populist radio station and making such outlandish statements. Although those anti-English words may have been lapped up by some of the more rabid members of Ally's Tartan Army, they were used in utterly light-hearted fashion by MacLeod as simply another excuse for a joke. Ally and his wife had, in fact, made good friends among the English people they had encountered during MacLeod's five years with Blackburn. The couple had thoroughly enjoyed their time in England, and they had godchildren there. MacLeod had even been on the verge of going into a business partnership with David Whelan, a team mate at Blackburn, but had decided against it at the last minute. Whelan, as it turned out, would go on to build up the JJB Sports business and would eventually own Wigan Athletic FC; he helped guide them into the FA Premier League in 2005, by which time he was worth an estimated £235 million. 'Ally wasn't anti-English,' says Faye MacLeod. 'I don't think he was anti-anybody to be perfectly honest. His was not that kind of nature.'

The former pharmaceutical sales rep was in his element in early 1978, enlivening the quiet months between Scotland's qualification and the beginning of the World Cup. 'For years,' recalled Ally in a thoughtful moment after it was all over, 'the SFA had been considered a staid, stuffy kind of organisation, lacking in the razzmatazz to really sell the game.

'It seemed to me the public demanded and deserved much more and I aimed to provide it.' Ally felt that the game in Scotland required some 'drum beating' and that he was 'just the man to generate the publicity that every successful team needs'.

The continuing carnival found Faye MacLeod roped into the ring with her husband. 'They said Ally did a lot of adverts but he didn't,' she says. 'I think he did two, the carpet one and one for a video thing. When he went for the interview for the Scotland job and he mentioned the salary they said to him, "But Ally, there are all the things you can make on the side as well." Then he gets criticised for it. I did one – that's another one where he lands me in the soup. He said, "Would you do an advert?" I said, "I suppose so. What's it about?" He said, "I don't really know."

'I had to go down to London to do this advert. It was the one for the *Daily Record* and the *Sunday Mail* about shopping at the Co-op and winning tickets to go to Argentina. I had to meet this chap I had never seen in my life before who would have a paper under his arm. I felt it was like the Secret Service kind of thing. I didn't know what I was doing until I got down there.

'I'd thought I might be working with an Oxo cube or something like that. I had to say something like, "I've been to my Co-op and I've got my copy of the *Daily Record* and with a little bit of luck I'll soon be on my way to Argentina . . ." I finished the advert with this wee bit, "Just to keep my eye on Ally . . ." If I had a pound for every time someone, in the years after that, said to me, "Are you still keeping your eye on Ally?" It became my catchphrase. It was fun. I'd never done anything like that in my life before so it was another experience for me. It went over all right.'

There was more than one troubadour attached to the Scottish team who was prepared to offer vocal support to Ally and his army. Andy Cameron and his down-home blast had an international-class rival in the shape of Rod Stewart. Rod's support for the Scottish national team had first come to the fore in the mid-seventies at around the same time as he was being transformed – like a butterfly from a chrysalis – from a sincere, gritty, blues, country, rock and folk singer into an international pop star playboy. Leopard-skin outfits and pneumatic blondes now clung to his skinny form as tightly as a drowning man to his rescuer. In the midst of the glitz Rod suddenly revealed himself to be a passionate partisan for Scotland's national side and he used some of his rapidly increasing wealth to jet around the world in support of them.

Rod Stewart, born in north London to Scottish parents, had chosen to adopt their country as his own when it came to football; a hint that romantic notions of birthright lay beneath his glittering reincarnation. A poster of the time had Rod, head and blond mane tilted back, expression pawky with shirt unbuttoned to his waist, beer bottle clutched tight to his chest and a well-worn Scotland rosette pinned over his heart. This was high profile, seventies rock laddishness writ large and enlisted in the Scottish cause.

The week before the Home Internationals Rod had been in London showing his face at Tramp in Jermyn Street – the trendiest nightclub in town. Now he had helicoptered to Dunblane to sprinkle some fairy dust over Scotland's World Cup effort. In mid-May, wearing the full official 1978 Scotland World Cup strip, Rod was allowed to participate with the squad in a bounce match played in the grounds of their base at Dunblane Hydro. With his blond bouffant flopping merrily around, the singer's face showed the most serious, rapt concentration as the Scottish players pulled out of tackles and let him waltz past.

The singer had dropped out of the sky to publicise his recently released *Ole Ola* – the official Scottish World Cup song – which sounded as though it had been conceived during a raucous pub evening and then recorded at the resultant lock-in. 'Ole ole', sang Rod languorously on the record, over a cacophonous samba backbeat, 'Ole ola/ We're gonna bring that World Cup back from over tha'. The song, which boasted of the prowess Scotland would display in the tournament, featured so many promises of things to come that listeners could get a sense of what it might be like to be a pneumatic blonde pinned against the wall of some opulent nightclub whilst being propositioned by the singer. The record's B-side featured *Mammy*, which is what a lot of people were exclaiming when they heard the A-side. 'We did the record at studios in Baker Street on one day in London,' recalls squad member Bruce Rioch. MacLeod and the players had sung their part, with the manager to the fore clutching a cardboard cut-out of the talismanic Rod for support; the star would add his contribution on a separate date. The record reached number four in the UK charts during June – two places higher than Andy Cameron's *Ally's Tartan Army*.

Another visitor to Dunblane in that mad, mad May was an English schoolgirl, Tessa Robins, aged twelve, who was welcomed by the Scottish squad after winning the BBC TV *Blue Peter* competition to design a picture in support of Scotland's World Cup effort. Tessa had won with her picture of the Loch Ness monster rearing its head out of the water, wearing a tartan bunnet and spouting a speech bubble saying, 'Good luck Scotland from its secret supporter Nessie!' Alan Rough was to take the picture and place it in his goal net during matches.

A more glitzy piece of television was an advertisement that hit Britain's screens featuring various Scotland players promoting Chrysler cars. For this, the starring players, wearing full Scotland strips, headed footballs over the cars then coordinated the synchronised opening of each car's driver's door from which they leaned out, smiling. 'They both run rings round the opposition', was the slogan for this piece of commercial chicanery. Alan Rough remembers the commercial being filmed in London, on one day, at the White City Stadium: 'We had all gone down the night before and had had a good night in town – the PR company took us out for a meal. It was quite a long day. You had to get the cars in a 'V' and everybody had to come out of their car simultaneously. I thought it was quite a funny ad; it was even funnier seeing everybody coming out of the car after having been on a night out, with blood-vesselled eyes and all that sort of thing.'

An accompanying newspaper advertisement making the same claim, 'They both run rings round the opposition', showed a team of eleven Scotland players standing, arms folded, round the Chrysler Avenger, a car which looked close to inseparable from any other modest, mass-marketed family saloon of the late seventies. The car may have been of its era but on close inspection the advertisement was already dated when it hit the press at the time of the World Cup; two of the players in the picture, Arthur Graham and John Blackley, had failed to make Ally's squad. Blackley had not played for Scotland during Ally MacLeod's time as manager and Graham had just one substitute appearance for Scotland to his name, against East Germany in September 1977.

'There were tons of other things,' says Rough. 'Like opening things, appearing at bookies, and a lot of wee Umbro appearances in sports shops because Umbro were our kit manufacturers. That kind of stuff. We had a pool; everything went into the pool. The divvy at the end of it? You'd be lucky if it was a thousand pounds each.'

It was reported that the Scottish squad would share at least £200,000 for their commercial work, with MacLeod reputed to be on the verge of receiving £100,000. Such figures seem fanciful. The players, to a man, testify that they did not enjoy endless riches from advertising and promotional ventures.

'All this stuff in the newspapers about players earning fortunes from the World Cup was embarrassing,' says Gordon McQueen. 'Only certain players got something from the Chrysler cars advertisement because quite a few players had sponsored cars from their clubs; I had a sponsored car at Leeds United. In total, I got a few hundred pounds from the players' pool. It probably wasn't even enough to cover the cost of phone calls home from Argentina.'

Sandy Jardine has similar memories of the matter. 'Any commercial opportunities were never going to make you a fortune,' he says. 'Everybody realised that. People in the media played it up and bandied big numbers about but the players knew that was totally unrealistic. There were no major commercial opportunities.'

As if to emphasise that lack of commercial opportunity, some of the ventures in which players became involved were almost outrageously low key. While the squad was at Dunblane limbering up for the greatest show on earth, Jardine himself, Tom Forsyth and Derek Johnstone took a trip to the Polaroid products' factory in Dumbarton to be presented with a sackful of Instamatic cameras which they were to hand out to the squad so that each could keep a personal photographic record of the finals. Polaroid employee Pat Gillespie also gave them each a pair of sunglasses to assist them, so she was reported to have said, 'to put all the other teams in the shade'. The visit encapsulated how this type of promotional activity sat more easily with some players than others. As Gillespie showed the Instamatic to her visitors Jardine, a gentleman professional to the core, displayed what seemed a keen, genuine interest in the camera. Johnstone, on the other hand – the young, sometime playboy – wry grin on face and every hair of his trendy perm in perfect position, appeared to be imagining the unlikely prospect of himself and his fellow teak-hard professionals frolicking around taking souvenir snaps of each other. And Forsyth, meanwhile, was paying no attention at all to the camera and was instead issuing a cold, hard stare towards the back of the room as if he had just heard someone there describing him as a 'big Jessie' for getting involved in something like this.

The wittiest of the commercial ventures was a Heineken lager billboard advertisement featuring Joe Jordan. Heineken was running a successful advertising campaign during the seventies based around the slogan that Heineken 'reaches the parts that other beers cannot reach' and showing people achieving spectacular results through imbibing it. Jordan had lost four of his front teeth to a stray goalmouth boot after fearlessly challenging for a ball inside the penalty area, a loss on which the advertisers capitalised; their billboard cartoon pictured the player gap-toothed before downing a glass of Heineken yet after supping the beer, his four front teeth had been restored, gleaming.

A more serious matter than anything connected to the squad's advertising exploits did begin to bubble to the surface while the squad was at Dunblane. The ugly, internal dispute over team members' bonus arrangements would hover like a scowling, unwelcome gatecrasher over the Scotland squad during the forthcoming weeks. Memories of the dispute remain seared into the mind of Joe Harper and he associates one individual in particular with that episode.

'They told us what the bonuses were,' recalls Harper. 'Now, to be honest, most of us didn't listen. You weren't there to make millions of pounds and the bonuses weren't that great anyway, but they came out with the bonuses and Lou Macari came out with the statement, as far as I can remember "This is rubbish. I could make more from my fish and chip shop outside Old Trafford on a Saturday night than I can from going away for four weeks and playing for Scotland."

'Maybe that was true but if he didn't want to play for Scotland and the jersey, why go? What Kenny Dalglish got from Adidas, or whoever it was, compared to what I got was probably twenty-fold, if not more, but that didn't bother me. I was going there [to Argentina] to represent my country.

'Lou Macari said this, and that he wanted it resolved, but there wasn't anything to resolve. All Ally said to him was, "If you do the job and we get through to the next phase, you'll get what you're worth." That was it.

'We were sickened by it. Myself and Bobby Clark got up and walked out. I don't know who else came out after us but we weren't interested in listening to it. If he [Macari] was going to go and start shouting and bawling about bonuses, he could do it on his own; he certainly didn't have my backing.

'To me, it wasn't something that Ally MacLeod should have dealt with; it was something the SFA should have dealt with. They were the ones with the coffers. They were the ones charging people to go to Hampden Park and making money off it.'

Confusion reigned over the bonus issue. Ally MacLeod met with the players' committee – Bruce Rioch, Don Masson, Sandy Jardine – at Dunblane, and remembers giving them 'the broad outline of what was on offer'. The Scotland manager also 'explained why I could not be definite [about the bonus figures], in view of the tax question. It is therefore quite true that the players were still in the dark on this when we arrived [in Argentina].' The 'tax question' to which MacLeod refers was whether or not the players might legally avoid paying tax on any bonuses they would earn in Argentina.

MacLeod would later suggest that there had been a lack of clarity from the SFA, insisting that the SFA had told him they would investigate the possibility of the players being given tax-free payments; SFA officials cannot recall having agreed to make such an investigation. In a report to the SFA's international committee shortly after the 1978 tournament's conclusion, Ernie Walker, secretary of the SFA, did accept that the matter of bonuses had become problematical from Dunblane onwards.

'It is fair to say,' wrote Walker, 'that a measure of uncertainty relating to tax matters clouded this aspect of affairs at the time. The outcome was that whilst the committee and the administration were of the opinion that the manager had given the players the necessary details, subsequent events proved that not to be the case, as certain players, after arriving in Argentina, claimed only to have a very sketchy idea of what their rewards might be.'

That their bonuses may or may not be liable for UK tax seems to have been a sore that festered within the squad. With the high rates of income tax levied in seventies Britain, the players' bonuses would be worth considerably more to them if they could be paid exempt of UK tax. From the time when the issue was raised at Dunblane MacLeod continued to hold out hope to the players that the SFA might find a way to pay the bonuses free of tax. Those who have been employees of the SFA and who know the internal workings of that punctilious and proper organisation, suggest that it was never likely that the SFA would be party to such an arrangement, even if some sharp accountancy were to make it viable.

Lou Macari, suggested MacLeod, was particularly

disgruntled because he had turned down the chance of a short-term playing contract abroad that summer and the World Cup bonus was insignificant compared to how much he might have earned had he taken up the contract. Macari suggested to the manager that, with his rate of income tax, he would be as well giving away his bonus payments to charity if they were to be taxed.

Willie Johnston also recalls the bonus dispute and Macari's part in it, and, in common with Harper, was uninterested in its outcome: 'Mr "I get more playing for Man United" Macari,' quips Johnston. 'We could always beat Man United . . . they were hopeless. I thought that was shit. You were there to play for your country.

'I played with West Bromwich Albion; he played with Man United. Man United were a bigger club; it doesn't make you a better player. I wasn't caring about bonuses. I would have played for nothing. I had wanted to play for my country in the World Cup finals since I had been a wee boy.

'Man United were always money orientated. Lou was a professional, he wanted more money, but I didn't want to get involved. If Scotland had won the World Cup and you had got twenty thousand pounds, thirty thousand pounds or forty thousand pounds, it would have been good but that wasn't why you were there. And if you did win it, things were bound to follow on from there.' Although some of his players objected to Macari's attitude towards the question of money, MacLeod was more sympathetic and understanding of the player. The bonuses on offer were, MacLeod stated, a mere 'flea-bite' to a player of Macari's standing and MacLeod never at any time before or after the tournament lost faith in the Manchester United midfield player.

'The bonuses still weren't sorted out by the time we went

to Argentina,' states Sandy Jardine. 'We had a meeting in the training camp to try and get the thing resolved but that was badly handled as well. That should have been sorted out well before anybody set foot on a plane but it was allowed to drift, and it wasn't as if we were talking about fortunes.'

The bonus issue remained unresolved as the Scottish squad swept across the Atlantic to Argentina. For some players the matter was an irrelevance; for others it was a grudge they were nursing and keeping warm as they hit the trail for South America.

5

Political Games

Crazy coincidence saw the Scottish national team career to the forefront of international football just as a mania for Scottish nationalism took hold. Both enjoyed a dangerously potent run of power, albeit one that always seemed only one wrong move away from disaster. That only made the years of their respective successes all the more heady.

The ability of the Scotland team to strut the world stage boosted the boasts of the Scottish National Party (SNP) that the country could succeed as a politically independent nation. Success on the field, one of the few places where Scotland maintained an expressly separate identity, produced instant independence without all those messy arguments about political detail: why worry about economics or industry in the late-20th century when you could sport a banner at Wembley telling everyone to 'Remember Bannockburn – 1314'.

The Scottish team and the Scottish National Party had each begun the seventies in a state of inertia. Scotland had failed to qualify for the 1970 World Cup and Scots could only claw the stuffing out of their armchairs as England, the only British representative, battled in epic encounters with Brazil and West Germany in the suffocating heat of Mexico. The Scottish National Party was also struggling; in its thirty-six year history it had never won a seat in a General Election.

Soon, however, the fortunes of both these national institutions would change – almost in parallel. England's exit from the World Cup at the quarter-final stage (despite having been 2-0 up against the Germans) signalled a decline in their team that would last the length of the new decade, and that would dovetail – with quite amazing precision – with the rise of Scotland as the dominant British team in international football. The SNP, in June 1970 – the month of England's defeat – finally snatched its first seat at a General Election. Four years later Scottish Nationalist politicians would bask in the warm glow of the feel-good factor generated by Scotland's fine World Cup performance in the summer of 1974, and in that October's General Election their party would go on to win 30.4 per cent of the Scottish vote. That gave the SNP eleven parliamentary seats; never again would the party be so strong, although in the District Council elections in '77 – just as Ally's Army was setting out on its march – they garnered 24.2 per cent of the vote.

As a nation, Scotland had always preserved a separate identity even after the Union of the Crowns between England and Scotland in 1603 and of the Act of Union in 1707, through which Scotland would be governed from Westminster. The name Scotland may have been replaced on many maps, often military ones, with 'North Britain' during the second half of the 18th century, but a distinct and romantic identity of Scotland was constructed, nurtured and preserved through the poetry of Robert Burns, the novels of Sir Walter Scott, even the kilted, music-hall lampoonery of Harry Lauder – a predecessor, in spirit, of the raucous Andy Cameron.

The arrival of organised sport helped to crystallise further a Scottish identity and nowhere more so than in the country's national football team which, increasingly during the 20th century, became a gathering point for mass demonstrations of loyalty to Scottishness.

'It was part of the whole business of Scotland at that time,' says Margo MacDonald, an influential SNP policy maker and MP for Glasgow Govan in 1974, as she thinks back to the seventies. 'We had an explosion of performing arts in Scotland; we had *The Cheviot, The Stag and the Black Black Oil* and the 7:84 [theatre] company. All sorts of things were happening in Scotland that were positive and up and exciting in a way that they hadn't been ten years before and football was most certainly part of it.

'It's very hard to pin down the exact part that football played in it. In the SNP we used to print leaflets and stuff that made reference to the football because it was such a big part of Scottish life, Scottish social life, Scottish cultural expression. It burnished the pride in being Scottish but it didn't carry them over the hump of feeling somehow inferior or dependent on England; I'm talking about the whole of Scottish society. We'd have been independent if it had.'

Long before Ally MacLeod had become the charismatic manager of the Scottish national team, the SNP had opportunistically spotted his potential as a man around whom Scots might rally. MacLeod, in his first post as a manager at Ayr United, was already a figure who knew how to rouse people with wit, warmth, charm and humour. His wife, Faye, on welcoming Ally home of an evening, would often remonstrate gently with him that he really had gone right over the top with his latest exercise in applying Cecil B. De Mille-type showmanship to the task of trying to attract a few more faces through the creaking turnstiles of Ayr United's Somerset Park to watch the part-time players who represented the small seaside resort and market town. It says much about politics that the SNP saw a great deal to admire in Ally's expert exaggeration of his team's abilities – and that they believed such brazen braggadocio could quite easily be transferred from the rough-and-ready world of football to electioneering for a seat at Westminster.

The SNP duly asked MacLeod if he would be willing to stand as a candidate. It was a possible point of departure for MacLeod: the chance to strut around the great talking shop that is the House of Commons as one of the well-loved 'character' members of parliament with a potential nationwide audience. But MacLeod was a football man to the tips of his toes and had no strong political feelings for any party. He politely declined the Scottish National Party's opportunistic offer; he would not even so much as vote for the party during his lifetime. Margo MacDonald believes MacLeod would have made a 'rotten' politician. 'I don't think he was political,' she says, 'that wasn't his style at all. Ally wasn't a dissembler. He was upfront with everything and trusting; very trusting, I think. I think he was doing the job that he should have been doing. There's no doubt about it, he did inspire.'

Ally MacLeod may have been able to separate football from politics but for many of his countrymen the line was blurred. The discovery of oil in Scottish territorial waters in the North Sea and the arrival of the first barrels onshore in June 1975 had fuelled hopes of economic self-sufficiency and for self-government in Scotland after almost three centuries of being governed from England. The Scottish National Party stickers that appeared across the land on lamp posts and cars during the seventies claiming 'It's Scotland's Oil' never looked so fresh and radiant as on those mornings after the Scottish team had scored another of its great successes of that decade.

'The explosion of pride and self confidence started in Scotland in the seventies,' says Margo MacDonald. 'It was sufficiently removed from the World War that people were confident in thinking in national terms rather than pan-national. On top of that, the tradition of the Scots being part of the UK and feeling themselves a minority partner and somehow inferior to England was overturned when the strongest feeling – that of just being too poor, of being the fag end, being the recipient of English largesse – was turned on its head when oil was discovered, because that knocked the economic argument out of the window.

'We wanted to be independent and we could afford to be independent. The debate was carried on, really, in those terms. The debate wasn't carried on in terms that would have been understood by liberation movements elsewhere, which argued on the principle of the right to self-determination and on the sheer nobility of determining your own future, taking responsibility for yourself, having the responsibility of interacting with other sovereign bodies and so on. Our debate didn't really take that on. It was whether or not we could afford to be independent – which tells you something about Scotland.'

It is certain that the success of the Scottish national team provided a rush of energy to the SNP but it is impossible to gauge the full extent to which the party fed off of that success. During the seventies the SNP had defined itself as a left-of-centre, social democratic party and that definition allowed it to fit in with the ideas of Labour voters at the same time as proposing a nationalist agenda. By the spring of 1978, with Ally spurring on the masses in the cause of Scottish football, there was a chance to feed off the fanaticism that he had fanned among the followers of the working person's game.

At the height of that fanaticism, though – six days after the squad's send-off to Argentina at Hampden and three days before Scotland's opening World Cup match with

Peru – there was a by-election in Hamilton, contested by Margo MacDonald, who had lost her Govan seat at the 1974 General Election and gone on to become SNP vice president. With support for the national team never higher, this would be a sterling test of how far football's popularity might sway voters towards the Scottish National Party; it was estimated that MacDonald required a swing of only 4 per cent to take the seat. The impact of the 1978 World Cup in Scotland was even reflected in the day of the by-election being moved from its traditional Thursday to Wednesday 31 May, to avoid a clash with the tournament's opening game, between Poland and West Germany.

'You had to crack Lanarkshire if you were talking about independence,' says MacDonald, 'so I was adopted as the candidate and, very unexpectedly, Alex Wilson, who was the Hamilton MP, died. Now there had never been any intention that I would fight a Westminster election. The assumption was that we would have a Scottish Assembly before then. That was why I was drafted into Hamilton and that was me; I had to fight a by-election and it was a dreadful one to fight because Scotland was just collapsing into itself. De-industrialisation had started, only most people weren't willing to call it that.

'What people didn't realise was that the ground had already started shifting and it was shifting towards Margaret Thatcher and Thatcherism. On top of that, the SNP made a very, very stupid tactical decision and that was not to back the nationalisation of a part of the shipyards, just to keep them open, on the Clyde. The reason they decided not to was that every nationalisation in the UK had been followed by a rationalisation, which meant that jobs had been transferred out of Scotland; what the SNP had wanted was a Scottish shipbuilding corporation. The SNP were painted as anti-trade union, anti-nationalisation and in those days that meant anti-Scottish. So the SNP had started going down the slope.'

MacDonald won a third of the vote, of which she was proud, but lost the by-election to George Robertson and Labour. The Ally MacLeod effect, at its height, had not been sufficient to divert the current of opinion in Scotland towards the SNP just when it needed it most. The sense of patriotism and the feeling of independence that surrounded the national football team and that appeared to have caught almost everyone, young and old, in its wake was not strong enough to exert influence once people had taken off their tartan scarves and were standing soberly in the ballot box. The only thing likely to change that would be Ally carrying home the World Cup itself.

The SNP's problem of converting ninety-minute patriots into sentient supporters of Scottish independence looked like a parlour game when compared to the political reality that was taking place in Argentina. Scots, within Great Britain, enjoyed every democratic right and people could ignore or involve themselves in politics as they wished. This was not true of Argentina, where politics invaded life at a most visceral, terrifying level. Eight thousand political prisoners crammed Argentinian jails as the World Cup neared. A military junta under General Jorge Videla had seized control of the country in 1976 and had embarked on a 'dirty war', whereby they used torture and execution as a means of eliminating opposition to their regime.

Thousands of people had disappeared, snatched off the streets or taken from inside public buildings by secret police wearing dark glasses and cruising the streets in their Ford Falcons. The military were in the process of murdering, in cold blood and without trial, anywhere between 10,000 and 30,000 individuals; the exact figure would never be known because of the secretive and insidious nature of this terror.

The staging of the 1978 World Cup had been allotted to Argentina long before the emergence of that military regime, but falling as it did in the midst of this dirty war it would be hijacked by the junta. The 1976 coup had received widespread support from Argentines wishing an end to a campaign of terror by the Montoneros, a left-wing guerrilla group who had plagued the country with a stream of kidnappings and killings of their own. The backlash from Videla's military was enormously and excessively out of proportion to the actions of the outlaws. 'All the necessary people will die,' Videla had said before embarking on his quest to hunt down anyone who might disagree with his extreme right-wing policies; most of his victims were in their twenties, contemporaries of the footballers in Argentina's national team. Many were dropped to their deaths, drugged, from aircraft into the River Plata in Buenos Aires. The early enthusiasm of the Argentinian populace for the hard-line government had diminished by mid-1978 after a purge of subversives that left few people entirely untouched. After two years of the military dictatorship, it had become clear that the army had the power to pick on and kill anyone they wished; guerrillas formed only a fraction of their victims and people wholly innocent of any crime could be erased by the state's killers, on a whim.

At the opening ceremony for the World Cup Videla used his speech to talk repeatedly of peace and freedom. But when Monsignor Juan Carlos Aramburu, the archbishop of Buenos Aires, got to his feet to relay some words from the Pope, who had priests numbering among the political prisoners in predominantly Roman-Catholic Argentina, the microphones suddenly failed. Technical difficulties can occur, but it is worth bearing in mind that in a land where

Roman Catholicism is the major religion, Catholic priests numbered among the political prisoners.

The mass distraction of the World Cup was needed to help Videla shore up his regime; he was due to present the trophy at the final on 25 June and if he was presenting it to a fellow Argentinian it would unleash a wave of patriotism that would wash over the entire country. That ensured that the 1978 World Cup would be the most politicised in the tournament's history and that the tainted tentacles of the dictatorship would become entangled in every aspect of the tournament.

6

Holiday Camp

Time was ticking away before Scotland faced Peru and Rod Stewart was becoming more and more distraught by the minute. It had been out of the question that he should reside in provincial Cordoba where Scotland's opening match of the 1978 World Cup was to be played. Instead, Rod – a man who could flounce in and out of the world's premier establishments with flunkies bowing to his every request – had been playing his customary role of boule-vardier at a top-notch hotel in the Argentine capital, Buenos Aires. His plan had been to catch the Scots' ninety minutes of World Cup action on the day by flying the 445 miles to Cordoba from Buenos Aires but on presenting himself at the capital's airport the star suddenly found mundanity and low-wattage reality assaulting him from all sides. The jobsworths at the gate to the flight were, unbelievably, telling him that he was to be prevented from lending his support to Scotland. Rod had left his passport at the hotel and, with minutes to go before his flight flew, it cut no ice with these minions that he was one of the most high-profile rock stars in the world: no passport, no flight. Rod was one 'blond' who, at this particular moment, was having rather less fun than he had anticipated.

Alongside him, the singer had Andy Roxburgh and he, then a youth coach with the SFA, sprang into action as a baffled Rod pondered hazily how the lack of a mere passport could prevent his carriage to his rightful place at the side of the Scottish team as they took their first steps in the 1978 World Cup.

'I had my accreditation on,' says Roxburgh, 'so I asked who was in charge and explained that this would cause an enormous diplomatic incident and headlines around the world if he missed the match. They bought the story and let him on. He was really pleased and was singing away and signing autographs.'

At Cordoba, Roxburgh and Stewart parted: the coach was flying on to Mendoza to watch Holland play Iran. Theatrical hugs ensued as Stewart draped himself over the SFA man and profusely thanked Roxburgh for his help, then teetered off the plane, thankful that disaster had been narrowly averted . . .

For Rod Stewart, there had been a hazardous overture to that incident when, the previous evening, on a visit to La Cantella restaurant, he had been forced to dodge flying bullets after a gunfight had erupted. It may or may not have cheered Rod to discover that inconvenience had also become a way of life for the Scottish footballers he idolised. They had found themselves at the end of the line from the moment they had arrived at their base in Argentina: Alta Gracia, the sedate, well-ordered town of 40,000 inhabitants, twenty-five miles south of Cordoba, was the final stop on the railway line that the British had built. The Scots would be staying at the Sierras Hotel, constructed in 1908 and which, in its whitewashed pristine prime, had attracted the wealthy Argentinian middle classes to visit Alta Gracia for long, languorous sojourns in the country during the twenties and thirties, when Argentinians had been confident in their prosperous, booming economy.

The town had even been home to a young Ernesto 'Che' Guevara, whose middle-class parents, on the advice of a doctor, moved there during the mid-thirties in the hope that the thin, dry air there would help cure the asthma that afflicted him as a child. At the Sierras Hotel, Guevara's father, a womanising bon viveur, would mingle with the elite of Argentinian society, down for a few days from Cordoba or Buenos Aires, and the young Che and his brother would entertain the drink-sodden dilettantes by rattling off the eleven names of the Boca Juniors team. Those heady days of rich gadflies flocking to the Sierras Hotel were well behind it by the late seventies. The hotel's past stature was still recognisable – it was three times the size of Dunblane Hydro – but the service at the Sierras made Fawlty Towers look like a haven of Teutonic efficiency. The last word in luxury during its heyday, by 1978 it had become not so much tired as asleep on its feet.

The first thing that hit the squad collectively when they had arrived at the Sierras was that the swimming pool had no water in it. This blocked off one avenue to light relief during their stay; one that could have been used productively in the pleasant Argentinian climes. Despite it being winter time in the southern hemisphere, it could become exceptionally humid during the day, with temperatures that matched a Scottish midsummer; although it could turn bitterly cold in the evening. During the two days prior to Scotland's opening match the heat and humidity would increase so considerably that the players barely trained at all; in such circumstances a fully functioning pool would have been invaluable. The hotel staff, throughout the Scots' stay, promised that the pool would be filled 'mañana'. But tomorrow never came.

Martin Buchan and Lou Macari, on repairing to their quarters on arrival, had to be transferred immediately, as the first room to which they had been allocated was found to have plaster peeling from the ceiling. Bruce Rioch recalls finding his bed less than comfortable, principally due to there being no springs in the mattress, which rested on a slab of hardboard. 'It was like a run-down Butlins,' says Willie Johnston.

Joe Harper, the forward, was another Scotsman less than enamoured with the hotel that would be the team's home from home for close to a fortnight. 'The sleeping conditions were terrible,' recalls Harper. 'The rooms were horrible – very dark and dingy. The swimming pool had no water, the tennis court had no net and there were no rackets. We had taken somewhere in the region of a dozen videos to last us a minimum of a month and they were done in three or four days.

'We went for a game of golf, maybe ten of us, and we had one set of clubs between us and it wasn't a full set. The only way we could spend our time having any fun was in playing head tennis and when you're there looking forward to a World Cup, you don't want to be playing head tennis when you're training every day as well.'

Alan Rough was another who was far from enchanted: 'The main problem was the accommodation. It was horrendous. The room didn't have any windows; it was sort of dormitory-style, all of them backing on to each other. It was just a wee poky room with a cupboard in it and a bath. That was it. You couldn't swing a cat in it.

'The swimming pool would at least have provided some relaxation. You get up, you go to training at ten, you're back at half-twelve; you've got a whole day to fill and although we trained sometimes in the afternoon, often we would just spend the days sitting about. At night time we would just watch the telly or sit about and everybody was just fed up.'

The food, one thing that can pep up players' morale, was less than enticing. 'You got something you enjoyed and you stuck with it because the rest of the stuff wasn't all that great,' says Hugh Allan of the food at the Sierras. 'They had talked about it as being the Gleneagles of Argentina, before we went out there, but having been to Gleneagles I'd say our hotel in Argentina would probably get a three-star rating.' Tough horse steaks and ropey-looking salad were on the menu every evening.

'Diabolical' is how Gordon McQueen describes the arrangements with which he and his squad mates were confronted. 'Scottish players got a lot of stick for complaining about the food but every day it was soup, and chicken or steak. Now that might sound good to some people but when it's what you're getting for lunch and dinner every single day it's just not good enough.

'You would have thought after being to one World Cup in '74 they would have learned about preparation but the thing was that in 1974 the Germans looked after every-thing in terms of accommodation and facilities. That wasn't the case in Argentina.'

It is never the best thing for a group of football players to find that their hotel facilities are not of the highest standard. What can happen is that one or two will soon leave their room to complain to other players, who may have been feeling unconcerned about the conditions. Under the influence of their displeased team mates, those players can then also start to see the drawbacks. 'Players are fickle,' as one high-profile Scotland international from that time puts it. 'We players only have an attention span of about two minutes. After that, if someone is giving you a team talk or something, you start scratching yourself or laughing with your pals. Then, if things go wrong, players are always looking for somebody else to blame.'

A robust defence of the choice of hotel is made by Ernie Walker who, together with MacLeod, had scouted around

Argentina to arrange accommodation in the early part of January, prior to the draw for the tournament. 'The manager of the hotel refused an offered bribe by the Iranians to move in and jump ahead of us,' says Walker.

'We had gone all around Argentina, as you must do, before the draw, because when it comes out of the hat, you must know which hotels are in which cities so that you can go – you have to have made a deal with the manager of the hotel that if you are in a group at that venue you want that hotel. It was the best available to us.

'Ten minutes after the draw was made, the Iranian people came to me and said, "Where's Cordoba?" I told them where it was, that we were staying in the Sierras Hotel, and then said I would mark their card and told them which hotels had been our second and third choices. We went to the hotel in Alta Gracia the next day and the manager met us and told us that the Iranians had come before us, had gone straight to our place and had offered him money to kick us out and let them in.

'It's not where you would normally stay – it's not the Sheraton or anything like that – but we were not in that kind of country. We were in the wilds of Argentina. The hotel may not have been to everybody's taste but if there had been a better place we would have been in it, believe me.'

The Scotland squad had arrived in Argentina on Friday 26 May, eight days prior to their opening match with Peru. Crowds of local people welcomed them to their base and a pipe band led them up the hill to their hotel. Unfortunately, the rousing reception did not prove sufficient to galvanise a great performance from the team bus. The wheezing vehicle screeched, groaned and gasped as it strained up the steep slope and, with such extreme demands on its engine, began belching out clouds of black smoke that eventually became so voluminous that the pipe band had to walk away. The smoke then began to engulf those inside and, as Joe Harper recalls, 'Roughie said, there and then, "We're going to die before we even play a game here."'

On eventually arriving at the hotel, Ally MacLeod announced that there would be no training until the Monday, although adding, 'If anyone really fancies a bit of training before then, they can. It's up to them.' Medical advice had been that it would be best not to do anything strenuous for two days after arrival, to overcome the effects of jetlag.

It proved to be an interesting weekend. The local pipe band held a raucous ceilidh at the hotel and Willie Johnston, Sandy Jardine and Alan Rough decided to head off to a neighbouring casino. As things turned out, this decision was to mark the beginning of the end for happy relations between the team and the press back home – not that Ally and the players knew that at the time. Other players spent a more sedate weekend, enjoying the occasional kick-about; some took an even more relaxed approach by simply wandering the grounds and drinking coffee. 'Noo's the day and noo's the hour' read a banner that had been erected in the players' lounge, but the urgency of that call to action lost some of its gusto as the minutes and hours dragged along inside the Sierras.

That lazy weekend after arrival in Argentina afforded Ally the opportunity to hold court and crack a few jokes about the blanket, supposedly undercover, security that had been supplied courtesy of the Argentinian junta. They were extremely nervous about the prospect of sabotage from guerrilla group the Montoneros destroying their tournament. 'Security is quiet but efficient,' commented MacLeod. 'I saw a dog lift his leg against a tree and the tree ran ten yards. And what about the gardeners? They pull out the flowers and leave the weeds.' The bulges underneath the jackets of some of the waiters suggested that they packed more than an order book and zealous guards had locked out Dr John Fitzsimmons, the Scotland squad's medical man, on the first day after he had dropped his bags on arrival and gone straight out to look for a church.

The light mood extended to Ally's decision not to travel into Cordoba, despite all the time on the Scots' hands, to inspect the playing surface and surroundings at the Chateau Carreras stadium, the venue for the opening match. 'Why go and see the pitch?' asked Ally as he lolled in the grounds of the hotel. 'It only gets players into a little state of tension so why bother? It's a waste of time – we all know why we're here anyway.'

Once it became time to train properly, the Scottish squad encountered a major problem. The training pitch close to their hotel lacked an even, flat surface, was on a slope and was bare in parts. The Argentinians had promised to reseed the pitch but the seed had not taken and the pitch had become rutted and treacherous, its surface presenting an ever-present possibility of strains and stresses on muscles and bones. It was not the only pitch in Argentina to suffer from this problem; those inside the actual World Cup stadiums at Mar del Plata and River Plate were in an equally appalling condition.

Four days prior to the encounter with Peru, on the Tuesday after the Scots' first weekend in Argentina, MacLeod finally relented, like a father giving in to a repeated request from his children to take them on a special holiday outing, and took the squad to the stadium and to decent training facilities in Cordoba. 'It was good to get out of the camp and on to a proper practice pitch,' he said. The Scots would now begin travelling half-an-hour each way to go training in Cordoba, work up a sweat and then come back on the bus before getting a shower back at their hotel.

Two dead horses lay on the side of the road from Alta Gracia to Cordoba and remained there from the day the Scottish party arrived until they left; bent-over shanty houses lined the route – another reminder of how the glitz of the World Cup was only temporarily glossing over the realities of life in the third world. The gentility and prosperity that European emigrants had experienced in Argentina at the beginning of the 20th century had been whittled away gradually in a country that had since experienced much political turbulence and now, in the late seventies, a military dictatorship.

In Peru, too, where the military also held sway, the national football team was run by a government who understood the importance of sporting victory to keep the people happy. That was underlined by the fact that for five months the members of the Peruvian national team – all but one of whom, Juan José Muñante, played in their native country – had been removed from their club sides, even though the League season was continuing, and sequestered together to prepare intensively for the finals. Muñante, too, was eventually brought home for these preparations, the Peruvian government paying a fee to his Mexican club, UNAM, for his release.

Muñante and his team mates had played together in fourteen matches between February and May 1978 to perfect the blend of football that they would take to the tournament. Half of the Peruvian side had been part of the national team since the early seventies. Five of the team that would face Scotland were with Alianza Lima; four were with Sporting Cristal. All of these factors suggested the players' knowledge of each other ought not to be a problem. Peru had been characterised as a team of old players but this was completely untrue. Hector Chumpitaz, the captain, was thirty-four but was in the side on merit, on the basis of his exceptional talents and leadership qualities. The remainder of the team were in their mid- to late-twenties, with the sole exception of Jaime Duarte, aged twenty-three.

However, the Peruvian Football Association faced one major problem before the 1978 World Cup: they could not afford to go. The Peruvian government was effectively bankrupt and FIFA had to provide a loan of 100,000 US dollars, to cover the team's expenses, before they could travel to Argentina.

Peru had been treated with something close to disdain by MacLeod. His super-confidence with regard to the chances of his team demolishing the South Americans had taken root in the cavernous San Martin theatre in downtown Buenos Aires when he had escaped the Scottish winter for summery South America to attend the draw in January 1978. Initially, sitting in that enormous edifice, MacLeod's confidence had plummeted when, during rehearsals, the practice draw in advance of the grandiose, televised spectacle of the real thing had seen Scotland shuffled into a group featuring Brazil, Austria and France; a tough group when viewed from any angle. The gloom into which MacLeod plunged during that trial run was, minutes later, lifted – like grey mist being burned off by bright sunshine – when he found his team grouped, in reality, with Iran, Peru and Holland; a 'dream' section, was what MacLeod thought of it.

The contrast between rehearsal and reality must, for the Scotland manager, have felt like exchanging a pair of miner's boots for a pair of sandshoes midway through a marathon. Not only did the draw seem much better but also Cordoba and Mendoza, where Scotland would play their matches, were the twin centres that MacLeod had wanted. 'Ally, your luck is in,' he had thought to himself as he witnessed the names that joined that of Scotland in group four.

'When you saw the draw coming out and we had Holland, Peru and Iran you thought, "My goodness!"' reflects commentator Arthur Montford. 'You were feeling it was not a bad draw and it was possible to finish second in the group to Holland – and when it began to become close to the World Cup I think we were all a wee bit party to the hype. Then, when we got to South America, I said to Ally, "How much work have you done on Iran and Peru?" and was surprised and disappointed that his home-work on those two countries had been limited.'

Prior to voyaging forth to Argentina for the finals, MacLeod had confidently stated his belief that the games against Peru and Iran would be matches in which Scotland would 'chase goals' and he had suggested that Lou Macari and Joe Harper could be introduced as extra forwards at some point during those fixtures for that very purpose. He compared the matches with Peru and Iran to the one with Zaire in 1974, but six days prior to the Peru encounter a jarring note of caution descended, seemingly from nowhere, on MacLeod's pronouncements. He stated of Peru, 'I think they will turn out to be a better side than most have been saying.'

As is the case with most managers, MacLeod was not greatly given to self-analysis so it may have gone out of his mind entirely that he had been one of the leading demeaners of Peru. Perhaps it was a little bit of homework that helped change his mind. Having watched the Peruvians on video at home in the days immediately before departing for Argentina, Ally now declared of Teofilo Cubillas, their forward, who had shone at the 1970 World Cup, 'Though he's short and tubby now, he's a wizard on the ball.' The Scotland manager also showed some prescience in stating, 'I am convinced that this World Cup will be won from these dead-ball situations. It is as important for us to be prepared for those "surprise" elements our opponents may introduce as it is for our own moves to be well rehearsed and ready. This, in fact, will take up most of our training time.'

Anyone seeking serious anonymity in the summer of 1978 could have done little better than to procure themselves the position of assistant to Ally MacLeod, Scotland manager. Such was Ally's overwhelming persona and snaffling of all press attention that few people outside the close circle involved with the national team would have even realised that he had with him an assistant in Argentina. He did, though, and that man was John Hagart, a former manager of Heart of Midlothian, who had been handed the post specifically for the 1978 World Cup. MacLeod had decided against taking as an assistant Alex Ferguson, a fiery up-and-coming manager who moved from St Mirren to Aberdeen in the summer of 1978, the cantankerous Jim McLean of Dundee United or even the domineering Jock Stein. MacLeod believed that serious disagreements would inevitably arise if one of those men had been his assistant and were to tell him that he was making mistakes. Hagart, proclaimed Ally, would be at his side but would know 'just who is the boss, who has the last word'.

The experience was one that Hagart enjoyed but he did, at times, find MacLeod to be an unpredictable figurehead. 'We would be going to training, this is in Argentina, and Ally would say to me, "What do you think we should do today?" I would say, "We'll have a good warm-up and then, maybe, I'll take the forwards for some shooting or if you want to take them, I'll take the defenders and we can drill the back four." He'd say, "That will be great."

Then the bus would stop at the training ground and one of the boys would say, "Ally, what are we on today, boss? What about a game for half an hour?" And Ally would say, "Aye, John, a good warm-up and then we'll just have a game."

'He could change what he was going to do so spontaneously and they loved him for it. I don't mean, saying what I've just said, that you could almost think that they loved him because they could manipulate him. I didn't mean it like that; I just mean that they loved him because a wee suggestion could get a good response; he didn't turn round and say, "You'll do as I bloody well tell you." He didn't just agree either; he would be so enthusiastic. To a suggestion like that, he would say, "Great, we'll have a game. That'll get everybody buzzing."

'Nine times out of ten the training routine that had been planned would change. I would sit down at night and I would write out what I was going to do at training the next morning and, although I did always realise that I could be wasting my time, I would never say, "I'll not bother." I liked to be organised just in case I was left to run the training and would always say to myself, "This'll be the morning where he wants to go and blether to somebody." Ally was a spontaneous guy and very successful with it. One must never forget that he kicked the ball off at Aberdeen. Billy McNeill and Fergie did so well at Aberdeen but Ally started the ball rolling.'

The nation waited and anticipated the opening game although not everyone in Scotland was right behind Ally. On the eve of the World Cup, and three days prior to the Peru match, MacLeod, of Corsehill Place, Ayr, was fined ten pounds for speeding at forty-four miles per hour in the town in March 1978. He admitted the offence by letter and had his licence endorsed but there was, in Argentina, little sign of a slowdown at the team hotel. On the Thursday evening, two days before the Peru match, Ally allowed the players to relax and have a couple of beers at the bar inside the hotel. Most were happy with this but four players absented themselves from the company, went to a room, and instead traversed in and out of the bar one at a time. The first of their group through to the bar asked for four bitter lemons. Twenty minutes later, the second of them was through for another batch. Ally MacLeod was beginning to wonder what was up, especially when, shortly afterwards, a third player swayed unsteadily through the lounge, stumbling against a couple of items of furniture, and planted himself at the bar where he asked for eight glasses of bitter lemon to take through to the room – presumably to prevent himself or another of his party having to repeat such an inconvenient and precarious journey too soon. MacLeod asked him what was going on and was told that the four players were just having a wee game of cards in their room so wanted to take their drinks through; the player in question omitted to mention that the bitter lemon was being topped up with gusto from the contents of a large bottle of vodka.

That evening the players gathered in the Sierras Hotel's television lounge to watch the opening match of the World Cup: West Germany versus Poland at the Monumental stadium in Buenos Aires. John Robertson, looking every inch the holidaying Scot with his tracksuit top unzipped to the navel to reveal a hairy chest, discussed with Kenny Burns the odds on the match. 'I think West Germany, easy,' said Burns. Robertson's response, 'Poland are certainties.'

Don Masson, perched happily on his back-row seat beside Joe Harper, chipped in, 'Lou's the bookie – get your money on with honest Lou.' Macari, turning, pen in hand and with the authority of a man in his natural milieu, responded with clear seriousness about doing some business amid the friendly banter, "Well, what do you want? Name your score.' Harper responded, 'One-nil Poland.' Macari, with the cobra sharpness of an on-course, sheep-skinned bookie, took two seconds to respond, 'One-nil Poland; ten-to-one . . .' Willie Johnston, at the back of the room, grinned widely as he flicked a pair of dark glasses on and off. As it was, the game ended 0-0, with Joe Harper failing only narrowly to make a killing.

It was, says Bruce Rioch, the Scotland captain, a realistic bunch of players that plunged into action for Scotland against Peru in Cordoba on 3 June 1978. Ally's boasts as to their being there to take home the trophy cut little ice with Rioch and the other seasoned professionals in the side. 'I didn't take too much notice of it,' says Rioch, whose English accent betrays the fact that he was born in Aldershot and brought up south of the border. His mother originated from Skye and his father, a Scots Guard, was from close to Stonehaven. 'Then again,' he adds, 'you're not going to go there not to win it and if your manager says that you are there to win it, you've got to do your best to back up his words. It's like going out of the dressing-room door and not thinking you are going to win; you might as well not bother. Coming off the '77 tour we had felt confident about ourselves as a team but as players you know it's going to be tough to win the World Cup in South America.'

The view of most players was that Scotland were good but probably just short of the type of quality required to fulfil Ally's stated view that they would return with the trophy. 'The players never thought that way,' says Gordon McQueen, 'but we were confident we would have quite a successful World Cup.'

It was a positive group of players, recalls Joe Harper, that travelled from Alta Gracia to Cordoba for the Scots' opening match. 'We had a week of acclimatising before the serious stuff started; getting the group together; bonding. We used to get massages off Jimmy Steele and Jimmy would tell stories and all the boys would be there laughing and joking. So we were pretty upbeat when we went out against Peru.' MacLeod, though, must have been feeling the heat. For him, finally, the moment of truth had arrived.

Management of an international football team is a relaxed existence; most of the time. There are usually only eight to ten matches to be tackled per season – an average of one a month. Ally, for example, had had to deal with only one fixture – a friendly with Bulgaria in February 1978 – in the seven months between the victory over Wales in the qualifier at Anfield and the beginning of the Home Internationals in May 1978. An international manager does not get the players fit – that happens at their clubs – and he does not have to scour the transfer market looking to bring players in on a budget he can afford. In comparison to the daily grind of a club manager, then, an international manager appears to have an easy time of it.

There is, though, one area in which being the national boss puts much greater and more pressurised demands on a manager: the specialised area of team selection for the annual handful of key games, when a manager brings all his experience, ruthlessness and judgement to bear. At club level, a manager has dozens of competitive fixtures in which to get his team blend and selection correct; not at international level. There are only a select few matches that really matter and it is vital that, for those matches, the manager justifies his selection with Swiss-watch precision.

Only two matches had really been of vital importance for Ally MacLeod in his first year as Scotland manager: those against Czechoslovakia and Wales in the autumn of 1977, and in those games his team selections had been flawless. He now faced a bigger test. He had problems at full-back: Danny McGrain was injured and Willie Donachie suspended. Gordon McQueen, the centre-back, would also miss the match – his knee still injured since the Welsh Home International when he came off second best to a Hampden Park goalpost. Bruce Rioch and Don Masson, the experienced midfield players, had been automatic selections throughout MacLeod's initial year but both had been off form at Derby County; so much so that Tommy Docherty, a Scotland manager in the early seventies and now in charge at Derby, had opted to place both players on the transfer list in May 1978, hours before the players had joined the Scotland squad. 'They go on show in the World Cup,' said Docherty.

'My form going into the World Cup wasn't particularly good,' admits Rioch, 'and Derby County's form wasn't particularly good. There had been an awful lot of changes at Derby after Tommy came and there was a little bit of disharmony inside the club and that affected our form.'

There were, for MacLeod, viable alternatives to Rioch and Masson in Lou Macari, Graeme Souness and Archie Gemmill, all of whom had been in excellent club form during the 1977-78 season. Macari, in scoring eleven goals from midfield for Manchester United, had outscored and outshone Joe Jordan, who had arrived at Old Trafford in January 1978 but who had hit only three goals between then and the end of the season. Gemmill had been the driving force in the Nottingham Forest side that had topped the Football League in England. Souness, most impressively of all, had been essential in lubricating Liverpool's midfield engine en route to collecting the 1978 European Cup. MacLeod had to balance the cases for Souness, Gemmill and Macari against the extensive, sturdy service given to him by Rioch and Masson. And it would appear he was wholly comfortable with this sometimes troublesome aspect of the manager's job. 'I don't shirk decisions. That's a side of me people don't know.'

There were also imponderables as to who should accompany Kenny Dalglish in the Scotland attack; questions were hovering over the head of Joe Jordan who, together with his paucity of goals for Manchester United, had scored only twice for Scotland in his sixteen games since the 1974 World Cup, while Derek Johnstone, Jordan's chief rival for a starting place, had scored forty-one goals for Glasgow Rangers in 1977-78 and had headed two fine goals in the Home Internationals against Wales and Northern Ireland. Dalglish, who had hit thirteen goals in thirty-three games since the 1974 tournament, was an automatic choice as one of the front two. In Jordan's favour, both he and Dalglish had scored at crucial times in the qualifying matches for the 1978 tournament; something that none of their competitors for striking positions had done.

Dalglish, in a purely footballing sense, was the most charismatic member of the squad but was a superficially dour character who remained true to his Glasgow roots despite having been elevated to the top stratum of elite European footballers after his doings with Liverpool in the 1977-78 season. At one gathering of the Scotland squad at the luxurious Gleneagles hotel in the Perthshire countryside, Dalglish had requested 'square', Lorne sausage – known in Glasgow as 'pink lint' – for his pre-match meal and, with masterly efficiency, the staff at Gleneagles had produced a foodstuff that few of their other guests were ever likely to request. Culinary finesse to one side, his sophisticated, cosmopolitan footballing skills had attracted representatives of Juventus, who were with the Italian squad at the World Cup, to fly to Cordoba to watch this exquisite footballer do his stuff in the match with Peru.

Dalglish's intricate style had more in common with that of a cerebral, deep-lying continental forward than with the more physical, aggressive approach that had traditionally been associated with the British game. As such, he was expected to shine in the company of the finest footballers in the world, although the one skeleton in his cupboard was that Dalglish, aged twenty-seven in 1978, had, as a younger man, failed to register much of an impact at the 1974 tournament despite being selected for all three of Scotland's matches.

Loyalty and continuity, on the day, proved to be MacLeod's guiding factors in choosing the following team to go head to head with Peru: Alan Rough, Stuart Kennedy, Tom Forsyth, Kenny Burns, Martin Buchan, Bruce Rioch, Don Masson, Asa Hartford, Kenny Dalglish, Joe Jordan and Willie Johnston. It was, with the exceptions of the missing Jardine, McGrain and McQueen, the team that had taken out Czechoslovakia at Hampden Park nine months previously – and if McGrain and McQueen had been fit they, too, would certainly have featured against the Peruvians, at the expense of Kennedy and Burns.

It was a team selection that made its own specific sense. Any international manager wants his team to have knitted together and to know each other scrupulously well and MacLeod's selection contained its own internally consistent logic: players' past performances for Scotland, in matches that mattered, were his form guide rather than what they had been doing for their clubs over recent weeks and months, or for Scotland in friendlies and Home

Internationals. He had been rock-solid in his selection: he had not been dilatory and he had not mixed good past performers with arrivistes. The manager would stand or fall by his judgement.

'I'm a loyal sort of person,' MacLeod had said when naming his squad in early May. 'I remember what players have done for me and I tend to stick with them.' At the beginning of April 1978, MacLeod had written out twenty-two names and put them away in a drawer; in early May he had retrieved that piece of paper and nothing had convinced him to change any of the original twenty-two names written on it when naming his squad for Argentina.

The origins of Ally's team for the Peru match went back even further; all of thirteen months to his first victory in charge of Scotland – 3-0 at home to Northern Ireland on 1 June 1977 – only a fortnight after he had been appointed manager and only his second match with Scotland. On seeing the style with which his team had played against the Irish that evening, he had decided that that team would be the one he would use at the World Cup, if Scotland were to qualify. Of that side, only McGrain, McQueen and Donachie would fail to take to the turf against Peru, all for reasons outside of Ally's control.

It was a side that looked better from the front than from the back. In defence, Scotland looked almost experimental. The full-backs, Buchan and Kennedy, had never played together and the Peru match would be Kennedy's initiation into fully competitive international football after a couple of domestic jousts in the Home Internationals; he had won his place in the team after performing well against Wales and England. Buchan was a natural, and quite exceptional, centre-back, where his steady approach to the game was more valuable than on the flanks. He had come into repeated conflict with Tommy Docherty, his manager at

Manchester United for five years, when Docherty had forced the player, against his will, to play as an overlapping right-back. Against Peru, Kennedy would be on the right and Buchan on the left; Buchan had never previously in his career played a full match at left-back.

Tom Forsyth and Kenny Burns, the centre-backs, would be starting only their second full match together. Burns, after being dropped for the England match in 1977, had turned to Willie Johnston after the match and, as Johnston recalls, said he would not now go on that summer's tour of South America. In fact, the official reason for Burns missing the 1977 tour was somewhat strange. As MacLeod explained, 'He called off from the tour with a telegram which made what sounded like a far fetched excuse at the time – that he had fallen off a horse and strained his back. In fact it was a genuine, and unlucky, injury. I accepted that, but it is not my way to go back on statements I have made to players.' Missing the tour had excluded Burns from MacLeod's plans for the subsequent year – now, McQueen's injury forced Ally to use the centre-back Burns, who looked permanently like a furious nightclub bouncer who has simultaneously been stung on the neck by a wasp and had a particularly scruffy student stand on his foot. Behind the back four, Alan Rough, the six-feet-one-inch-tall goalkeeper, would be his usual languid self, coming off a season in which he had been in mixed form for Partick Thistle.

Things looked better further up the team tree. Most Scottish supporters had not witnessed Rioch and Masson struggling for form; they remembered instead the Rioch and Masson who, since being given belated – both players were nearly thirty – international debuts in the mid-seventies had jointly cut a swathe through a variety of top-quality opposition sides for Scotland. Rioch retained his place mainly because Ally believed that Rioch, rather than Gemmill, was closer to how the manager believed the game should be played. Masson, possibly to an even greater degree than Kenny Dalglish, was the player on whom MacLeod depended desperately. As the fulcrum of the team, Masson – a 'sly player' according to one Scotland team mate, who means it as a compliment in relation to Masson's footballing know-how – would be stationed at the back of midfield to take the ball from defenders, turn and set up play with swift, sharp passes. 'I've built the side round him,' MacLeod had stated shortly before the tournament. 'Most of our attacks start and revolve around this man. If he plays as well as he can, the whole team plays as well as it can.'

Rioch and Masson were complemented by the intelligent, industrious Asa Hartford and the quick-fire, explosive Willie Johnston on the left wing. Johnston's approach to full-backs was similar to that taken by a jet-skiing billionaire playboy buzzing a slow-chugging pleasure cruiser. The winger would leave scorch marks on the turf as he zipped past yet another distraught defender.

Of the front two, Dalglish, at the peak of his powers, had proven himself a top-class player with Liverpool: in the fifty-nine games in his debut 1977-78 season for them he had scored thirty goals, the most recent of which, a crafty chip, had won the European Cup for the Anfield side just three weeks previously. Alongside Dalglish, Jordan was something of an anomaly: he was not as ordinary a player as his many detractors would have it but not as good as those who championed him believed him to be. Some suggested that he was little more than a clumsy, blunt instrument who failed to complement Dalglish with the necessary style, but two wonderful headers from Jordan, both against Czechoslovakia, had been vital in directing

Scotland towards the 1974 and 1978 World Cups. Nor did it explain why Bayern Munich and Manchester United had been determined to attain his services.

The striker was renowned in England's top division for having a pair of elbows that clicked in and out throughout a match like those of a man operating a pair of garden shears and he was widely feared by Scotland's opponents because of his physical presence and ability in the air. The high ball into the middle of the penalty area was a tactic alien to many non-British nations and opposition defenders were expected to quail as the flint-faced, taciturn Jordan launched himself skywards with arms and elbows repelling all boarders.

That supposition of foreign trepidation at the Scots' aerial ability tended to sway Scotland team managers towards always playing a tall target man. With Scotland's tactics in attack and midfield dictated by exploiting their supposed superiority in the air it would have gone against all Scottish instincts to play the in-form Macari with Dalglish, even if MacLeod had wished to. MacLeod's studying of Peru on video had also led him to the conclusion that the Peruvians were especially vulnerable to the high ball into the box; a specific weakness in what he regarded as an all-round brittle Peruvian defence.

It seems puzzling that so many Scots who earned their living from football – not only Ally MacLeod – could have ever even considered underestimating the Peruvians. It was difficult to see how they could ever be rated as anything other than highly talented, dangerous opponents. Peru were among the leading South American nations and had played some magnificent football during the 1970 World Cup, having eliminated Argentina in the qualifiers and falling only to eventual winners, Brazil, in the quarter-finals.

Some of the Peruvian players who had glittered at that

tournament, such as Hector Chumpitaz, the captain, Teofilo Cubillas and Hugo Sotil, were still part of Peru's plans for 1978. Although they were now eight years older they were still due respect for keeping on top of their game to such an extent that they remained key players for the Peruvian team. They did not always ply their trade at the world's very biggest clubs – Cubillas had spent chunks of the seventies at Basle and Porto – but that merely kept them more refreshed and dedicated when it came to representing their country. Peru were also, in 1978, South American champions for only the second time in their history and they had lost just once – 1-0 to Brazil – in their six qualifying matches for these finals. Despite all this, there had been a belief in Scotland that the Peruvians would simply fold under the Scots' force. The truth, after all the months of talk, was about to be discovered.

7

Mastering Disaster

If Marcos Calderon was concerned about his Peru side meeting Scotland in their opening World Cup tie he wasn't showing it. Calderon, the most successful coach in Peruvian football history, had moulded his team into the reigning South American champions and stated he was not fazed at all by the prospect of joining in tactical battle with Ally MacLeod. 'Scotland, I think, have a strong defence but their side is not flexible enough,' he said. 'We will try to wear them out with short passing and hope our attacking ploy pays off at the end.'

As the game drew closer, Kenny Dalglish sounded a cautionary note: 'A defeat would not be a disaster but we want desperately to win. If we lose, I hope the fans don't start to complain that we are useless because we will be putting everything into it.'

An unwelcome intervention occurred in the Scottish dressing room prior to kick-off when Harry Cavan, a vice-president of FIFA, from Northern Ireland, entered and stressed to the Scots that referees at the World Cup were going to be extra tough on discipline. During the Home International Championships some Scottish players had been criticised for placing too much emphasis on the physical side of the game, so this crass and unnecessary piece of 'advice' irritated the players as they limbered up for one of the most important matches of their lives.

Madness accompanied Scotland's players as they emerged from the tunnel for their opening match. Alongside them, stepping out on to the turf at the Chateau Carreras in Cordoba was 'El Loco' – 'The Madman' – Peru's Argentinian-born goalkeeper, Ramon Quiroga. Quiroga was a man who appeared determined to invite trouble on to his team. The goalkeeper, who stood at all of five-feet-eight-inches-tall, habitually wore the number thirteen on his back and was renowned for his crazy dashes to the halfway line where he would not only take on opposition players but would also occasionally leap to head the ball. Quiroga was the smallest goalkeeper in the World Cup and in front of him Peru fielded José Velasquez, a centre-back who was even smaller than the goalkeeper, at just five-feet-six-inches. This was the man whose task it was to help combat the aerial threat of the Scottish attacks.

There were 46,000 inside the Chateau Carreras stadium, filling a ground that had been purpose-built for the World Cup, on wasteland on the edge of Cordoba. A pocket of a few hundred Scots and another of a similar number of Peruvians could easily be picked out in a crowd composed almost entirely of locals. Peruvians generally rubbed along easily enough with Argentinians even though the inhabitants of the host nation were sometimes seen as too haughty for their own good by their South American neighbours. One Peruvian joke had it that if an Argentinian wished to commit suicide he would take a leap off his own ego. Still, for the next ninety minutes, most of the crowd would be firmly on the side of Peru, jeering Scotland and cheering their fellow South Americans.

The match kicked off at a quarter to five in the afternoon local time, making it a quarter to nine in the evening when it was broadcast live in Scotland. Scotland wore their traditional blue tops and red socks, but with blue shorts to help television viewers distinguish between them and the

Peruvians, who wore white shorts. Peru, with a red diagonal sash across their white jerseys, looked like a collection of South American dictators ready to strut out on to the presidential balcony to survey the passing troops and armaments on national day.

A mere two minutes of the match had passed when Dalglish screwed an angled pass in between two Peru defenders but Asa Hartford, travelling like a train, miskicked as he met the ball eight yards from goal to splay wide his volleyed shot. Within a minute, a slick, quick move began inside the Scotland half, with Rioch finding Dalglish, whose curved pass to Jordan was headed smartly forward by the striker to set Masson free, but his angled shot from the edge of the penalty area lacked power and was held firmly by Quiroga.

Peru, at this early stage, looked lackadaisical as they ambled around, seeking a way into the game. Cubillas, Cesar Cueto and Juan Carlos Oblitas tried to get things moving forward for their team with dinky, sharp passes to feet, only to find that the Scottish defenders were always able to muscle them off the ball before their trickery escalated into anything approaching a scoring chance. Scotland, in contrast, were cutting cleverly through the Peruvian defence and midfield. After nine minutes, Hartford, on the left, flipped the ball past two defenders to find Dalglish inside the penalty area, and his cute pass allowed Masson to sway inside one defender and outside another before sending a shot from ten yards into the arms of Quiroga. Scotland were getting closer to the goal that would be necessary if they were to capitalise on their almost total control of the game.

Fourteen minutes had passed when Cubillas, in the centre of the park, attempted to meander forward once again. Burns's brisk tackle stole the ball from him and it rolled into the possession of Masson, on the right-hand side of the Scotland midfield, close to the halfway line.

Masson held off the flimsy attempt at a retrieving challenge from Cubillas before returning the ball to Burns who, in turn, switched it to Buchan, at left-back. Buchan curled the ball forward to Dalglish in the centre circle who, back to goal, swayed left, then right, shaking off his marker in the process, before sending a right-footed pass to Hartford on the left side of the midfield and just inside the Peru half. This was clever stuff – holding possession but not dwelling on the ball; and pulling Peruvians out of position.

Hartford, looking up, sent a left-footed pass down the line to Johnston, who eased backwards slightly and craftily shuffled the ball between his feet before zipping a pass forward to Dalglish, who had now crept stealthily forward into space outside the Peru penalty area. The pace of the passing now increased suddenly. Dalglish angled the ball, first time, to the running Hartford who, with one touch, moved it on to Rioch, whose left-footed shot, on the turn, from the edge of the penalty area, veered awkwardly across Quiroga, allowing the goalkeeper, as he lurched forward, to get only one hand to the ball, reducing drastically its speed. As the ball broke free, Jordan, alert on the right side of the six-yard box, squeezed a smart, well-judged, low shot between Quiroga and the goalkeeper's left-hand post. Scotland were 1-0 ahead through an excellent goal that had come about thanks to a display of patience, perseverance and painstaking skill. Eight passes had been linked together flawlessly to switch the ball from one side of the field to the other and, as the move unfolded, the mastery of it all had left the Peruvians as only the next best thing to the spectators in the stands.

A second, consolidating goal was now sought urgently by Scotland. Hartford's twenty-yard drive, one minute after the opening goal, was held low down by Quiroga, as was a pacy cross that went screeching into the six-yard box off the boot of Johnston. It took twenty-five minutes for Peru to get their first shot on target. A swift move that began inside their own half saw the ball whirled directly through the middle by Cubillas, who swooped towards goal, danced past two challenges – the second of which, from Burns, had the subtlety of an attack from a man with a meat cleaver. Cubillas then played a one-two with Guillermo La Rosa inside the Scotland penalty area, skipped free of the attentions of the Scottish defence and speared a right-footed shot at goal that Rough turned round the post. Cubillas, who had motored magnificently from halfway line to six-yard box within seconds, looked far from a spent force as the Scots took stock of this sudden jolt of electricity. Masson, Hartford, Burns and Forsyth had all been found wanting in the face of that surge of energy from their opponents.

A second save from Rough, minutes later, at close range from Oblitas, Peru's elusive left winger, maintained Scotland's lead but Peru had clearly awoken and were now very much on top. The Scottish defence was struggling to stay with the lithe movement and fluidity of the Peruvians as they used their intricate, close control to attack from deep. It was proving to be a first half of two halves, although there was still the occasional Scottish tryst with goal. Masson's pass from inside his own half found Jordan, whose header downwards freed Dalglish inside the Peru penalty area, but his attempt at propelling the ball over the head of Quiroga was thwarted by the goalkeeper who had rushed rapidly from his goal line to throw an arm into the air, with alacrity, and block the ball.

'Tight on him,' shouted MacLeod, wearing a Scotland jersey, and now leaning forward on the edge of his seat in the dugout, as Toribio Diaz the Peru left-back, under no pressure from the nearby Jordan, advanced to play the ball forward to La Rosa, on the half-hour. The anxious manager could see that Scotland were now conceding possession and space with alarming regularity. There was some relief for MacLeod when the Peruvians' initial spurt of synergy was followed by a lull, and as the first half entered its final five minutes it began to look as though the Scots might just reach the safe haven of half time with their lead intact.

Three minutes before the interval, another Peruvian move seared like a laser beam through the centre of the Scottish defence. Once again Rough was left exposed by his back four but this time he was given no chance of saving. Cesar Cueto controlled the ball with his upper body before, on the turn, jabbing a tidy, left-footed shot past Rough and into the right-hand corner of the net.

During the opening stages of the match Scotland had been composed, controlled and stylish and had lived up to the billing that Ally MacLeod had given them. The steep decline in performance that had been in evidence from the midpoint of the first half was reflected in the face of the Scotland captain; as he walked from the field at half time Rioch looked like a man wrestling to adjust mentally to a piece of particularly bad news. Inside the dressing room, MacLeod shouted at his players, 'You've no fire in your bellies. You are not playing like Scottish players.' He excoriated the number of square balls being knocked about – especially by the back four, and particularly by Kenny Burns.

The Peruvians had pulverised Scotland with their thrusts through central midfield and the Scots had been unable to match the speed and skill with which their opponents transported the ball. The start of the second half saw the Peruvians take a different tack, working the wings rather than making headway through the middle.

Oblitas – unusual for a wide player in being tall and elegant, and looking like a gentleman gambler – glided down the left flank, ensured that he got the break of the ball from an ineffective Kennedy tackle, and pierced the Scottish defence with a cross that dropped perfectly between Forsyth and Buchan for La Rosa. The striker, unusually chunky and deliberate amid his more free-moving team mates, squandered his 'free' header in front of goal and watched it putter softly wide before standing, hands on hips, bemused by his own lack of resourcefulness. A similar pose would be struck by Joe Jordan, at the opposite end of the field, minutes later. Masson's ball forward was met by Dalglish, expertly coming off his marker to knock a first-time ball to Hartford, whose quick, diagonal cross into the penalty area was met on the edge of the six-yard box by Jordan, whose header kissed the outside of the Peruvian post.

Johnston, switched early in the second half from the left to the right wing, was next to seek out the head of Jordan. This time, the striker nodded the ball down to Kenny Dalglish, whose shot was deflected over the bar by Chumpitaz. Masson's corner was headed into the six-yard box by Burns, finding Jordan with the goal gaping in front of him. But Jordan's left-footed volley was met by an exceptional, two-handed save from Quiroga who, from almost directly under his crossbar, tipped the ball up and over to safety.

Neither side, little more than an hour into the game, was displaying the cohesion that had been evident during their better periods of the match but Scotland were now at least taking the game to Peru, with dogged determination. The ball had remained in the Peru half for a sustained period when, after sixty-two minutes, a Stuart Kennedy cross from the right was met by Jordan, who headed the ball to the running Rioch on the edge of the Peru penalty area. The captain played the ball in front of him, into the box, then appeared to knock it too far forward for him to reach while, simultaneously, becoming the victim of an over-the top challenge from Hector Chumpitaz. Ulf Eriksson, the thirty-five-year-old Swedish referee in charge of only his eighth international match, was in no doubt that it should be a penalty and remained firm in his decision despite the protests of half-a-dozen agitated Peruvian players.

Quiroga hovered on the penalty spot as Masson prepared to take the kick. The Scot simply turned his back and bounced the ball up and down as he waited for the referee to assert his authority. Marcos Calderon – the Peru manager looking more than ever like Ray Charles, his outsize sunglasses now matched by a jazzy jacket that he had slipped on over his red tracksuit at half-time – delayed matters even further by taking the unusual step of carrying out a substitution – Hugo Sotil in place of La Rosa – before the kick could be taken. Back in the box, Quiroga had to be threatened with the possibility of a yellow card before he retreated to his line, still protesting, and Masson was finally able to place the ball on the spot.

Masson looked poised and prepared as he waited to take the spot kick. Standing with his hands on his hips, he watched the referee for the signal that would allow him to strike the ball. There was nothing about him to suggest that anything had intruded on his composure at such a vital moment. His kick, when it came, was of medium strength and went halfway between Quiroga and the right-hand post at mid-height; Quiroga, slightly off his line when Masson had struck the ball, leapt to his right to deflect the ball round the post before acknowledging the acclaim of the celebrating Argentinian crowd behind his goal.

Peru made the most of their narrow escape. Hector Chumpitaz, in the sixty-fifth minute, thumped in a free kick that was held at his near post by Rough; the Peruvians' first on-target effort of the second half. A Cubillas through-ball sent Muñante in on goal and only a desperate, combined challenge from Rough and Buchan stopped him slotting the ball in the net. Masson and Burns each gave the ball away on the edge of their own box and both were fortunate not to be punished severely. MacLeod, as he bobbed back and forth in the dugout, was wincing in the wake of Masson's penalty miss. A certain lack of conviction had now crept into his players and in seventy minutes Peru made the most of it.

A cross from Kennedy was caught by Quiroga, under pressure from Hartford, and, once the goalkeeper had distributed the ball, Scotland sat off the Peruvians as Muñante, on the right, slipped the ball to Jaime Duarte, who moved it on to Cueto, who found Cubillas, on his own, thirty yards from goal and slightly left of centre in front of the penalty area. No one was near him or thinking of getting near him as he took a touch to steady himself and get the ball on to his right foot, took another touch to push the ball forward and used his right boot to strike the ball smoothly and high into the left-hand corner of Rough's net setting off delirious celebrations in the Argentinian crowd, and, of course, its Peruvian enclave. As Cubillas's shot sped towards him, Rough had hopped to his right, hovered on one leg and extended a hand loosely in the direction of the disappearing ball – like a man stepping off the kerb to make a token effort at hailing a speeding taxi . . . something that Rough and some of his team-mates may have felt like doing in the wake of that goal.

An agitated MacLeod now told Macari and Gemmill to get ready to come on and two minutes after the goal the pair replaced Rioch and Masson. The newcomers had been sent on to add some attacking zest to the Scotland side as they attempted to retrieve the game but Gemmill, in one of his first actions on the field, was dreadfully short with a pass to Jordan that was easily cut out by Duarte, who fed Cueto, scorer of Peru's first goal. Cueto's curved pass, from twenty yards inside his own half, was as sharp as a guillotine's blade and found Oblitas, similarly unmarked in much the same place as Cubillas had been when he had scored six minutes earlier. Unlike Cubillas, Oblitas did not have any defenders between him and Rough. The way was clear for him to ease in on goal – until, that is, he was the subject of a crashing, clumsy foul from Kennedy, who by now appeared to be struggling severely to keep up with the pace and panache of international football. The offence had taken place only inches outside the penalty area, and although Kennedy had prevented a clear goal-scoring opportunity, that, in 1978, was not an offence automatically punished by instant dismissal. He was not even booked.

Cubillas seized the ball and placed it on the ground for the kick to be taken but Rough and the five men in the Scottish wall were confronted not only by Cubillas but also by three of his team mates, hovering over the ball alongside him. Of them all, Cubillas looked the most relaxed and the player least keyed-up to strike the ball. Muñante looked ready to hit it but he ran distractingly from left to right and over the ball, allowing Cubillas to run straight at it. It had been Masson's job to line up the defensive wall but with the midfield player now having been substituted, Macari was stationed on the end of the wall and Cubillas flighted the ball over the Scot's shoulder – Macari even seemed to move reflexively to his left to avoid being struck.

As if guided by remote control the ball veered inside the post, evading Rough's strenuous dive. The goalkeeper had done magnificently well to get a hand on the ball but could not prevent it crossing the line, high up between post and crossbar. Again the South American crowd got to their feet and greeted the goal with delirium. 'Ally didn't know, for example, that Cubillas took free kicks for Peru,' says Arthur Montford. 'When he lined up the free kick, I could see it coming, but the wall didn't.'

A lack of organisation had left Rough struggling to do his best behind a jerry-built wall. 'The wall didn't help me,' he says. 'At the Cubillas free kick, if the wall had stood up it wouldn't have gone in. There were three of the smallest guys in the team on the end of the wall – Lou Macari, Stuart Kennedy and Archie Gemmill – and when Cubillas hit the ball it was going at head height and they all bent their bodies to their left. That's why it went round them.

'The other one that he hit, the second goal, I thought was a good strike. You get them. No goalkeeper likes to get beaten by a free kick but these guys have got a lot of ability, they're not just any wee Joe from the SPL. It's Cubillas; a world-class player. They certainly could do things with a ball that you never experienced in the Scottish top division.'

The delicate right-footed shot that Cubillas had employed had required only the most feather-light back lift and follow-through but it exacted a heavy price from the Scots. Night was falling on Cordoba when the match – minus further major incident – drew to an end and as the team trudged off the field of play in the gathering gloom, it looked like a much blacker, bleaker World Cup for Scotland.

The aftermath of the match saw MacLeod explore virgin

territory: for the first time he had to face up to a significant defeat as the Scotland manager, a defeat that had
destroyed his reputation as the man who could do no
wrong. As the spectators drifted away into the chilly
Cordoba night, Ally MacLeod began seeking reasons for
his team's defeat. MacLeod had always been superstitious
to a degree – if his team won a match, he would wear
the same suit for the next match. Now, in the dressing
room, he raged as he threw around the blue shorts that
the team had worn, cursing them and insisting that
Scotland always performed poorly when they played in
them; he swore they were Scotland's unlucky shorts. The
team had worn blue shorts during the Home
Internationals – in the build-up to Argentina – which was
when MacLeod's Scotland first began to falter, and the
coincidence of wearing those new shorts once again would
have been enough for MacLeod to associate them with
bad luck.

MacLeod was, for the first time as manager of Scotland,
entirely subdued as he contemplated how his plans and
promises had been shredded mercilessly during the most
important ninety minutes of his career so far. 'We simply
didn't play well,' he told the press. 'Players did not play
to their strengths. Too many of them were off-form – and
they will tell you that themselves.' Arthur Montford recalls
facing a flummoxed MacLeod after the match as the
manager flailed around for reasons why it had all gone
wrong. 'He was stunned; absolutely stunned. "How did it
happen? What have I done wrong? I can't blame the ref."
He had written that first game down as a banker for sure,'
reflects Montford.

As a manager MacLeod felt instinctively that it was
better not to have too much detail on the opposition. He
wanted to know who made them tick and how they played

but was wary of overloading his players with information for fear that that would build up their opponents too much. That approach appeared to have worked against him in the Peru match. In MacLeod's defence it has to be noted that the South Americans had not watched Scotland, nor had MacLeod watched Czechoslovakia prior to his team's fiery 3-1 victory over them at Hampden in September 1977 – a victory that had done so much to push Scotland in the direction of the World Cup finals.

It was, believes Joe Harper, one of Ally's most admirable qualities that had punctured the efforts of the team. 'Ally, being a loyal, loyal man stood by the guys who got him there, whereas some of them were just over the hill – Rioch, Masson, you know, these guys were just beginning to get past their best. That was when the Sounesses and these guys should have come in. Bruce and Don were great players, I don't blame them at all for what happened. I blame, to a certain extent, Ally for picking the guys. I admire him for his loyalty but if there was a mistake by Ally MacLeod, it was that he stood by the guys that got him there.'

Bruce Rioch, himself, as he flicks back his memory to that eventful evening in Cordoba, points to other factors. 'It would be fair to say we didn't know much about Peru as players. I think we went out determined to try and do well but they proved to be a decent side and you can get beaten by a decent side. You have to remember they were playing in South America and players like Chumpitaz and Cubillas had played in previous World Cups. They had influential players but I don't think we underestimated them. I can't recall for one moment us underestimating the teams in the group.

'The reason, I think, we had done so well in the couple of years before the World Cup would really be because of the continuity of the team and the squad. From the time I was given my first cap, in the May of 1975, it did appear that the same squad was gathering on each occasion, with one or two new faces added to the mix. That meant that we were almost a club team; as far as you can get that at international level.

'There was also a long break between the match with Wales in late 1977 before everybody came back together again for the World Cup – there was only one international played in that time – and in the Home Internationals Ally gave other people opportunities to see what they could do. There were changes to the team in the matches before the 1978 World Cup, and results weren't quite as good going into the tournament. Maybe because there were such a number of changes, the continuity of the team dissipated a little bit. Ally was, I'd have to say, loyal to a fault – he continued to support his players at all times.'

Pointing up a couple of key factors that he feels contributed to Scotland's defeat by Peru Willie Johnston says, 'We weren't bad as a team against Peru but we didn't know that Cubillas would be the one to bend the ball round the wall; we knew they would do that but we didn't know which one of their players was the one. If Don Masson had scored with the penalty kick we would have beaten Peru. We played all right but, with the two goals that we lost to Cubillas . . . if we had known about the boy we would have maybe been better.'

The pre-tournament claims made by Ally MacLeod had, in the space of one match, begun to sound hollow and Sandy Jardine suggests that began to nibble away at the Scottish players' morale. 'Scotland were capable, maybe, if we played at our very, very best, of maybe getting a medal of some sort – but not of winning it – but you don't shout and blow your trumpet before you go. Everybody got totally carried away and that unrealistic expectation put pressure on everybody so when we got off to a bad start, what that did was created even bigger pressure.'

The ongoing issue over the players' bonuses hadn't helped morale either. It had muddied the players' minds before they even played Peru and had interfered with the fine-tuning of the team. 'We had some problems prior to the game,' says Rioch, 'where there were discussions on finance and that had an impact for three or four days for quite a lot of the players. That had a small part to play in the defeat; not a whole part, though.'

At Cordoba airport a downcast Rod Stewart was hauling himself across the tarmac towards the plane that would take him back to the comforts of metropolitan Buenos Aires. He met Andy Roxburgh, returning after having seen Holland defeat Iran 3-0 in Mendoza. Rod raised his scrawny, rock star fist. 'If it hadn't been for you I wouldn't have been at that game!' he yelled at Roxburgh, before falling upon his pal with the obligatory backstage-type hug. 'I think it is goodbye to the World Cup . . . endsville,' decreed Rod, in best LA seventies speak.

At his press conference on the morning after Scotland's defeat, MacLeod got proceedings underway with the words, 'The end of the world has almost arrived . . .' as he tried, in the cold light of day, to explain away his team's defeat by Peru and say what he planned to do next. Journalists were asking him when, not if, he was going to resign. MacLeod was genuinely puzzled over why so many people to whom he had given a story in the preceding weeks were now turning on him – a sea change he had failed entirely to anticipate.

As he sat in the courtyard of the Sierras Hotel a dog padded over and MacLeod began to pet it, throwing stones for it in a desultory manner and murmuring that the animal was now his only friend in the world. An apocryphal story would arise telling that just as MacLeod said those words the dog bit him. This was not true. This was a dog that, in common with Scotland against Peru, was lacking in bite.

8

A Positive Scandal

Distraught and desparing players sat with sunken heads in the Scottish team's desolate dressing room after a defeat by Peru. Ally MacLeod stood amongst them in that hour after the final whistle, desperately seeking something that he could use to begin to lift his own and his players' morale as they slumped amidst discarded tie-ups, boots, laces and pieces of strapping – a scene of devastation after one of the most significant setbacks in their careers. Inspiration soon came to the manager. Eventually, as Ally hovered helplessly in the dressing room amidst his disconsolate footballers in that hour of defeat, he was given news that Willie Johnston and Kenny Dalglish were the players who would be providing a sample of urine for FIFA to check for illicit substances. 'At least that will turn out all right,' joked MacLeod, attempting to lift his players after a match that had gone so wrong for Scotland.

The cataclysmic defeat by Peru would soon look like a gentle blip. Willie Johnston had popped a couple of pills down his throat prior to the encounter with the South Americans and when the man who wore number 11 on his back was selected to provide a urine sample, his number was up. He tested positive for traces of a banned substance called fencamfamin, a central nervous system stimulant that increases locomotor activity: it makes someone move more quickly. The fencamfamin had been contained in two tablets of Reactivan that Johnston had swallowed shortly before kick-off in Cordoba.

In a typical tablet of Reactivan, 6 per cent of the composition will be fencamfamin; the other ninety-four per cent comprises vitamins B and C. Reactivan increases drive and mental alertness, elevates mood and gives a general feeling of well-being and is often used in the treatment of depressive day-time fatigue, lack of concentration and lethargy.

Johnston was unaware on the Saturday evening after the match that he had tested positive. The following evening, Sunday, at the Sierras Hotel, an official reception was planned for the Scottish team. The guest of honour would be Denis Howell, Britain's minister for sport, who had often expressed his disapproval of the use of drugs in sporting competition. The Scottish players, spruce in their hundred-pound suits from Daks, looked as out of place as young, energetic footballers always do on such occasions. Don Masson larked around, smiling; Jim Blyth, a reserve goalkeeper to Alan Rough, stood impassively by; Kenny Dalglish, ultra alert, sat taking in the detail of all that was going on around him.

Willie Johnston, spotting a television camera turning its lens on him, put on a clownish face; he opened his eyes as unnaturally wide as possible, pinned his eyelashes back and manipulated his mouth into a gaping grin to reveal every gleaming front tooth. Here was a man without, apparently, a care in the world – he recalls that he had still not been told by that point that he had failed the test. It was only later that evening, as he sat smiling and nursing a nice drink at the reception, that Johnston was presented with the bad news. Trevor McDonald, then an Independent Television News reporter, sidled up to him – with a cameraman in tow – and, in his cultured tones, informed Johnston of his predicament and requested a comment or two for the soon-to-be-bemused British nation.

'I didn't know anything about it,' says Johnston. 'It was Trevor McDonald who told me, when I was sitting in the bar. He said something about me failing the drugs test. I went, "What? You're joking." He said, "Yes, you have." He wanted to know my reaction and then Ally MacLeod came and grabbed him and put him out. That was the first time I had heard about it. Somebody had leaked it. There were a lot of politics. Some Argentinian people must have told the media.'

MacLeod was furious at McDonald for descending on Johnston in such a way. The reception was not a media event but McDonald and his crew had been given special permission to film, at the invitation of the British government. For the duration of the reception, hosted by the British Embassy, that section of the hotel had been categorised as British soil. MacLeod saw McDonald's actions as a serious abuse of the privilege and twenty minutes after the Scottish players had arrived, they were told, on MacLeod's instructions, to depart en masse.

The defeat by Peru had been dispiriting but in the light of Johnston's drug test result it was now clear that a draw, or even a victory, would have been much worse for Scotland. If the team had managed to pluck any sort of positive result against Peru it would have been snatched away from them almost immediately: FIFA rules stated that any team with a player found guilty of a doping offence would forfeit, with an automatic 2-0 defeat, the match in which they had participated. That now seemed academic, following the Scots' two-goal defeat by the South American champions. More to the point, FIFA possessed the power to eject from the tournament any national team whose player had tested positive for a banned substance. Scotland now teetered on the brink of expulsion from the very World Cup that Ally MacLeod, Rod Stewart and Andy Cameron had confidently told the nation they were going to win.

In the wake of the devastating news, MacLeod and the team doctor, Dr Fitzsimmons, maintained that Fitzsimmons had asked the players, individually, prior to the match with Peru, whether they were taking any kind of tablets or pills, such as something for a cold, headache or any other mild ailment.

'We were aware, naturally, that there were going to be drug tests,' says Ernie Walker, the SFA secretary at that World Cup, 'and the doctor, John Fitzsimmons, went round everybody and told everyone that if they were taking any pills then he had to know. So that had been done and Dr Fitzsimmons assured us that he had certainly been round all the players.

'I remember Tom Forsyth saying to us that after the doctor had spoken he was scared to clean his teeth before the game in case there was something in the toothpaste, so there was no question about whether the message got through – to Tom Forsyth – but it appears that Willie, being Willie, went straight to his pocket and took out a couple of Reactivan pills and took them before the game, as he had been advised to do by the doctor of West Bromwich Albion, who had given these pills to all the West Brom players.'

It may even have come down to when and how the doctor's question was asked. MacLeod recalled that Dr Fitzsimmons had 'asked Bud [Johnston] at two o'clock on the afternoon of the match if he had taken any pills and the boy said he hadn't, which was true. Then he went and took them an hour later, ninety minutes before the game started.'

Dr Roger Rimmer, the club doctor at West Bromwich

Albion, admitted to having given Johnston Reactivan in
the past, describing it as 'a mild stimulant preparation
containing vitamins widely prescribed in the Health Service
at a time when a patient feels low or debilitated. Until
recently, it could be bought freely over the counter at any
chemist's shop.' There were, he said, no restrictions in the
UK on prescribing such potions. Johnston himself said he
had taken a dozen Reactivan pills with him – he compared
it to Aspirin – and said, 'There are over four hundred drugs
on the banned list but nobody ever showed it to me.'

Johnston, thinking back to that time, denies vehemently
that the process of warning the players about banned
substances was carried out prior to the Peru match; his
easygoing demeanour gives way to a quick flash of serious
anger at any suggestion that he had been well warned not
to take anything that might contain a banned substance.
'That's shite,' he asserts. 'No way; no how. Nobody was
told about drugs or anything like that; what to take, what
not to take. Because if half the squad had been drug-tested
there would have been a lot more than me. No, nobody
was told about drugs before the Peru game.

'I might be Jack the Lad,' he adds, 'but I'm not completely
daft. If I'd been told not to take it, I wouldn't have done.
I just took two tablets that they gave to everyone who had
had a cold or the 'flu. At West Brom, if you were off with
the 'flu or the cold they would give you a course of tablets
to build you back up. Everybody in England was doing it.
They weren't stimuli. After the way I played? They must
have given me the wrong stuff . . . if they doped me it
was the wrong way.'

The episode proved a severely testing one for Dr
Fitzsimmons. 'He was devastated,' says John Hagart. 'He
wasn't, by nature, the type of person to overreact or shout
and bawl or look as if it was the end of the world but he

was shattered by it all; that the whole thing had happened. Being the man he was, I always had the impression that he was annoyed with Willie and felt Willie had let us down but that he also felt a bit sorry for Willie.'

Only one player at a World Cup, Ernst Jean-Joseph of Haiti, in 1974, had ever been previously tested positively for taking an illegal substance so this was seriously big news, as Johnston quickly discovered. 'Next morning,' he remembers, 'I opened my room door, came out and there seemed to be about two million photographers and reporters. They asked me what I had done. I said I had taken two tablets called Reactivan and had failed a drugs test.'

A real crisis was now on the hands of the SFA and they met on Monday afternoon to discuss what their reaction should be. Johnston was brought before them and informed that he would never play for Scotland again. He recalls the succeeding moments well. 'I was told, "Go to your room. There will be a car sent for you. You're going home."' He would be on the next available flight out of Argentina.

The Scottish FA's reaction had to be seen to be swift and severe in the eyes of FIFA and they had to act to try to pre-empt the world body doling out their own harsh punishment, possibly expulsion. FIFA's subsequent edict, as the SFA had hoped, was softer than it might have been had the SFA not been so blatantly hard on Johnston. The player was banned by FIFA from international football for one year and they gave a 'severe' warning to the SFA on the matter of doping. There was clearly no need for them to hand out their automatic punishment of a two-goal defeat.

'I was bamboozled,' states then SFA secretary Ernie Walker, 'when they came to me and said, "Your player, Johnston, has been tested positive." The first I recall hearing of it was at the reception, when Harry Cavan, a Northern

Irish vice-president of FIFA, mentioned it to me. I thought, "What are you talking about?" It was much to Willie's amazement as well; he didn't know what we were talking about.

'We had never heard of drugs. We didn't use drugs. Whatever else our shortcomings or failings might have been, cheating in that way would not be one of them. We might be a bit brutal; we might be this, that or the other but we actually observed all the rules meticulously. We never tried to get the better of anybody in some nefarious fashion; certainly not giving players drugs. Nobody would have understood what you were talking about; the subject wasn't well known in those days.

'We called a meeting and the player was going to be suspended anyway, and we decided that in everybody's interests, particularly Willie's, the best thing would be to get him away to hell out of it and go home. His presence was going to be bad news around the place; we'd be hounded more and more by journalists as long as he was there. At least when they knew he was away they might get off our backs a wee bit and give us some peace. We arranged to smuggle him out of the camp by going the long journey by road to Buenos Aires. I'm not suggesting our hotel was like Gleneagles but it was in a huge area like that, with trees and fields and tennis courts, with a perimeter that was guarded by the Argentinian military. The media couldn't walk in or out but the place was besieged by them – it was a blockade, almost. However, we were advised about a back gate that you could get to through the woods.

'There was a massive, massive press conference on the steps of the hotel, when I was pushed up front to explain to the world that we don't cheat and it really stuck in my craw that I was conscious that I was talking, in many cases, to people who do cheat. I was apologising on behalf of my country that this awful thing had occurred but at the same time I was trying to make a defence of our situation, as far as you could, standing there rather naked.'

Johnston had actually trained with the squad on that Monday morning but early that evening he was bundled on to the floor of a Mercedes, a blanket placed over his head, and whisked out of Alta Gracia at speed – via the previously reconnoitred back gate. On the eight-hour overnight journey, along crater-pocked roads through the rough terrain from Cordoba to Buenos Aires, there was just one stop, at a transport cafe. The car arrived in Buenos Aires early the next morning and Johnston was booked into a hotel in the Flores district prior to catching a flight to Rio de Janeiro, then to London via Paris.

'They put a blanket over my head and I was like a criminal for eight hours in a car,' says Johnston. 'Peter Donald of the SFA was in the car; he was brilliant. I went to a hotel for a couple of hours and then I had to go to the British Embassy and a wee boy from Edinburgh in the British Embassy came in and asked me how I was doing. I was shattered. He said, "Are you wanting a bottle of beer?" I said, "I'd love it." He brought this big bottle of beer, like Newcastle Brown Ale, and I said, "Oh, that's great." We sat for two hours – me and him. He was great.

'I still felt like shit. After leaving the Embassy, I was taken to the airport and was put in the VIP lounge, on my own. An Argentinian came in with a machine gun, shouted "John-ston" and motioned for me to go out on to this bus to go to the aeroplane, which was a long distance from the terminal; there were only me and him on the bus and he had the gun and he was prodding me with it. I thought, "This guy's going to shoot me."

'We got to the plane and on the journey home I felt so

bad that I was just wanting the plane to go down. Someone said to me, "That's a bit selfish, what about all the other people on the plane?" That was how I felt. I went from Buenos Aires to Rio, Rio to Paris, and Paris to London – a twenty-six-hour journey – but I didn't want to go home. I chain-smoked all the way; I was chewing them.

'Wee Willie Henderson spoke to me on the phone. He said, "Bud, you've got more publicity than World War Two." At London I was met by big Ron Atkinson, my manager at West Brom. He said to me, "Have you got any of those tablets left? I'm knackered . . ." Then he said, "The good news is that I've negotiated a new contract for you . . . with Boots the Chemist . . ." Joking aside, it was actually terrible and that was the worst part; coming home.

'My wife couldn't get out of the house for reporters camped outside the door so West Brom took her and the kids away to Oxford. So I asked Big Ron to take me to Oxford. He said, "No, stay here. Go on *Nationwide* tonight, live, it'll a big thing." This was Big Ron getting a foot in the door with the television thing. So I went along with it but when I got to the TV studios Jock Stein was there. He growled at me, "What are you doing here?" Lawrie McMenemy was there too. He said, "What are you doing here?" They were there as part of a World Cup panel.

'Big Jock said, "Bud, you shouldn't be doing this." I said to them, "I know, but it's him. Big Ron is wanting me to do this." I got five hundred pounds for that. They couldn't pay me in cash so they gave me an air ticket to Calgary, which I had to go down to the travel agency to redeem. I felt like using it right away.'

To make things worse for Johnston, who believed he was simply on the *Nationwide* show to give his side of the story, he found himself being interrogated fiercely about why he had decided to take 'drugs' during the World Cup.

Commentating for Scottish Television, Arthur Montford was on hand in Argentina, watching the details unravel, and he suggests that Johnston's failed drug test episode brought out some of the best human qualities in Ally MacLeod. 'It was a perfect media story,' says Montford, 'a gift to the media. Ernie Walker's statement was not high-handed exactly but what FIFA would have expected, but Ally was quite reluctant to be overly critical of Johnston.

'I admire MacLeod very much for that because, with the way things were going, it would have been very easy for him to have pilloried Johnston and he was very reluctant to do so. He said Johnston was naïve and wrong not to tell the doctor but he did not take what would have been the easy step and try to deflect on to Johnston the blame for Scotland's troubles.'

Back in Ayr, Gail, Ally's teenage daughter, took the news badly. She had always liked the small, cuddly players best and had plastered her room with pictures of Johnston in the approach to the tournament. Faye MacLeod also recalls the compassion Ally showed for Johnston. 'Ally said, "How would Willie have felt if we had won and we had had the points taken off the team and they didn't go on and qualify? Willie would have had to have lived with that for the rest of his days." That was the kind of person Ally was – even afterwards he thought of how Willie Johnston would have felt.'

The crisis over Johnston had been devastating for MacLeod but it had been compounded, during those dark hours, by Don Masson, who shared a room with Johnston, casually strolling up to MacLeod to let him know that he had also taken Reactivan. MacLeod, stunned at Masson's news, had immediately advised the SFA that he believed Masson should be sent home, too. But on being inter-

Rod brought the house down at Wembley many times. After the 1977 victory over England he joined the Tartan Army in bringing the posts down

30,000 buy into the dream at Hampden. It only cost 50p after all

Training in the mornings in Argentina. Not much to look forward to in the afternoons

The perfect start. Joe Jordan celebrates putting the Scots 1–0 up against Peru

Minutes before half time, disaster. One–all

Penalty! 62 minutes. But it was to take another 162 minutes of football before Scotland scored a goal of their own in Argentina '78

Peru seal Scotland's fate

Ally playing for Blackburn in 1958

Prince Charles perfected the
Ally MacLeod look

The Faces. Willie Donachie, Martin Buchan, Ally MacLeod, Joe Jordan,
Sandy Jardine, Bruce Rioch, Derek Johnstone, Asa Hartford, John Blackley.
Ole Ola, Rod must have been over tha'

Johnny Rep dives; referee Erich Linemayr, in distant background, buys it, the Dutch still go one up

Kenny sweeps in the equalizer and Scotland are on a roll

Dreamland. One goal away from qualification …

… and the fans know it

COLORSPORT

Johnny Rep (far left) breaks Scottish hearts

MIRRORPIX

The dream is over

The Perms

A magic carpet ride ...

Which one's Nessie? 48,000 competition entries were sent in to Blue Peter

On the march with Ally's Army. This lot – Andy Cameron is on the left – would shake anyone up

Willie Johnston on his way back to Scotland ...

... while Ernie Walker explains Johnston's expulsion from the tournament for failing a drugs test

To the wild excitement of the fan(s),
Joe Jordan charges towards goal against
Iran ... to no avail

viewed by SFA officials Masson, under pressure, retracted his admission and stated that he had only been trying to ease Johnston's plight by showing solidarity with him. Then, just to show exactly how muddled his state of mind had become, Masson threw in an apology for missing the penalty against Peru.

As the craziness escalated, Johnston, about to become the first European expelled from a World Cup for failing a dope test, was called in by the SFA as nothing less than a witness for Masson and duly told them that Masson had not taken Reactivan.

It seems strange that the SFA should have accepted this story so readily, but clearly, at this point, it was what the SFA would have wanted to hear: having to send a second player home would not have been good news. Losing one player could be regarded as a misfortune; losing two as carelessness. That would hint at an escalating epidemic of drug-taking within the Scotland squad rather than the offence being portrayed as a single, isolated rogue element.

Had another team member been found to have taken drugs the likelihood of FIFA coming down on the Scots with an iron fist would have been strong. MacLeod's wish for Masson to be sent home was duly overruled by the SFA. 'Our instinct would be to try and shut it up,' confirms Ernie Walker. 'We were already the subject of international humiliation.'

That bizarre cameo, a play within a play, meant – even allowing for the sterling evidence offered by Johnston – that Masson's World Cup was effectively over. Masson was quickly told by MacLeod that he would not figure again in the tournament – surely an unnecessary thing to tell a player as opposed to simply not selecting him. Within hours, as a consequence, Masson, with nothing left to lose, had sold his story to the *News of the World* for publication on the morning of the final group match, with Holland. 'He left everybody with a bad taste in their mouths,' says Walker, 'principally through taking the shilling of the media. When things were at their worst, he was phoning home and reporting all the guff.'

Paranoia now invaded the Sierras Hotel. MacLeod and Dr Fitzsimmons stalked the corridors and scoured the players' rooms to discover that a number of other players had Reactivan in their possession; around two dozen tablets were confiscated when the manager and the doctor made their rounds. The fact that so much of the banned substance was found suggests either that Dr Fitzsimmons may not, as Willie Johnston alleges, have been as stringent as necessary in checking for such substances prior to the Peru match or that he was dealing with a number of footballers who were using Reactivan and were completely unwilling to declare it to the doctor.

His fellow players felt, in the main, only sympathy for Johnston. 'I think it was very, very unfortunate,' says Sandy Jardine. 'People think he had taken drugs and think of injections but what he took was a tablet that was quite prevalent in England and I don't think it was associated with being a drug. It was like a glucose drink; something that helped you to speed up reactions.

'I don't think he thought it was a drug and he then got hung out to dry by the SFA and everybody in the world media. I think the SFA could have handled it better. It obviously was an embarrassment to everybody concerned but it wasn't a major drug, like people think.'

The role of victim did not come in a size that would quite fit Willie Johnston. This was a player in the course of tallying up a quite majestic twenty-one dismissals in his career and who generally gave the impression of not caring a hoot about anyone's opinion of him. With West Bromwich Albion he would occasionally, when the ball went dead for a throw-in or free kick, taunt a particularly niggly opponent by using the index finger and thumb of both hands to pull out his shirt at the chest to create an imaginary pair of breasts just to show the opposing defender exactly what he thought of him.

'He was a typical Fifer,' says Hugh Allan. 'He wouldn't even go to the shop to buy shoes; his wife bought them for him. Willie didn't give a damn what anyone thought of him; he didn't hold anyone in awe. He just did his own thing; he was kind of harum scarum but he was a good player, a good attacking player.'

North Sea waves crash against the seafront wall in Kirkcaldy, spraying on to the coast road, as Johnston, now comfortably ensconced back in the safe haven that is his hostelry, the Port Brae Bar, settles down to consider the events that ripped a hole in a first-class football career that appeared close to its peak in the late seventies. West Brom had capped two fine years since promotion by finishing sixth in England's top division at the end of the 1977-78 season; they had qualified for the UEFA Cup and, with their new, young manager Ron Atkinson at the helm, the club looked poised for bigger and better things. Johnston, playing on the left wing, had been a vital ingredient in West Brom's success and that had won him, at the age of thirty, a recall by Willie Ormond to the Scotland squad for the friendly with Sweden in April 1977. It had been seven years since Johnston had been involved with the national team.

The winger had turned down a six-year contract at Rangers in 1972 to leave for England because he had felt that the walls were closing in on him in Scotland. Johnston felt that his disciplinary record meant that he had become a marked man for the SFA's besuited assassins – his most recent punishment from the SFA had been a ten-week suspension for a misdemeanour committed in Rangers' colours. He feared, in 1972, that his next suspension – and there would surely be one – would see him sidelined for six months. The only logical response was to leave the country. After a five-year gap he had gone back to Scotland to represent the national side and had been delighted to prove that he was an even better player than the one who had done such an enormous amount to land the European Cup-Winners' Cup for Rangers a few weeks before his departure from Ibrox.

'I was playing well at West Brom so I was hoping to get back in,' Johnston says of his long-awaited recall to the Scotland squad, 'but there was big Hutch [Tommy Hutchison], Arthur Graham, [Alex] Cropley and a few of them also playing quite well. But I got back in the team. I wasn't well liked at the SFA because of what had happened when I had been at Rangers: I got a few suspensions and they wouldn't pick me for Scotland. That was why I had been away from the Scotland team for so long.

'When I got back in the Scotland team, the manager was Willie Ormond and he took me aside at Largs and told me, "Bud, don't get into any bother because they are not wanting you in the team." He said, "I want you in the team because you're playing well at West Brom but the SFA don't want you in the team."'

Johnston had excelled in Scotland's key matches in 1977 but was less than happy with the performance he had turned in against Peru. 'I didn't play too well,' he says. 'I wasn't right. I shouldn't have played because I had the 'flu. I felt bad on the day before the game and took a couple of paracetamols and went to my bed and thought I would be all right, but when I woke up I knew I wasn't

– but I wanted to play for Scotland in the World Cup; everybody wants to play for their country in the World Cup. It's like a wee boy's dream, isn't it?'

The outside-left remembers sitting, crumpled, in the bath when it was announced that a sample had been requested from him. 'I didn't bother. I said, "Fine." I didn't think anything of it. I just pissed in the bottle with Kenny Dalglish, Cubillas and the other boy.

'Ally was shattered,' says Johnston of the resultant uproar. 'He just asked me what had happened and I told him the truth. I said I'd taken two tablets. He said, "Bud, you're going home." I didn't like the place anyway . . .'

The mood of jocularity is soon replaced by one of seriousness as Johnston recalls the sinister warning doled out to him after Scotland had drawn 1-1 with Argentina in their friendly in 1977 – a warning that might have sent more nervous players scurrying for the shadows. 'I had been there the year before,' says Johnston, 'and I was told not to come back by Luque, the big centre-forward for Argentina. I got sent off against them and he asked me to go out with him for a drink at night, after the game; he also wanted my jersey but I wouldn't give him it. He was a great fellow. He said, "John-ston, my friend, you not come back to Argentina. You very good; you must not come back. We win World Cup next year. You – do not come back." What did I do? I went back, didn't I?

'He was suggesting I was going to be a marked man. If we had played Argentina again it would have been world war three; honestly. There was only one team going to win that World Cup, and it wasn't Scotland. So when I went back for the World Cup and my name was selected for the doping test after the first game, I think that was what Luque had been talking about. I was a marked man, whatever they could do to get me away from there, they would do.'

Johnston is convinced that his positive test would not have been revealed by FIFA if Scotland had beaten Peru, and that because Scotland lost by the requisite two-goal margin FIFA could make an example of him without having to alter the course of the tournament. This also, he believes, enabled FIFA to issue a warning, very early in the tournament, to the sixteen participating nations of the possible consequences of taking illicit substances; a matter of growing concern for the world body. The implicit suggestion from Johnston is that players from other nations were taking similar substances.

That may seem like a conspiracy theory too far but as Johnston expounds on his belief that he was a marked man on his return to Argentina, he describes what do seem to have been strange circumstances surrounding his doping test. The two players from each team who provided a urine sample were supposedly chosen at random – using numbers drawn out of a bag. Following the Peru match, the two Scottish players beckoned immediately to provide a sample were Kenny Dalglish and, not Johnston, but Archie Gemmill. Gemmill duly traipsed off to the appointed venue but struggled to provide a sample. Only after he had been there for some time was Gemmill informed that he was not required and sent back to the dressing room to tell Johnston to return in his place; Johnston was soaking in the team bath when Gemmill went to fetch him. It does seem as though Johnston could have been a wanted man.

It is impossible to dismiss the possibility that in Argentina in the late seventies, where corruption was rife and where the government needed to nail a World Cup victory to bolster its popularity, that Johnston could have been targeted and specifically chosen to provide a urine sample. It would not have been difficult, for example, for one of the secret police – who crawled all over the country and who were prevalent in the Sierras Hotel – to discover that Johnston had Reactivan in his room. The player had, after all, been quite outstanding in the opening period of the friendly against Argentina one year previously and, with Johnston removed from proceedings, one more obstacle had been discarded from Argentina's path to a potential final appearance. Scotland had been regarded, pre-tournament, as one of the most potent teams in the competition.

There is sympathy from Joe Harper as he ponders the nature of the substance taken by the winger and Harper concurs that Johnston was always likely to suffer severely for his very presence in Argentina. 'It was what they call an upper; something like a halibut orange [Haliborange] tablet,' he says. 'We didn't have them in Scotland but the English-based players swore by them and used to take them before a game.

'Now whether it's a mental thing to make you feel better . . . but it doesn't make you run faster; that's what it doesn't do. Now in that particular game, I think about five of our players took them, English-based players, but Willie was always a certainty to get taken off for a drugs test because he'd been sent off the previous year. So he was always going to get done but, even at that, you didn't realise that there was going to be anything that he could get done for; then they tested him.

'That, more than anything, took the morale of the boys downwards. I felt absolutely sorry for Willie at that point. We didn't exonerate him – it was silly – but it was a legal thing to do here, in the UK, and Willie never thought about it; neither did the rest of them, the guys that took them. They could quite easily have been done as well. It certainly opened their eyes up but we felt sorry for him, we felt sorry for the way he was treated. He wasn't trying to cheat the system or anything. These were just different things that they do in England. It was a sad time and more ammunition and fuel for the press.'

Johnston is gripped by the conviction that he was dealt a bad hand, not only because of his perceived threat to the Argentinians but also because of his nationality. 'The SFA handled it shockingly badly,' he contests. 'If that had been an English player or a Dutch player or an Argentinian player, you would never have heard about it but because it was a daft wee Scotsman, you heard about it. If it had been someone from one of those other countries, it would have been all hushed up.

'Don't tell me that players from other countries weren't taking tablets. Once the test proved positive, the SFA could have just said, "Right, hold it." I wanted to appeal but they wouldn't allow me to appeal. I wanted a drugs test twenty-four hours later and they wouldn't let me do that. Twenty-four hours later, I might have been clear but I just got told to go.

'Maybe if it had been somebody else – maybe if it had been Joe Jordan or Kenny Dalglish – the SFA might have done more but because it was Willie, the bad boy, it was a case of "Just get him out of here." The other players stood up and asked for me to stay but the SFA said, "No, he's going."'

The after-effects of Johnston's ejection from the 1978 World Cup would linger on for a long time and would bring even this super-confident, devil-may-care player grinding to a sad halt during the subsequent season at his club.

'The West Brom fans were brilliant,' he says. 'I received thousands of letters from them. But I got a lot of hassle from opposition fans at away matches; it was "junkie" this and "junkie" that. I lost it after that.

'I was getting so much shit it was terrible and the kids, at school, were getting it too. It was bad. I had loved to go to Old Trafford, Arsenal, Liverpool – it had been great – but I could not shrug that off. It got to me. I was finished. The children were coming home from school and saying, "Dad, you're a junkie." Your confidence just goes in circumstances like that.'

The situation was compounded by a letter from the SFA that dropped on Johnston's Midlands doormat later in 1978, confirming that he was banned from playing for Scotland for life; he was also banned from participating in West Brom's run to the quarter-finals of the UEFA Cup during the 1978-79 season. Johnston's solution to all these troubles was to emigrate from English football and in the spring of 1979 he left West Bromwich Albion in a £100,000 transfer that took him to Vancouver Whitecaps in the more relaxed, less intense surroundings of the family-friendly North American Soccer League.

Suspicion and unease pierced those who remained in Alta Gracia. 'About four days later, after Willie had gone away,' says Joe Harper, 'myself, Derek and Alan were lying on our beds after a training session and the Doc came in and said "What is that there?" We looked around and couldn't see what he was meaning and it was a nasal spray that Derek had been using just to clear his nostrils but within it there was a banned substance so he could, quite innocently, also have been banned for drugs.'

The Scotland squad reeled from the dull dual blows of defeat by Peru and Johnston's removal from their midst. An enormous cloud rolled over players, officials and management that would sit there for the next few days, with the match against Iran looming on the horizon.

'Johnston will be a sensation in Argentina,' Ally MacLeod had stated prior to the 1978 World Cup tournament. The Scotland manager had never been more correct.

9

A Lesser Nation

The calamities and clamour that had surrounded the Scotland squad had left their followers jaded after a mere week of the World Cup. The tournament that had promised so much had delivered nothing more than a blast of failure. Now, seven days in, it was as if a brilliant and intuitive personal physician had suddenly materialised to prescribe the perfect tonic: a match against Iran. The disappointments of the previous days would never be forgotten but Scots were sure that their team's second match would ensure that this, at least, would be no bad news day.

That cold Wednesday morning in Argentina Scottish fans, awakening in Cordoba's boarding houses, threw off their cowls and embraced the day. Porridge was eaten and delicious Colombian coffee savoured in anticipation of better things to come. At home, Scots prepared to see on their screens a routine, even a rousing, win. Victory, the nation was sure, would be a mere formality and would set up a do-or-die fixture with Holland. A presentable performance against Iran, topped off with a few goals, would wash away some of the bad taste that still lingered in the mouths of Scots everywhere. Their team had been tossed around by Peru and laughed at around the globe after the Willie Johnston affair. Now Scottish fans were revelling in their intended role reversal – they would bully Iran.

There was good reason for confidence. The Scottish

national team had never, in its 106-year history, lost or even drawn a match with a minor footballing nation from outside the British Isles. One good reason for that was that the Scots had rarely deigned to face the minnows of world football – the country that had done so much to give the world the game felt such competitors beneath their status. On those rare occasions when Scotland had confronted the smaller footballing nations, the matches had turned out to be like taking tea in the park.

In the ten years prior to the 1978 World Cup the Scots had thrashed Cyprus twice, by 8-0 and 5-0, and had beaten Zaire competently at the World Cup in 1974. Their only other brushes with the world's registered whipping boys had been back in 1947, when Scotland had lashed out with a 6-0 defeat of Luxembourg in their own rich, tiny duchy, and in 1952 when they had thrashed the United States 6-0. So there were no unexpected slip-ups to look back upon as the Scots contemplated their first encounter with Middle Eastern opposition. As one Scottish interna-tional of the time succinctly puts it, 'We thought, "Iran – that's all desert and rocks – how can they be any good at fitba?"'

Throughout the seventies, representatives of Africa, Asia and Oceania were still widely regarded by Europe and South America as token presences at the World Cup. Such teams were there to ensure that it could justifiably be described as a global tournament, but were seen as being really just baubles whose status was almost on a par with the opening and closing ceremonies; there only to add a bit of variety and lightness to the spectacle before stepping aside to allow the serious players to take over as the tournament reached its climax.

These supposedly lesser nations were prized opponents in the opening, group, stages – a match against any one of them was seen by European or South American nations as a promissory note of two points. Iran, in 1978, were one of only three representatives from outside Europe and South America – the others being Tunisia and Mexico – to participate in a World Cup that would see three South American nations jostling with ten from Europe for world supremacy.

There had been occasional shocks in previous World Cups. Cuba had beaten Romania to knock the Eastern Europeans out of the 1938 tournament. The US, captained by Eddie McIlvenny, a Scotsman from Inverclyde, defeated England 1-0 in 1950 – after the Americans had enjoyed a night out on the town in the belief that they had little hope in the following day's match. North Korea, in 1966, were reported by Italian scout Ferruccio Valcareggi to be a team of Charlie Chaplins but they defeated the Italians 1-0 in Middlesbrough; later in that tournament the North Koreans were 3-0 up on a superb Portugal side, Eusebio and all, in a quarter–final before losing 5-3. Set against those sporadic warnings from history, though, there were far more numerous examples of emphatic trashings of such sides: Cuba's 8-0 loss to Sweden in 1938, Poland's 7-0 drubbing of Haiti and Yugoslavia's 9-0 defeat of Zaire, both in 1974.

Scotland's own 1974 experience had featured a 2-0 victory over Zaire, in the Westfalen stadium on a sweltering evening in Dortmund. The Scots were, as it turned out, eliminated from that World Cup on goal difference: the received wisdom was that the only error made by the Scots was when Billy Bremner, the captain, defied managerial orders to pursue further goals and, instead, told his team mates to conserve their energy. That, however, did nothing to put off those optimistic about beating Iran in 1978. Zaire, in 1974, were expected to be the victims and so it had proved.

The Iranians who turned up for duty in Argentina were perceived to be disorganised. Those who had viewed one of their initial training sessions in the days before the tournament began had come across what they saw as a directionless rabble wearing multicoloured kit, aimlessly fluttering around their training pitch. The Iranians' opening match had done nothing to change the opinion that they were losers: they had been beaten 3-0 by Holland and it was suggested that if the Dutch had switched the power on full, it could have been by many more. Heshmet Mohajerani, the Iran manager, stated, 'All we want to do is represent our country honourably. Everything else will be sheer fantasy.'

Nevertheless, Iran's form prior to the World Cup had been impressive. They had qualified unbeaten from a gruelling set of matches that had required real dedication from them simply to fulfil their far-flung fixtures: they had faced Australia, Hong Kong, Kuwait, Syria, Saudi Arabia and South Korea. Iran had won ten and drawn two of those twelve matches, home and away, scoring twenty goals and conceding only three. Their most recent friendlies had seen them go down 2-1 to France and draw 1-1 with Bulgaria, whom Scotland had beaten only 2-1 in February.

With odds of 500-1 to win the World Cup Iran had begun the tournament rated as the second-least-likely nation to be successful; Tunisia at 1,000-1 were the rank outsiders. Even then, the Tunisians had defeated Mexico 3-1 in their opening match and had been unlucky not to achieve a draw with Poland, going down only 1-0 to a nation that had finished third at the 1974 World Cup.

If there were few worries among the Scots as to the capabilities of Iran, there were tensions inside the team hotel that threatened to create irreparable fissures in morale. The dissatisfaction that some players had felt since Dunblane about the situation with bonuses continued to linger. Shortly after the squad's arrival in Argentina, Bruce Rioch, as captain, had approached MacLeod to ask for a meeting with SFA officials to establish the detail of the bonuses to be paid to the players. MacLeod had told him, in some anger, that the players should be focusing on the match with Peru.

The issue would not go away, and after the Peru match Rioch, on behalf of the players, again asked for a meeting to discuss bonuses. This time, SFA officials agreed to the meeting, which was interesting as the SFA had had the opportunity to discuss the bonus situation in previous weeks but had declined to do so, instead opting to leave it to the manager. Now, with the Scots' second World Cup fixture on the horizon, Willie Harkness, the president of the SFA, agreed to a meeting to get the players 'into the proper state of mind for the game against Iran'.

Facing the players that evening were the graven figures of Harkness, chairman of the international committee Tom Lauchlan, SFA vice-president Tommy Younger and SFA secretary Ernie Walker. Money was not the first item on the SFA's agenda. Instead, the players were told by Younger to remember how proud they should be to be representing their country. The fallen figure of Johnston was mentioned as an example of someone who had strayed and who had let down badly the SFA and the nation. It was implied that the players somehow shared responsibility for Johnston's actions. That did not go down too well.

Then, and only then, did the SFA officials decide to mention money. Harkness requested that Walker should read out the bonus sums agreed and that was duly done. The SFA had agreed to pay the squad £40,000 collectively if they reached the second round; £75,000 for finishing fourth; £95,000 for winning the third/fourth place play-off; £120,000 if runners-up and £210,000 if they won the World Cup. Questions were then allowed from the floor but by the time the SFA officials shuffled out of the meeting, the players' tension over the bonus question had been exacerbated still further.

The players felt they had been patronised and it had finally become clear that there was no possibility of extra money now coming their way. This was a severe blow for MacLeod – he had never wanted the meeting to take place but the SFA had insisted on it. Lou Macari would soon be telling MacLeod that he wanted to go home. 'The reason it was raised,' says Rioch of the bonus issue, 'was because we didn't know what we were playing for. We didn't feel that that was acceptable.'

Regular meetings about bonuses are recalled by Gordon McQueen as 'terrible, drawn-out affairs. Those meetings dragged on and on, especially so for me since, as I was injured, I knew it made no difference since I wouldn't be playing and wouldn't get the chance to win the bonuses. The problem, I remember quite clearly, was that we never knew what the bonuses were. They had been promising in the long build-up that they would tell us what they were and we kept asking.

'Really, people like myself – even if I had been fit to play – and Joe Jordan and Asa Hartford and Willie Donachie couldn't have given a monkey's. To us, the amounts were of no importance but they were to quite a few people in that squad and that was one of the reasons there was some disharmony.

'I didn't think it was a particularly happy camp. Some people who weren't in the team thought that they should have been and after the first result, which was supposed to be a walkover, the flak started flying from the press.

People were also stirring it in the squad, making a big issue out of money, keeping that alive, when all that the others were wanting to do was get down to preparing for the matches.

'Tommy Younger said, "Why are you bothering about bonuses? You should be proud to play for your country." The players took offence to some of that attitude. It annoyed me. I don't know what Tommy Younger's business was but he wouldn't have carried out any transaction for nothing, for sure. That annoyed everybody, being talked to like that, regardless of whether the bonuses were terribly important to them or not.'

Ernie Walker suggests of the ongoing rumblings in Argentina about payments, 'It's a bit late in the day then, if somebody's moaning. Within the limits of these days, it was a generous enough package. Nobody was trying to steal money from anybody.

'The meeting [with the SFA in Argentina] was led largely by Macari – he was to the fore. And Kenny [Dalglish], of course. Kenny thought it wasn't right that Umbro should pay the SFA for the strips; that that should go to the players and not the SFA. He said that the SFA don't need that. Every national association in the world engineers a deal but Kenny thought it should be for the players and not for the national association.

'It was explained,' continues Walker, 'that the association has to run all kinds of football and refereeing and coaching and needs income from every source it can get; the age-old argument. Kenny was never far away whenever the subject of money would crop up. As always, it was two or three players that were doing their turn; the rest were sitting embarrassed.

'Bruce Rioch, as the captain, would have spoken but I don't remember him demanding anything. He was quite a conciliatory type in that role. Macari, Kenny – I certainly can remember Kenny speaking. It became almost a kind of joke: "The SFA doesn't need money; we need money." As if he was skint . . .'

The SFA, in fact, had been desperately, almost disastrously, short of money prior to the 1978 World Cup. 'So his remark that we didn't need any money was a wee bit off the mark,' says Walker.

The issue regarding the team's kit had arisen to a large degree because the 1978 World Cup was the first at which the commercialisation and sponsorship of football, into which the SFA had begun to delve deeply in the mid-seventies, would show itself in the very strip that the Scottish team would wear. The symbol of Umbro, kit manufacturer for the team, was a diamond, and the sponsor's logo had become an intrinsic part of the strip's design – solid diamonds across both shoulders of the jersey, down the sides of the shorts and across the tops of the socks. Obliged to wear the strip at matches and in training, the players became all-action clothes-horses for Umbro and were, in addition, required to make promotional appearances on behalf of the company.

Willie Allan, Ernie Walker's predecessor at the SFA, had refused to believe that any company would pay the association a significant sum of money for players to wear its kit but, in the new era of sponsorship, Walker was much more in tune with the potential for high fees. It was against this background that players had begun to question whether they, as chief models for Umbro, ought to receive a cut of the proceeds.

'It came up and was dealt with,' adds Walker of the bonus dispute. 'It was turned down. More money was what they were wanting. The bonuses were there and that was it. There was no question of paying any more than they had been promised beforehand. That was the type of background that caused me to suggest that Ally didn't quite have the resilience for the job at that level. It was great when it was all singing and dancing and everybody was on your side but life's not like that all the time.'

The line-up for the match with Iran found Willie Donachie back in defence; a player, MacLeod had noted privately, with a slapped, backhanded compliment, who 'always plays to his limitations'. Burns would still growl his way through the game in central defence but now with Buchan beside him in the middle, and Sandy Jardine replacing Stuart Kennedy at right-back. It would be the first time Buchan and Burns had ever played together as central defenders.

Gemmill took the place of Masson, a significant move as MacLeod had in the past been hesitant to select him. The manager had worried about Gemmill's tendency to play too many square balls which worked against the high-tempo, attacking style of play that MacLeod wanted from his team. During the 1977-78 season, though, MacLeod had gradually changed his opinion, having watched the player drive Nottingham Forest on to become champions of the Football League in England. This had still not been enough to make him a regular for Ally as long as Masson and Rioch were in place. But with MacLeod refusing to play Masson after his part in the Reactivan debacle, and Rioch injured in training the day before the match, Gemmill now had his chance to show what he could do.

Another midfielder available to MacLeod was Graeme Souness, of whom the manager had said, pre-World Cup, 'He tackles and he opens up play, more even than Don Masson. Obviously you wouldn't play the pair of them.' Again, MacLeod's refusal to play Masson had opened up an opportunity to field Souness in his starting eleven.

Souness, a hugely self-confident twenty-five-year-old – six-feet-one-inches tall and more heavily built than his fellow midfielders – was different in style to Gemmill and MacLeod's other available midfielder, Lou Macari. Both Gemmill and Macari were just five-feet-five-inches tall and both were hard-working, scurrying players who would snap at opponents and snaffle opportunities. Souness, in contrast, would make more stately progress through a match – pinging passes, long and short, here and there, with exceptional accuracy and, on best form, swaying a game entirely in his side's favour.

Had Souness been included in the side facing Iran, it would have been a calculated gamble. Souness had won only six caps in four years and was unproven at international competitive level. He had not featured in any of the World Cup qualifying matches but he had enjoyed a very good 1978, helping Liverpool to the European Cup after his transfer to Anfield from Middlesbrough that January. There was a commanding, aggressively arrogant air about Souness and in the hours prior to the match John Hagart had tried to steer MacLeod towards including the player in his side. This was a match in which Souness had the potential to add a degree of control to the Scotland midfield that had frequently been missing against Peru.

'The night before we played Iran,' says John Hagart, 'Ally said to me, "Let's have a wee blether" and we went into his room. He said, "What do you think about tomorrow?" I said, "Well, I don't know . . ." You had to approach things carefully because you couldn't say to Ally, "Listen, Ally, you're being daft. Take this player out of the team and put this player in. That's what you've got to do." If you said that to Ally there was no way that the player you had suggested would be in the team.

'I found with Ally that the best way was to say, "I don't know but is it maybe an idea to try this player? What do you think yourself?" He could say, "I'm not too sure about that." Or he could say, "Yes, that's a great idea. We'll play him." He would then say, at the press conference the next morning, "I've had a wee bit of inspiration. I'm going to bring in so-and-so . . ."

'Now, on the night before the Iran game, we went through the team and I led him into the Graeme Souness area, suggesting Souness for the team. Graeme was coming to the fore then and I always thought we were missing something and he was too good a player not to be in the team. Ally agreed to that and there were two other changes; one of them a player Ally wanted in and another one we had agreed on jointly. When I left his room that evening, Graeme Souness was in the team for the match with Iran.

'On the morning of the game we were going for a light training session and Ally was sitting at the front of the bus and I was sitting beside him. We stopped at the training ground and he jumped up and said, "Right, all sit where you are just now. We're just going to have a nice, wee, light warm-up, practise some ball skills and that will do us because we want to have a wee sleep this afternoon; and I'm going to tell you what the team is, now." And there were three changes from the team he and I had agreed on the night before and Souness was no longer in the team.

'Of course, I never said what had happened to anybody, not to any player, anybody. We came back and had our lunch and I didn't say to him, "I want to see you" or anything like that. We just happened to be going out of the dining room together and were walking along a veranda and I had a wee look behind. There was nobody there so I said to him, "You've changed the team from last night

. . ." He said, "Aye, I know, I know, I know; I think this'll be better." The decided impression was, "John, I'm the manager." I wasn't even questioning him as such; I was just interested to see what his thinking was but he didn't tell me. That was that subject closed.'

Instead of Souness, MacLeod chose Lou Macari to partner Gemmill in central midfield. John Robertson, a twenty-five-year-old earning only his third cap, replaced Johnston on the left side of a midfield quartet of which only Asa Hartford had survived since the match with Peru. Dalglish and Jordan remained as the front two but Macari and Robertson were required by MacLeod to supplement the two strikers by bursting into the Iranian penalty area at every opportunity – and it was anticipated that there would be plenty of chances for them to do so.

The Iranians were expected to be a defensive side and it was the duty of the Scots, as per MacLeod's instructions, to panic them with plenty of high balls into the box. The team that took to the turf to face Iran comprised: Alan Rough, Sandy Jardine, Martin Buchan, Kenny Burns, Willie Donachie, Asa Hartford, Archie Gemmill, Lou Macari, Kenny Dalglish, Joe Jordan and John Robertson.

Arthur Montford commentated on that fateful game and he states now, 'When I looked at Iran's record and compared notes with my colleagues from Iran – you always exchange information with your opposite numbers at international matches – they expressed surprise to me that Ally hadn't sent somebody whose judgement he would respect to the Middle East to look at Iran.'

Despite the sting of the surprise defeat by Peru, MacLeod remained dismissive of an Iranian team that he had never seen play. He had even passed up the chance to watch them train prior to their match with Scotland, as John Hagart recalls.

'I remember we went to train at the stadium in Cordoba and who was coming in to train after us but Iran,' says Hagart. 'I can remember saying, "What about staying to see Iran?" He said, "Och no, no, what are you wanting to watch them for? Listen, if you want to watch them, just you stay. Get one of the Argentinian guys with the cars to wait for you and you can come back with him."

'So I watched Iran and came back to the hotel and said to him, "Listen, they're all athletic-looking guys and they're slim and they're good movers . . ." He said, "Och, we don't need to worry about them, do we?" I said, "But teams are getting better and better." He recognised that but he replied, "Oh, surely we'll have a wee bit too much in our armoury for them." Ally was always pretty much focused on what we did; not on the opposition.'

A plethora of microphones was thrust towards MacLeod – close enough for his mouth to munch – by journalists seeking his thoughts on the match. 'We have to treat the next two matches like Bannockburn,' the manager told them, 'for nothing less than victory over Iran and Holland will do.' Reclining at the Sierras Hotel, wearing a Scotland top, he looked refreshed and re-energised.

'At the moment,' continued MacLeod, 'I'm very happy with the squad. I'm just not happy with the way we played in these two spells against Peru but, as I say, the battle's lost but the war's not over. That's the saying and I'm quite sure,' he added, breaking into a natural smile, his head tilting characteristically lightly to one side, 'that we might be having a more pleasant press conference after Wednesday.'

An equally bullish attitude could be found in Ali Parvin, the Iranian captain. 'We will not be beaten easily by anyone,' Parvin boasted. 'We have some very good players and Scotland will be surprised by the calibre of our play. If they underestimate us they will be in trouble.'

The people of Cordoba showed their appreciation at having thrust upon them a World Cup tie between Scotland and Iran by clubbing together to create one of the smallest attendances at any World Cup match ever. A mere 7,938 were present and most of those had opted only for the ground's cheap sections, behind the goals. Thus, as the two teams sauntered on to the field at the halfway line they were confronted by a vast expanse of deserted seats, which helped to give the occasion a surreal feeling. Iran were all in white, which meant that, once again, Scotland had to wear their dreaded blue shorts.

It was Iran to whom the first half-chance fell. Twelve desultory minutes had passed when Hossein Faraki's less than powerful shot spent several seconds trundling in the general direction of goal until it was cleared. A free kick from Robertson and a header from Dalglish produced good saves by Nasser Hejazi, the Iranian goalkeeper, but there was little fluidity from either side in a match that spluttered and stuttered. The only other significant chance of the first half fell to Parvin when, after half-an-hour, he came close to scoring from a free-kick, but the ball slipped over the bar.

With one minute to go until half-time the spectators – in common with Ally MacLeod, who, on the bench, looked entirely scunnered – were anticipating the interval and blessed relief.

The game had slowed to walking pace in those final seconds when Burns picked the ball up inside his own half and knocked it to Hartford, inside the centre circle. The midfielder prodded a long, hopeful punt into the Iranian penalty area but it veered away from Jordan, its intended target, to well within the sphere of goalkeeper Hejazi and Andaranik Eskandarian, the centre-back.

It seemed a simple ball for the Iranians to deal with as Hejazi advanced, fifteen yards from his goal line, and Eskandarian did the right thing by inserting his body solidly between the ball and Jordan. As the ball arrived, the two Iranians decided to break into what looked like a well-rehearsed, smoothly worked, clownish comedy routine. It would have been no surprise to see Eskandarian pull out a Klaxon and sound it a couple of times as he, completely unnecessarily, bounced forward to collide with his goal-keeper, forcing the ball up and out from between them.

Hejazi extended his right hand in an attempt to gather the ball but, like a wriggling hen evading a slaughter-hungry farmer, it squeezed free before Eskandarian, still in the mood for fun, intervened yet again. The ball rolled off his shoulder and, as it bounced, he was ready with his coup de grace; he would cap the laughter by smacking the ball away as quickly as possible in the direction he was facing. Unfortunately for the Iranians, he was facing his own goal. And so, from just behind the penalty spot, Eskandarian planted a graceful, left-footed volley right into his own net.

Dalglish and Jordan turned away from the scene, not even celebrating – they both looked decidedly sheepish and possibly even embarrassed at having to rely upon such inspired idiocy for Scotland's opening goal. Hejazi, continuing the comic theme, turned his back on the grounded Eskandarian and proceeded to put his hands behind his back, bow his head and cast his eyes to the ground in the manner of a ham actor looking for sympathy from his audience. He then slapped his palms together and turned to yell at the prostrate Eskandarian while gesticulating in the direction of his goal, just in case the defender needed reminding of the outrage he had just visited upon his nation.

The comedy continued after the break. Five minutes into the second half Donachie accidentally kicked Buchan in the head, leaving a wound that required several stitches and which forced MacLeod to replace him with Tom Forsyth. Forsyth quickly got in a fankle with Burns and Faraki took advantage to come close to equalising.

An hour of the match had passed when Jardine's pass was intercepted easily inside the Iranians' half. MacLeod rocked back and forth in frustration, lamenting his team's continuing lassitude with a forced smile of resignation and some mutterings to Hugh Allan who sat beside him. Ibrahim Ghasempour, in a meadow of space on the right wing, had time to find the skilful Faraki inside the penalty area and he dribbled past three Scots before returning the ball to Ghasempour, whose cross was headed clear by Jardine.

The ball dropped to Iraj Danaifar outside the penalty area, who showed it to Gemmill before going round the Scottish midfielder's right side, easily evading the limp attempt at a challenge and finding time and space to steady himself before driving a low, left-footed shot between Rough and his near post.

Among those watching from the stand that night was Bruce Rioch. 'When that goal went in, it was a dagger in your heart,' he says. 'It was not just the fans there and the people back home and the Scottish people around the world; the players felt it too. It was a really awful moment.'

Rough accepts that he should have stopped the goal. 'The boy came in and I anticipated him cutting it back. There were three of them waiting on it. The thing you never do is anticipate and move and I did. It was a bad goal from my point of view. Their boy did well to get there but any goalkeeper losing a goal at the near post is going to be disappointed.

'The Iran game was just a nothing, probably the worst game I've ever played in; an all-time low. You had a lot of characters, and Ally in there as well, but nobody could get lifted for that game at all. Some of the supporters were having a go at us before that game; some of them were still reeling from Peru.

'It was just one of these games, on the back of Peru, where nobody produced anything. We just couldn't get that killer second goal.'

It had been late in the second half when Joe Harper finally got a taste of World Cup action, as a substitute for the injured Kenny Dalglish. 'With my first touch of the ball I picked it up on the halfway line,' remembers Harper, 'at the dugout, and hit a great ball across the park right to the far side for Sandy Jardine to pick it up and I thought, "That's a good start." After that, I had a couple of shots at goal that were blocked.

'It passed very quickly. Iran were not better than we had expected. Sure, they were physically fit, organised, but I think they only had one shot at goal and they scored, and that was a [Scotland] mistake. They just didn't give you any time on the ball. They weren't a great team. We had an off-day; it was as simple as that.

'On the day we should probably have beaten them about 4-1; the chances we missed . . . It just didn't happen. We didn't play well; a lot of players didn't play well, especially in midfield, that day.'

Neither side created much after Iran's equaliser and the match wound a weary way to its end; the 1-1 draw left Scotland's World Cup campaign in tatters. 'It was one of those situations you get in sport where you can't change gear and become a good side halfway through a match,' says Arthur Montford.

The inclusion of the young, hungry Souness – the most composed playmaker available to Scotland – might have made a difference, even if he had been introduced as a substitute after Ally's late change of mind had left him on the bench. Instead, it was an occasion that most Scots who had witnessed it wished to erase from their memories as quickly as possible. 'Other than that goal, I can't remember much about the match with Iran,' says Bruce Rioch. 'It was like watching a bad movie – once it's over, the first thing you want to do is forget all about it. You felt it was the end of our World Cup but then we suddenly discovered we were still in it if we could go through on goal difference.'

This had been Scotland's nadir, and a match that left anyone who witnessed it with the unforgettable image of a bedraggled, befuddled MacLeod on the bench during that second half, looking close to tears before burying his head in his hands as the match unravelled before his eyes. 'I never felt so helpless as when I watched him on television and saw him with his head in his hands,' says Faye MacLeod. 'I just thought he looked so alone, very much alone. I slipped out of the house and took the dog for a walk. I couldn't watch it any more.'

MacLeod looked like a man nursing a migraine while listening to the world's worst school choir all hit all the wrong notes at once. The bubbly ebullience with which he had cheered the nation had gone. 'You could see that evaporate once results started going wrong,' says Gordon McQueen. Alan Rough also observed the dramatic change in his manager's outlook. 'By the end of the game he was distraught,' reflects Rough. 'He was absolutely destroyed after that.'

At the press conference following the game, MacLeod was visibly wilting under the merciless gaze of the reporters and TV men. 'He would have just liked to have not gone,' says Arthur Montford. 'He faced it well; took it well. He was still reluctant to criticise the players. He looked like someone who had been sandbagged and the change in him was just awful – he became a different person.

'The jovial, cheeky-chappie persona had gone. He wasn't cracking jokes. He was trying to explain it away. He acknowledged later to me that it had been an error for him not to see Peru or Iran. He later admitted, off-camera, he should have put much more work into examining the opposition and he acknowledged that the opposition were much better than he had thought.'

Following the match, an unexpected delay brought about by Sandy Jardine struggling to provide a doping-test sample, meant that the players, management team and officials had to sit in their bus for 15 minutes while, around them, the supporters dissipated their anger. 'By the time we reached our hotel, most of the players were as near distress as I have ever seen grown men,' was how MacLeod later remembered that bus journey.

Bruce Rioch, who would go on to become manager of Arsenal, among other clubs, is sympathetic to the predicament in which MacLeod now found himself. 'Ally was loyal to a fault,' says Rioch, 'and he continued to support his players but it must have been a terrible time for him. Until you go into management yourself, you cannot understand just how lonely it can be, and Ally must have been feeling very lonely at that point.'

Advertisements for the Chrysler Avenger car, featuring the Scotland team, appeared in the press the day after the Iran match – clearly planned to cash in on an expected, safe victory for Scotland. The advertiser's jargon described the car as 'extremely competitive' with 'everything you need in performance and style', along with 'toughness and Championship performance'. Within hours, Chrysler had announced that they were ending their association with the Scottish national side.

Scottish bookmakers were equally merciless – the team was immediately demoted to 500-1 to win the tournament, pegging them alongside Iran. Only Mexico were experiencing a more disappointing World Cup than Scotland; their two defeats, to Tunisia and West Germany, had seen them score one and concede nine goals.

Following the dreadful debacle in Cordoba, copies of Andy Cameron's *Ally's Tartan Army* singles, normally sixty-five pence each, were on sale in a Dundee record shop for one pence. Customers were being encouraged to purchase as many discs as they wished, then to use the hammer provided to smash the platters to smithereens on the counter, under the approving eye of the shop's owner. The hammer blow of the defeat by Iran had ensured that Ally's Army had not only stopped marching but also that its supporters were now in a state of open mutiny.

10

Rough Stuff

Perms graced the heads of several members of the Scotland squad in the summer of 1978 but only one brought notoriety to its owner. It seemed acceptable for Graeme Souness to have adopted that most chic of seventies hairstyles – nicknamed Champagne Charlie he was living it up at Liverpool and had won the European Cup three weeks prior to Scotland's Argentinian adventure. Nor did a perm seem out of place atop the head of Derek Johnstone, a treble winner with Glasgow Rangers in 1978 and that club's glamour boy throughout the decade – it seemed only right that he should try out any passing fashion. Asa Hartford, a UEFA Cup regular with metropolitan Manchester City, also seemed to have the right to sport the hairstyle that was making waves in the late seventies.

The one place where the perm seemed out of place was in Maryhill, Glasgow, where it balanced precariously on the skull of Alan Rough. Goalkeepers were supposed to be frills-free protectors of the posts but Rough's blond frizz-bomb looked like a neon-lit super-halo designed to draw attention to his star quality. It could equally give him the look of a giant dandelion. This was not the style expected of a Scottish goalkeeper, especially one who earned his corn routinely amid the down-at-heel tenements off the Maryhill Road – as last line of defence for Partick Thistle, a club that relied almost entirely on part-time players, with Rough one of the rare full-time exceptions.

Scottish footballers had embraced enthusiastically the trend of long hair throughout the seventies but by 1978 the permanent wave – or perm – was separating the men from the boys in the preening stakes. Growing hair down to the collar had demanded little of the wearer but establishing a perm meant spending hours in a hair salon, wearing a plastic gown and sitting under a blow dryer with your hair twisted around the dozens of tiny rollers being used to frizz each and every strand from its root to give the impression of a giant bubblehead. Such pampering seemed more redolent of the court of King Louis XIV than of muddy goalmouths. 'Quite ordinary men in regular jobs are having their hair permed now,' cooed Michael Strum of Crimpers, a London salon, in mid-1978. 'A perm is trouble-free but you shouldn't put any tension on the hair, especially when wet, because it breaks easily.'

It was Taylor Ferguson, a hairdresser with a salon in Glasgow's Bath Street, who had approached Rough with the idea of him trying out a perm, shortly before the Argentina World Cup. 'There was a new hairstyle fashion coming out,' recalls Rough, 'and he thought that if he got three footballers sitting getting rollers in their hair then the punters would say, "It's not that much of a hardship. I'll do it as well." There was me, Derek Johnstone and Danny McGrain went to Taylor's and it kicked off from there. I don't know why I'm the only one that gets labelled with it because a lot of people had one. I seem to be the only one that people remember. A lot of people had them, even Keegan, with England, had one.

'Mine just got out of hand; I just couldn't control it. Other people had theirs quite short but mine seemed to be bushier than others. It was great because when you've got a perm you just get up in the morning and wash it and leave it; you don't need to brush it or anything.'

Rough was an unassuming, well-built, easy-going individual who had languidly kept goal for Thistle throughout the seventies, earning a League Cup winner's medal in 1971 thanks to the Firhill side's stunning 4-1 victory over Celtic in the final. By the time of the 1978 World Cup, Rough, by then aged twenty-six, was in his prime and seemed out of place with Partick Thistle who in the late seventies were symbolic of a malaise that had affected Scottish club football more seriously with every year of that decade. Thistle, despite being a Premier Division club, were accustomed to their players trotting on to the pitch to be confronted by expansive stretches of empty terracing at home matches, except for when the Old Firm came visiting. Other than those occasions the two ends of their oval ground would habitually be close to deserted. Most of their 5,000 or so supporters – huddled together like survivors coming to terms with some terrible natural disaster that had culled most of their number – would be gathered in the main stand or on the terracing opposite. Thistle were doing well on such meagre gate revenue merely to remain in the Premier Division, where they veered between the occasional spurt of good results and dances with the danger of relegation.

It was an unusual set of surroundings for the man who would keep goal for Scotland at the World Cup finals – he was the only member of the Scottish squad who played for such a modest club – but Rough had shown real character in making the Scotland goalkeeping position indisputably his own since his debut, while a First Division player with Thistle, against Switzerland in the spring of 1976. He had gone on to play in all but two of Scotland's twenty fixtures in the subsequent two years, stepping aside only for a couple of friendlies. In the latter of those two matches, a game in East Germany in September 1977, David Stewart, a goalkeeper from Leeds United, had produced what Ally MacLeod noted privately at the time was the best display he had seen from any Scottish goalkeeper during his period in charge of the national team.

Stewart, formerly a player at Ayr United under MacLeod's management, would have been given the chance to challenge Rough over a more sustained period if he had retained his place in the Leeds United first team but he failed to do so that season and subsequently dropped out of contention for the Scottish squad. There may have been questions in MacLeod's mind as to whether he could find a better goalkeeper than Rough, but he was still moved to describe Rough as 'world class' and had stated prior to the tournament that he expected no goalkeeper to acquit himself better in Argentina than his number one.

'Fortunately for me, I never got affected by crowds,' says Rough, now long rid of his perm but with copious blond locks testifying to the benefits of his perennially mellow approach to life, as he pads around the Lanarkshire riding stables that he leases and where he spends much of his time.

'It never, ever put me off, playing in front of 5,000 and then going to 100,000, or people saying, "Why's that goalkeeper from Partick Thistle playing in a Scotland team?" The English, in particular, would ask how you could play for a part-time club and play for your country. That egged you on to try and prove people wrong. I never felt inferior, because the guys in the squad were great; although I was playing with Partick Thistle and there was Kenny with Liverpool and others with Manchester United, they never, ever made me feel anything less than equal with them.'

Scepticism among the English did not stretch as far as

David Coleman, the BBC television commentator during Scotland's opening World Cup finals match with Peru. Coleman was effusive about the talents displayed by Rough as he made vital saves to prevent the Peruvians opening the scoring after their attacking players had flooded through a porous Scotland defence. Rough was still vilified by others, though, who adopted him as their pet scapegoat for Scotland's on-field failings, his critics screaming in protest at how a goalkeeper playing in front of such a humble backdrop as Firhill could be regarded as even halfway fit for the World Cup finals. Even Coleman's commentary made note of Rough being from a 'part-time' club and painted the picture of him training two nights a week with his club in preparation for going head to head with Teofilo Cubillas and Johnny Rep. All this suggested Rough to be the equivalent of a Territorial Army recruit pitched into the front line of battle.

The actual truth about Thistle was even more curious than the fiction. During Rough's seventies heyday he was one of only three full-time players on the club's books and he and his two team mates would prepare for matches by tearing up and down the pitch under the eye of the manager, with the outfield duo enjoying concentrated shooting practice or necessarily small practice drills, with Rough in goal. Not for nothing was Firhill seen as one of the great bastions of eccentricity in the Scottish game.

'When you look back on it now,' says Rough, 'it was scandalous. It was just unthinkable that this could happen. I trained during the day and then went back one night a week with the part-time players. It was very difficult for us to train when there were only three of us and the manager there during the day.'

During those agent-free days, players were tied closely to their clubs; those who wanted a transfer had to agitate hard to get one and that was not particularly Rough's style. He knew, as he left Scotland for the World Cup, that Partick Thistle had turned down a bid for him from Middlesbrough and he stated in those pre-World Cup May days at Dunblane that he would be happy to join another northern English club, Newcastle United, if they were willing to follow up their interest in him. At twenty-six and approaching his peak as a goalkeeper, he felt the need to break free from the part-time confines of Firhill. If not England, then, said Rough, he would be interested in opportunities in the new, booming North American Soccer League which in the late seventies was rapidly becoming regarded as the footballers' Mecca.

Familiarity had bred contentment for him at Firhill but he wished to develop his game at a bigger club with better players. 'There had been chances for me to go to England,' he says. 'On the Wednesday after the League Cup final in '71, when I was only nineteen, Terry Neill and Tommy Docherty, who were the managers of Hull City, came up to buy me and Partick Thistle just turned them away. After Argentina, Everton and Man City wanted to buy me, but in those days you didn't have agents so if the phone went at Partick Thistle, the manager would pick it up and say, "You want to buy Alan Rough? No, he's not for sale." He'd put the phone down and that would be the end of it. It wasn't in the papers or anything like that – nobody ever knew.

'It was only when wee Bertie Auld [the manager] left Thistle that he told me that he could have sold me three or four times but that the club didn't want their best player leaving. It was a hindrance – playing at the top level makes you a better player – but I enjoyed the twenty-odd years I had playing in Scotland.'

It was almost inevitable that if Scotland started to falter

the baggage surrounding Rough would result in blame being attached to him, but he assesses that only one of the goals that he lost at the finals – the one against Iran where he was caught out at his near post – was due to a serious misjudgement on his part. His approach to life, which would make Roger Moore look like a hyperactive neurotic, ensured that he was well-equipped to deal with everything that was thrown at him after the action.

'The goalkeeper always gets it,' says Rough. 'Everyone looks round at the goalie – "what happened there?" You just get hardened to it; the good ones respond to it. The others buckle and never come back. I think one of Ally's biggest quotes, that I was the best goalkeeper in the World Cup, didn't help me any, even though he was sticking up for me.

'People were obviously questioning him as to why he had a part-time goalkeeper playing in the Scottish team in the World Cup finals and he has gone right overboard the way he does. That had no effect on me, though. Honestly, nothing affects me. I'm so laid-back it's unreal. Obviously, when you have time to yourself, you reflect on how you could have done better but nothing puts me off. I just go out and do it. I'm lucky enough to have that approach to life.

'I think you have to be very single-minded to be a goal-keeper; whereas outfield players are part of a group, goal-keepers are individuals. It stems back to being a wee kid at seven or eight and wanting to be a goalkeeper. That's what you want to be and they shove you in big goals and you can't even reach the bar. Wee footballers know that if they hit the ball high it's a goal so you're standing there losing goals left, right and centre and everybody's shouting at you and I think that's when you start to realise how you're on your own.'

Nine goalkeepers – all from bigger and more prestigious clubs – had tried and failed to make the position of Scotland goalkeeper their own during the seventies before Rough came along and bettered all their efforts by beginning a ten-year association with the Scotland squad that stretched from 1976 to 1986 and won him fifty-three caps. Such an achievement hints at a cast-iron core of determination behind his easy exterior. Even some fellow members of the Scotland squad at the 1978 tournament could not resist joining in with the sniping about a player of Rough's standing being entrusted to keep goal for his country but the goalkeeper refuses, with characteristic dignity, to offer even a cheep of criticism of those individuals. All he has to do is glance at his record with Scotland to remind himself that he lasted a lot longer at the highest level than any of his detractors – or that fleeting fashion, the perm.

11 Story Time

Vivid picture-painting through words made Ian Archer one of the premier football writers working in Scotland during the seventies. Archer helped drive Scottish football journalism into new territory, expanding match reports and features beyond the matter-of-fact to highlight the event and incident that surrounded the game. Already highly respected for his contributions to the *Glasgow Herald* he was by mid-1978 writing for the *Scottish Daily Express*. Other reporters might be putting together formulaic, join-the-dots reports but Archer would dash off the equivalent of a quick watercolour in words to describe the beauty and grace of the great game. As Arthur Montford puts it, 'He could sit down and make a blank page sing.'

A Glasgow-born man who had travelled south as a boy to receive an education at the exclusive Rugby school, Archer spoke with the voice of an educated, upper-class Englishman but he possessed a great zeal for Scottish football that perhaps found extra zest because of the stark contrast between his privileged upbringing and the national game's grittiness. Archer's considered prose usually provided distinguished context amid the maddening maelstrom of events, so it was strange for readers in Scotland to peruse Archer's first despatch from Argentina in 1978. 'We've been on our way to Argentina for six months,' he wrote from South America. 'Now we're here. We shall not be moved.' This was more in the style of a quickly scribbled, beer-stained postcard home from an enlisted private in Ally's Army than expert picture-painting from a gifted journalist.

The artistry expounded by Archer on behalf of Scotland's rough-hewn national game could sometimes lead him to airy flights of fancy but he was not the only media commentator banging the big drum on behalf of Ally and his army.

Players in the squad who signed up to 'write' a newspaper column had their words transformed magically to follow a flamboyant house style that had been laid down by Ally's expansive expressiveness. 'Ever since I was a wee boy my dream has been to collect European and World Cup winners' medals,' were words attributed to Kenny Dalglish, shortly after arriving in Argentina. 'The first part has come wonderfully true with the great Liverpool team. Now I'm all set to march with Ally's Army in pursuit of the second.' Anyone even fractionally aware of Dalglish's supremely rational outlook on life would have found it an interesting task to match these fantastical words to the man.

It had been on a cold, January day in England when MacLeod had first warmed to the task of really turning up the heat under Scotland's forthcoming assault on the World Cup. Qualification had been obtained three months previously and without any fixtures between then and the draw, things had been quiet; perhaps too quiet for Ally. He and Ernie Walker had been in Argentina for the best part of a fortnight to attend the draw for the finals and to check on hotels, and as they disembarked from their flight from Argentina at Gatwick airport on 21 January 1978, they were greeted by a posse of pressmen who caught MacLeod at just the right time to set them off on one of the biggest stories of their lives.

Journalist Rodger Baillie recalls, 'The league programme had been wiped out that day because of the weather, so about six of us descended on Gatwick. I was on the *Sunday Mirror* at the time. We went into the British Caledonian VIP section and when he came he was excited at seeing everybody and he said, "We will win a medal."'

Baillie suggests that the quote was picked up by people as Ally meaning that Scotland would win the World Cup and that, instead of pulling back from that in any way or clarifying exactly what he meant, Ally 'went with the flood' of popular opinion.

'The impression now,' adds Baillie, 'is that he almost had a screw loose but I think he was quite shrewd, in a way. He knew how to work the press but by May he was totally swept away by this Niagara of hype. It was like a collective insanity that gripped the nation.'

MacLeod, once ensconced at the Sierras Hotel in Alta Gracia in late May, revelled, initially, in the attention he received from the world's media as they sought stories to fill their ink-thirsty pages prior to the tournament getting underway. There were, on occasions, he estimated, 200 journalists from a ream of nationalities hanging on his every word. Many would have been drawn there, as if to the feet of some legendary prophet from a far-off land, after hearing second-hand tales of this most unpredictable of managers, one they hoped would be guaranteed to give them better copy than their own dutifully dull equivalents. They would not be disappointed; there was no dampening down of Ally's glittering promises on arrival in Argentina.

It would have been ridiculous, MacLeod believed, for him to have become cautious or pessimistic about Scotland's prospects after saying publicly for so long that Scotland could win the trophy. The relaxed informality of holding open-air press conferences on the terrace outside the Sierras Hotel helped to encourage an initially friendly, free-and-easy atmosphere as Ally engaged with the press in the week or so before Scotland got down to action.

There had, prior to departure for Argentina, been a chance for Ally to use the media to take some of the heat off himself and to smother the expectation that had been transmitted rapidly across Scotland like some feel-good plague. The Scotland manager had, though, decided that he could not accept the opportunity to deflate this ballooning expectation. The sheer force of his personality prevented him doing so.

'*Scotsport* used to be on a Sunday afternoon in the days of Arthur Montford and Alex Cameron,' recalls John Hagart. 'A week or two before we were due to leave, Alex Cameron was going to interview Ally and Arthur Montford was going to interview me.

'We were sitting having a cup of coffee before the show and Alex Cameron said to Ally, "Let's try to get a bit of reality into today's piece. Every man, woman and dog in Scotland thinks we're definitely coming back with the World Cup." Ally said, "That would be great, to do that, but, Alex, it's got to come from you to me. I can't come out now and say, 'Wait a minute, we're not going to win this.'"

'He was dead right about that because it would just have been bursting the bubble for him to have said, "Listen, we've got to be realistic about this – all this hype has been misplaced." At that time, if you went into a supermarket, there would be two old women talking about the World Cup coming up; everybody was completely hooked and captivated by the whole thing.

'Alex Cameron said, "I suppose you're right but if we can try and get that in . . ." So they then got started on the interview but Ally was being his bubbly self about this and that, time went on – so much so that there wasn't the opportunity for Alex Cameron to come in with this, "Let's get a bit real" kind of thing and they simply ran out of time to do it.'

Arthur Montford had frequent contact with MacLeod in the months prior to the tournament and in Argentina and thinks that MacLeod may actually have convinced himself that Scotland had a realistic chance to seize the World Cup. 'I think he may have believed it,' says the commentator, 'but I'm sure most experienced TV people and scribes didn't think that. I was slightly anxious about it and I tried to express that in the build-up reports I sent back from Argentina for *Scotland Today* before the matches began.'

Montford, who, when commentating on Scotland matches wore a tartan scarf together with a rosette under his jacket, could recall the two error-prone attempts the Scots had made on the World Cup in the fifties. Those memories had chiselled their way into his thinking during the Ally era and made him less susceptible to the fanaticism that had swept away many of those among the nation's youth, whose only reference point for Scotland in World Cups was the close-but-no-cigar effort of 1974.

Modest hotels housed the press during their stay in Cordoba although the press centre, in the Anglophile Jockey Club, provided plush, ornate surroundings when they were working. The gold and mahogany decor was complemented by white-gloved waiters attending to the journalists' every need. 'We were treated like rajahs,' says Rodger Baillie, who recalls well the contrast between the Jockey Club building and the Sierras Hotel, where he and his colleagues would visit the Scotland squad. 'It was a real cowp of a hotel. You went into the bar and there were flies buzzing all over the place; it was a gloomy kind of place, slightly down-at-heel.'

To begin with, relations between the press and the Scotland party were amicable. The *Daily Record* had initially flown out copies of that newspaper to the SFA at the Scotland hotel every day, as a PR exercise. That particular enterprise would cease early on in the Scotland squad's sojourn in Argentina, once the paper realised that the stories that it was printing were unlikely to make pleasant reading among the Scottish party. It was one relatively innocent remark by Ally that started a trickle that soon became a flood of stories alleging indiscipline inside the Scotland squad.

The incident that sparked it all off was the Jardine, Johnston and Rough casino trip on the Scots' first day in Argentina. They exited via the front entrance to the hotel, which meant they had to take a circuitous route through Alta Gracia to get to the casino. On their return, rather than walking the long way round from the casino to the front of the hotel, they decided to take a shortcut across a lawn, then through some orange groves to the rear of the hotel, where they hopped over a knee-high stile and into the grounds.

As they dropped down, an Argentinian guard, with gun, confronted them but the situation was resolved swiftly and would have rested there had Ally MacLeod, surrounded by familiar press faces who had always been benevolent towards him, not decided to make a joke about the incident at his press conference the next morning. On the following day, the Sunday, Ally's slip resulted in scandalised front page headlines back in Britain.

'It was the page one splash so it must have been given a bit of topspin,' says Rodger Baillie, who reported the incident for the *Sunday Mirror* and who suggests that he wrote it up as an event that had happened but one that ought not to have happened. Fierce editorials followed about indiscipline in the Scottish camp and how the country had been let down. The stile, in some reports, became an electrified fence several feet in height. Through tackling this obstacle, according to such coverage, the Scottish players had placed themselves in severe danger. Mention of the casino – with the dissolute associations that can be attached to such establishments – was played up heavily. A seed had been planted in the public mind.

By the end of his stay in Alta Gracia, MacLeod had been forced back from the expansive to the defensive. Journalists who had initially arrived to hear Ally give them a new angle were now pressing him to confirm or deny any one of a series of snaking rumours associated with the Scottish squad. Because of all the bad press that had been flooding back home as the tournament unfolded it became harder for newspaper and television reporters to get into the team's headquarters in Alta Gracia. That was despite journalists being assigned drivers from the Argentinian equivalent of MI5; such drivers, with the weight of the bullying Argentinian regime right behind them, could usually open doors for the media almost everywhere they went.

When the tide turned against him and his team, Ally was baffled at the media backlash whipping him and his players; he had, after all, been so helpful in accommodating the press and Scotland's World Cup was helping to sell thousands of extra copies of newspapers. He had enjoyed excellent press relations for more than a decade in Scotland – as manager of Ayr United he had held a weekly Friday press conference, at the Press Club in Glasgow, at a time when no other provincial manager did such a thing. Ally was regarded as being always good for a story – he understood the importance of using the press to build momentum behind a football club. Within a few days in Argentina the relationships that he had constructed so painstakingly disintegrated into dust. MacLeod could not understand why this had happened.

It was an inevitable twist though, because Scotland's World Cup story, as relayed by the media, had to go somewhere once the tournament began. Ally had promised a magic carpet ride and had fanned the flames of expectation by telling everyone how Scotland would catch fire at the finals. It was inconceivable that, after such a build-up, the press would simply drop the story when things went wrong. Reporters who knew and liked Ally may have wanted to go easy on him once he was under pressure but their editors back in Scotland were demanding stories that explained why the team that had been going to skip to the final was, after its encounters with Peru and Iran, looking leaden-footed.

'I was friendly with the guys on the *Record*,' says Rodger Baillie, 'because I had worked with them, and they were put under great pressure from the [sports] desk in Glasgow. I'm sure they were not the only ones; I'm sure that applied to every daily paper. It was, "Why? Why? Why?"'

Unlike in the fifties, when World Cups had been contested largely out of sight of the Scottish public, the 1978 tournament was being despatched directly into living rooms on colour television. There was now a demand from sports and news editors that the journalists in Argentina provide the public with stories to explain the chasm that had emerged between what they had been promised and what they were seeing on their screens.

'The drugs story broke on the Sunday night,' recalls Baillie of the Willie Johnston affair. 'People had filed and we were all sitting having dinner in this Jockey Club and a German journalist came in and said, "Ah, have you heard – one of your players has been found guilty of a drug." Everybody laughed. Nobody believed it . . . Then all hell broke loose . . .

'The place was in uproar with messages going backwards and forwards. Demands were coming from Glasgow to journalists out there. I think they were probably only reflecting the feeling back home where there was a massive U-turn – and not just from the supporters but also from dear old ladies who had never seen a football match in their lives.

'I've never been on a trip where there was such a hothouse atmosphere. It got to the stage where if they had said, "Ally's flying to the moon tomorrow", we would all have been out to see it. The most improbable stories suddenly became reality, starting with the drugs, and on the Sunday night there was a "do" and the story went around that Ally had called Trevor McDonald a "black bastard". People were swooning.

'There had been a row with Trevor McDonald where Ally had accused him of trying to get players to say things, but he had never used those words to McDonald.'

MacLeod had actually ejected McDonald from the reception at which he had confronted Johnston by saying, 'You're pushing your luck. I'd just rather now you'd leave the company.' Then, raising his voice in response to McDonald's protests, 'You *are* stooping to low tactics.' This was an angry side of Ally MacLeod that had rarely been revealed. Then again, he had rarely been under such pressure.

There was good reason why the press would also seek out drinking stories, to go with the one about drugs. Scottish footballers had 'previous'. Jimmy Johnstone, prior to the 1974 World Cup, had rowed drunkenly out to sea from Largs in a boat during the early hours of one morning. Johnstone and Bremner had, days afterwards, almost been sent home after another drunken escapade. Five Scotland players, Bremner included, had been banned for life by the SFA in 1975 after an evening of high abandon in the nightclubs of Copenhagen.

Such stories from the relatively recent past helped convince many pressmen that there would be similar tales to reveal about the 1978 tournament, if only they could get their hands on them. Foreign journalists, whose sketchy knowledge of Scotland extended little further than it being an exporter of tartan and Scotch whisky, were quick to make the connection between the county's national drink and the players who had looked so unsteady on their feet in their opening two matches.

'It kind of all started with the local newspapers,' says Bill Wilson, press officer for the Scottish Football Association at the 1978 tournament. 'We were given a local press man to look after us and then we found out that he was feeding all sorts of stories out to the Argentinian papers.

'Stupid things were happening like *El Gráfico* [the biggest weekly sports paper in Argentina] giving big headlines to a story saying that the hotel had had to send out for more drink – for containers of whisky – because the Scottish players had drunk the hotel dry. It was such a pack of lies. The other one was that we were getting girls in every night for the players; again a lot of rubbish. Now we never knew about this because we weren't buying the Argentinian papers but, of course, some of the media were. They were getting this at home and then asking their own boys why they hadn't got these stories.

'I remember Stuart Kennedy, the Aberdeen full-back, a teetotaller I'm sure I recall, was celebrating a birthday and the local papers asked for a picture. They asked for a picture of him with a birthday cake and a glass but I told them he could only be pictured with a Coca-Cola bottle; the story was then written up that Kennedy had started off drinking Coca-Cola and had then quickly put down his Coke to start drinking whisky. Initially, the whole party laughed about it because it was so ridiculous; it quickly turned serious.

'Once all these stories were reported back home, Ally didn't want to meet the press. We got to the stage where he was doing it under duress because he didn't know whether he would be quoted correctly. He was very unhappy, latterly.'

There were, eventually, so many rumours swirling around of drunken Scottish footballers that the players were forbidden to leave the grounds of the Sierras Hotel after the Monday on which Johnston was sent home; being forced to remain in accommodation that so many of them considered to be substandard was an unpleasant, harsh side effect of this unwanted media attention. In addition, the press coverage that some players themselves encouraged began to cause friction within the squad. 'There were fallouts at the World Cup between the players,' says Bill Wilson. 'Some factions thought that others weren't playing the game. Some had secretly done deals with newspapers to do diary columns and didn't involve their colleagues [in the pooling of financial rewards for such enterprises] and that wasn't popular with the majority of the players. That caused a lot of unhappiness.'

Joe Harper still feels anger at the manner in which ordinary events were twisted to be used against the Scots. 'On the first day we arrived in Cordoba we went to the press centre and there was a table as you went in where you gave a guy all your details: name, date of birth, etcetera, etcetera – had your fingerprints taken, a photo taken. The whole team had to go through that process and after an hour you would get the wee identity tag for your lapel. Everybody couldn't do it at once so when you were not having your details taken, you would go to the cafeteria inside the centre.

'Now, they had around two hundred to two hundred and fifty girls doing the typing and telephoning; absolutely beautiful women. So we were in the cafeteria having tea, Coke, coffee, orange, whatever and this guy came in from *El Gráfico* and asked Ally if he could have a picture of some of his players meeting the local people. Ally agreed, so we had three of our players with three of the local girls: with a player, then a girl sitting in between him and the next player, another girl sitting in between him and the next player and then the other girl.

He took the picture and we heard nothing more about it but after the Iran game that picture was on the front page of *El Gráfico*, with the headline, "Scottish players – wine, women and song". On the table were Cokes and that was supposed to be the drinks. Now that's the shit that you got over there.

'Mexico came to Cordoba for one game. So they came to our place to stay. Being so close to America they speak English, so we joined in with them. We ate together, all got on well, exchanged things, trained together and had wee games with them. They were there for three days and it was fine. They went out on the Tuesday and got beaten six-nil by Germany; we went to the game and watched them and they left on the Thursday.

'On the Friday morning, a young, local girl, an interpreter, came in and she was laughing. She had this *El Gráfico* again and on the front of it the headline, "*Escocia*, blah, blah, blah . . ." We were saying to her, "What's this all about?" She said, "The Mexican coach accuses Scotland for six-nil defeat: Scottish players and officials were running

about the corridors with crates of whisky, chasing women."
Again, this was just rubbish.'

Harper states that one journalist, whom he particularly
despises, was going round with photographs of every player
and saying to local women, draped on street corners, 'Have
you seen him?' 'Has he been here?' Says Harper, 'Now you
know what these guys are like – they'd sell their granny
for two pennies. So if he was offering them a few pounds,
they would say, "Yes, I see him", and he's got a story.'

Harper remembers himself and several other players
surrounding this journalist, forcing him against a wall and
warning of the retribution that would be carried out if he
continued to write such scurrilous stories and upset the
families of the players at home. 'Some of the stuff going
back was way out of order,' says Gordon McQueen, 'about
women being involved, and when your family is picking
up stories like that, that is when it gets serious.'

Numerous tales were reported of players being out on
the town and becoming inebriated to a degree that would
not be expected of professional athletes. These were the
early days of football fans wearing team jerseys – most
spectators still turned up in everyday clothes and some
older fans even wore collar and tie to matches – so when
Argentinians saw young men wearing Scotland tops and
consuming beers and spirits in the bars and cafes of
Cordoba and, occasionally, Alta Gracia, it was frequently
assumed that these were members of the Scotland squad,
off the leash. And members of the Tartan Army tend not
to restrict themselves to one or two quiet beers.

'Half the fans here have been strolling around wearing
blue Scottish jerseys,' commented Ally MacLeod in the
midst of the mayhem. 'We love to have them showing
that sort of loyalty but they've been getting bevvied and
getting into bother and the local papers have been saying

it's the players. That's what has happened. I've seen fans signing autographs in Cordoba when they could hardly hold a pen.'

One supporter even managed to bypass the junta's security at the Sierras by strolling up to the gate of the hotel in his Scotland shirt and signing the register as Willie Donachie and immediately being given entry. Some non-players among the official party may also have contributed to the players' mistaken identity crisis. 'I know for a fact that there were SFA committee members walking up and down the streets of Alta Gracia in official Scotland tracksuits,' says Gordon McQueen, 'and who were going into bars.'

Had Scotland's results been good, then any stories of misbehaviour would have been regarded as a little bit of devilment on the part of highly strung young men; when results went wrong, the players were portrayed as irresponsible wastrels. 'A lot of stories were coming out back home,' says Bruce Rioch. 'There we were, sitting in a training camp, and if you rang home and spoke to your families you couldn't believe what was being read. That had an effect on morale.' Scottish journalists would also mix with the fans in downtown Cordoba and, through such mingling, the stories were spread to those who had followed the team all the way to Argentina, making it very hard for the SFA to keep a lid on things.

'We were the only British team there,' says Bill Wilson, 'so there was no England to concentrate on; a lot of the English media exaggerated stories. I remember the story about players "scaling electric fences". It was a lot of rubbish; it was a wee garden fence but they had to build up this story.

'I remember the BBC came out of it terribly. There was a Scottish freelance journalist sent over and the only way he would make money was to get more sensational stories than everybody else. Then, of course, the desk editors at home were seeing this on the BBC and their bosses would say, "This must be true. You'd better find out what is happening. Why haven't you got this story?" So there was a lot of trouble internally within the press corps. But there was no story. I know there was talk of throwing this guy out of the Football Writers' Association because of this. It was kind of fraught.'

The rumours concerning the players' misbehaviour were regarded by Arthur Montford as 'fragments of disintegrating rocks'; inevitable results of the wreckage of Scotland's World Cup campaign. 'We never found it to be the case,' he says of the stories of outrageous behaviour on the part of Scottish players. 'I think it was just one of the extra arrows to be fired at the manager. One aspect that did disappoint me was Lou Macari doing an interview for ITV about things that were going wrong in the camp.'

The interview Macari gave exclusively to an independent English television station on the day after the Iran match was regarded as being so severely critical that the SFA would decide to end his international career. Macari, looking wide-eyed and woeful, like a child who has just been told there is no Santa Claus, was resplendent in a red shirt as he punched out words that he must have known would only drag Scotland down further and stir the fury of those at home after the disappointment of the results with Peru and Iran.

He began his ramble through Scotland's World Cup affairs by offering an intriguing slant on a matter close to his heart, 'I was a bit annoyed last night when I heard Scottish fans shouting, "You're only here for the money." The money we're getting paid is not worth talking about. We all feel differently about different things. Some people are interested in money; others are interested in good accommodation. So there's something on this trip has affected everybody in this squad; be it accommodation, be it money, be it different things, be it freedom. When you're talking about the accommodation and the food, whether it's the best available, I don't know, but it wouldn't do an England team.'

In that final statement, Macari was entirely incorrect; England teams at World Cups prior to and after Argentina have had to make do with the type of inconveniences – and much worse – surrounding their accommodation to which the Scots had been exposed in Alta Gracia. More to the point, Macari would have known that his sideswipe would touch a raw nerve with its implication that whatever those from the land of his birth might think, do or say, they were always destined to be second-rate in comparison to those from south of the border.

'The twenty-two players who came here,' continued Macari, as he confessed all to the camera, 'rightly or wrongly regard themselves as better players than England because in Scotland that's what it's all about – Scotland and England – and you come here and you think, "Well, this is it. This is the biggest occasion of your life." And I don't think you're in the same league as England. Unfortunately, we came here and we couldn't lace England's boots as far as the way you're treated off the pitch and as far as the rewards at the end of the day are concerned.'

England, Macari conveniently overlooked, had failed quite spectacularly in their efforts to qualify for the World Cup finals in Argentina.

Even the Scotland supporters were roped in by the papers to boost their negative version of events once the tide turned against MacLeod and his team. A picture appeared on the front page of the *Scottish Daily Express* on Monday

5 June of half-a-dozen weary-looking Scotland supporters after the Peru game, portrayed as if taking the first steps home in apparent disgust at their team's efforts. The picture was captioned, 'We've had enough: Disgruntled fans start the long trek back to Scotland.' John McKenzie was one of the fans photographed and he admits that he and his fellow supporters were part of a fabrication.

'That wasn't true,' says McKenzie. 'That was just a photograph for the paper. The *Daily Express* got us to pose for that. We did that for the money. They always paid you money for any photograph or any wee article that you did; and they paid your drinks bill. There was no way we were going home; the furthest we were going was to Mendoza, a few days later, to watch Scotland play Holland. There was no way we were going to head off.'

Something similar happened after the match with Iran, when Scotland supporters had been egged on by representatives of the BBC to harangue the team. As the players and staff left the dressing room area to go to their bus, supporters were told by television crews to shout abuse at the players and management so that when the cameras swivelled on to them to capture the moment they would be seen by girlfriends back home. Bill Wilson accepts that much of the anger vented at the team after that match was real but suggests that, outside the ground, it was initially stage-managed.

Across the Atlantic, Andrew MacLeod, Ally's son, then aged sixteen, was offered the princely sum of twenty-five pounds by one newspaper if he would reveal how things were proceeding inside the MacLeod household during the darkest days of Scotland's Argentinian excursion. He turned the fee down even though it would have provided him with a substantial addition to his weekly pocket money.

'Everyone used to think that Ally courted publicity when

he was Scotland manager but he didn't,' says Faye MacLeod. 'The phone just used to go non-stop and we were brought up to try and help people, in our generation, and to try and be kind and if you could try and make somebody's life a wee bit easier, you did it. So he tried not to refuse anybody.

'One reporter, who is now dead, phoned every day and wrote about Ally non-stop but he then turned on Ally after the World Cup and wrote something pretty nasty and I said, "Next time he phones, I'm going to hang up." But he never phoned the house again so I never got the satisfaction of hanging up on him.

'One story said that we were besieged when Ally was in Argentina and that our windows had been broken, which was a lot of tommy-rot. In a way we were under siege; but only from the press.

'My two sisters came down to see me to check that I was all right and with them and some friends, we staged an impromptu party – there were about eight of us. Next day I noticed that the drinks' cupboard was a bit low on supplies so I went to a place where we had an account. I was standing waiting for it to open and I could see the headlines, "Ally's wife takes to drink."

'People were actually very good. I can only remember getting one dreadful letter; I don't know why they were swearing at me but they were. I got a boxful of lovely letters from people. I think they were so annoyed at the way the press had turned.'

The SFA, once their main representatives were back in Scotland, took legal advice on whether to sue for damages one journalist whose reporting they had regarded as particularly objectionable and inaccurate. Some of the excesses of the BBC had been so severe that, after the tournament, Ernie Walker and Bill Wilson went to BBC headquarters to view the worst of the footage it had broadcast. 'It was all such lies,' says Wilson. The SFA was considering legal action but it transpired that there was a legal situation where individuals would have had to sue the BBC – the SFA couldn't do it as a body – so the matter was dropped. 'Nobody had ever experienced that kind of thing,' says Wilson. 'We had been puzzled at the time. "Why are they doing this to us?"'

MacLeod, on his return to Ayr, slowly picked through a collection of newspaper articles and watched video-taped television recordings of the tournament with a growing sense of bewilderment at how people with whom he had believed himself to be on friendly terms had turned against him once the team's affairs had begun to take a turn for the worse. Even as Ally mulled over the matter, some sections of the press had still not had their fill.

'I remember, when we came back,' says John Hagart, 'Alex Cameron, who was chief football reporter with the *Daily Record* at that time, phoned me up and said, "John, we were wanting to do a three-day thing on Argentina and what went wrong and what happened and what didn't happen. We'd pay you for this but the only thing is, John, you've got to criticise Ally." I said, "Honestly, Alex, forget all about it. I would never get involved in that; I couldn't look at myself in the mirror if I was doing that."'

The SFA would later, in an official report, condemn the role of the press in sowing disharmony among the Scotland squad. 'That's fair,' says Bill Wilson of that official verdict. 'The players were getting bad results, which is number one, but lies were being printed about them and their families were reading all these things; they were upsetting wives and children. That kind of thing reduced morale greatly.

'Naïve as we were at the time, we couldn't understand

why they would do that to us, why they would not try to support us. I would say it did have a great part to play in reducing morale in the players. Not all of the media – that would be grossly unfair – but the media had a role to play in the disharmony in the camp.'

Six hundred Brazilian journalists had scrutinised every move made by Claudio Coutinho, their manager, in Argentina, eventually pressurising the Brazilian Football Association so greatly that Coutinho had been usurped from his position mid-tournament. Ernst Happel, the Dutch team manager, refused to speak to his own country's press. Almost every word from Helmut Schoen had been met with disbelieving looks from German journalists as his team faltered in Argentina. The style of play adopted by Cesar Luis Menotti, manager of the Argentina team, was doubted openly by the host nation's journalists. The Austrians were criticised by their own press for allowing wives and girl-friends into their hotel during the tournament.

Press pressure came with the World Cup. The difference was that the Scots had not been ready for it. It was only after they had been wearied by the most outlandish press stories of the tournament for the best part of two weeks in Argentina that the Scottish squad arrived at the correct response. As their third match, with Holland, drew closer, the squad drew on the negative energy provided by the media coverage to fuel their feelings of injustice. That created a desire to show that they could still turn on its head every story that doubted their worthiness as World Cup contenders.

12 Army Manoeuvres

It seemed appropriate that the tartan-trimmed terracing troopers who followed Scotland in the late seventies should be christened Ally's Army. A nickname with half cuddly, half confrontational connotations suited them well. Manager MacLeod may have been a fun guy who would dissolve into thin air at the sight of a fight but many of his foot soldiers struggled to match their leader's effortlessly friendly charm offensives – a number of Ally's followers were happy to be offensive without an accompanying onslaught of charm. On Ally's arrival as Scotland manager in 1977, a warlike element still bristled among the Scotland support, many of whom possessed an aggressive energy that could quickly spill over into confrontation. Their idea of a good time, when outside Scotland, often translated into hooliganism in the language of the local population, especially when that language was English and the locals were those in central London. The denizens of the capital city could survey a trail of wreckage and destruction in the wake of the Scots' supporters' biennial trip for the England-Scotland encounter.

In those days it was close to inconceivable that the Tartan Army would ever become a peacekeeping force that would become well loved across the world for their bombastic bonhomie, but the World Cup in Argentina would go some way towards hastening that seemingly unlikely process. It would simultaneously be one of the last stands of the unreconstructed Scotland football supporter: these foul-mouthed fanatics were as vicious, easy to rile and ferocious in mouthing their anger as they ever had been. Not for these guys an easy acceptance of defeat as being all part of the fun of being there.

It had seemed especially unlikely at Wembley on 4 June 1977 that the Tartan Army could ever be regarded as a friendly force by anybody other than those who belonged to it. Following the 2-1 victory over England, Scottish fans flooded on to the turf and began clawing at it with the relish of battle-high warriors picking over the booty on the bodies of the dead enemy on some ancient battle-field. Their seventies-style long hair, matted under the sweating sun of that June day, and their tartan garb now bedraggled after several days roughing it in the south added to the effect of them being an unkempt, uncontrollable, simmeringly violent, rebellious Highland mob. Jimmy Hill, the English television commentator, fumed with besuited rage that the Wembley groundsman would now have to work on the Jubilee Bank Holiday, the following Monday, to repair the damage. Some wondered how, in the work-to-rule seventies, the Football Association had managed to discover an employee who would give up his statutory holiday so readily. Middle England, if watching at all on television at home, shook its head sadly over a half-pint of bitter early that balmy June evening.

The topping-off ceremony took place when some Scots, tired of despoiling the turf, sought elevation and began to climb the Wembley goal frame. More and more of them ascended until, under their collective weight, the goalposts shuddered, shifted, swayed and then, finally succumbing to the weight of those who were pouring on to the goal in a frenzy of fun, the crossbar and its posts crumpled and fell to the ground. It was hugely symbolic for those who were there: England had been toppled, just like those goal-posts, and the sheer rarity value of the event made it worth celebrating as long, hard and dramatically as possible. Argentinians, way across the Atlantic, saw these pictures and pondered just how they might cope with such seemingly Neanderthal supporters if Scotland were to arrive in their country.

Those Scots back home who loved their football were fairly forgiving of the fans, seeing it as a vast outpouring of generally harmless fun. Scottish supporters had, after all, formed the vast majority of the crowd at Wembley that day and had paid most of the gate receipts – although a fair number, as usual, had managed to dispense with the frivolous frippery of engaging in a transaction at the turn-stiles and had mounted the sheer walls of the stadium to pour in through the windows set high in the Wembley facade as if scaling the battlements of an ancient enemy fortress; which is, after all, what they were doing. The Football Association could, surely, put up with the costs of the repair to the pitch, which would consist of only a fraction of their profits from the afternoon.

Football lovers also knew how invaluable the supporters were to the Scottish team. These may have been hearty, heavy drinkers and the type of people who would tip over a trader's stall if he tried to charge them excessive prices outside Wembley but whenever they were formed into serried ranks by the tight confines of a football stadium and turned the full force of their vocal artillery into support for Scotland and disdain for their opponents, they created an inspirational atmosphere that would set alight with passion all but the most ice-hearted of professional foot-ballers. That had been the case inside Hampden against

Czechoslovakia in September 1977, when the noise arising from the swirling mass of 85,000 inside the ground had helped sweep the Scots on to their 3-1 victory in the World Cup qualifier; a match at which even before kick-off some Czechoslovakian players were visibly shaking in the face of the wall of sound that was crashing down on them.

If the supporters had helped drive the Scotland team down the road to Argentina, which they surely had, then, as the SFA's Ernie Walker suggests, they also played a huge part in the decision to hold the grand send off from Hampden when 30,000 Scots turned up to cheer men in suits as they traipsed on to the turf. It was, Walker suggests, not so much another fantastical event of its time but rather one that was a practical measure to try to contain the sheer fanaticism of the Scottish support; a fanaticism that in 1978 could bend as easily towards misbehaviour as towards great celebratory goodwill.

'The departure from Hampden was really quite an innocent thing,' states Walker. 'It was not, as people suggested afterwards, a celebration of winning the World Cup before we'd even left Scotland. That was not true.

'When we qualified at Anfield against Wales, the game finished in something of a riot. We had tens of thousands of people down there. The mood of the crowd, although drunken, was peaceful, because we'd won. The team went into the dressing room but the crowd were going nowhere. They wanted the team to come out and go round the stadium and never moved. The Liverpool police started to panic; I'm sure the Glasgow police would have handled it differently because they're more used to our mentality.

'The Liverpool police refused permission for the team to come out. The feeling built up and built up and then there were announcements and the supporters started throwing bottles and anything that they could lay their hands on, at the police. It was really ugly. I don't recollect that anybody came on to the field but there was a hail of missiles flying and it was remarkable that nobody was killed. They felt they had been denied the chance to acclaim the team. Had the team come out it would have gone perfectly. It was a celebration; nobody was wanting to fight anybody.

'That had occurred and that only added to the feeling among supporters, "The boys are going away and we want to send them off." Normally, we met in the North British hotel in George Square and left from there but the police made it known to us that there was no chance of us doing that. The feeling was that the whole city would have come.

'When we arrived back from West Germany four years earlier, having failed to qualify for the second phase, it was like the end of the war in George Square. It was unbelievable. The bus had to inch through – you'd think we had won the World Cup. It had been an incredible scene. So, in 1978, the police said they weren't having that. They said, "You're not leaving from the city."

'I don't know where the idea started from but somebody came up with the suggestion that the place to meet would be Hampden and that we should leave from Hampden. Of course, that was picked up by the public and there were thousands of people at Hampden. It was perfectly peaceful. It was women, kids, whatever, and the players went round in a bus waving to the public. It was an incredible thing.

'Now, everybody was really startled at how wonderful this had been and how nice it was at Hampden. Nobody but nobody wrote one word that this was big-headed rubbish. It was a demonstration of nationalism the likes of which I had never seen before or have seen since. Scottish nationalism was high at that time, too, and that was part of it.'

The tournament in Argentina was the first time Scotland had been involved in a World Cup outside Europe and the distances involved in attending the tournament ensured eccentric excellence came to the fore. One student supporter, from Stirling University, desperate to attend the matches in Cordoba and Mendoza, even put forward the idea of commandeering a submarine to take him and his pals from the River Clyde to the River Plata. That would have been a world first: an 'army' hiring from the Navy an underwater stealth craft for transportation to a series of football matches hosted by a military junta. Not for nothing did Stirling University have a reputation in the seventies as a hangout where mind-altering drugs were as easy to come by as the bountiful student grants of the time.

The remoteness of Argentina, the expense involved in getting there, and the romanticism attached to any expedition undertaken to ensure attendance at that World Cup were guaranteed to produce outlandish stories and that helped hatch a new, benevolent image of the Scotland football supporter as happy-go-lucky eccentric. A fun-loving Tartan Army, though, was still very much in its infancy and, as such, was experiencing some growing pains – and not a few tantrums.

'We ended up in the local jail on the day of the Iran game,' says John McKenzie, one of several hundred supporters who made it all the way to Argentina. 'On the day before the match with Iran we had decided, in a pub we called the 'hole in the wall' because it was a wee sort of dive, to make a banner chastising the SFA, an idea unanimously accepted by all of our group. I think we probably did it because we had heard the rumours about the players drinking; in Cordoba you kept hearing rumours that players were being spotted out on the town and drunk although I never saw any.

'We'd heard about Willie Johnston [failing his doping test], which had been met with disbelief, especially as Willie Johnston was a bit of a hero because of the way he played football and he was a guy whom a lot of the fans had met and had liked. I think there were also rumours going about that all the office-bearers of the SFA were very much on a sort of junket; that it was all a great holiday for them, all paid for by us. It probably led on from there to making this banner.

'We found a white sheet and, with paint provided by an Argentinian friend, laid the sheet down on the concrete pavement in the main square in Cordoba and proceeded to paint a banner that said "Fuck the SFA", on the day of the Iran game. We hung that up in the 'hole in the wall'.

'We were in there drinking before the game and an Argentinian woman came along and took offence at the banner. I think she thought "the SFA" was something to do with Argentina. Anyway, she got into an argument with Mad Rab, one of our company, which escalated into a shouting match, with both of them swearing profusely in English. Eventually, she went away and came back about ten minutes later with a policeman, brandishing his pistol, and about seventeen of us were led off to the jail, where we spent the next three or four hours.

'As we all looked a bit similar – we had beards and we were hairy – the woman couldn't, or wouldn't, identify the one that had been talking to her and had got into the argument. The British consul came and told us we would get out if we would identify who the one was but we said we were all in it; we were all responsible. It was quite scary. We were in a cell but the door was open so one of us, a

Welsh guy, said, "Come on, let's go." As he started walking out and down a lane beside the police station, we were confronted by an officer who appeared to be in charge. He levelled his pistol and said, "One more step and I kill." That was enough for us – we returned to the cell.

'We were eventually released and we rushed to a taxi stance and crashed into several taxis but we had missed the whole of the first half of the Iran game. On arrival at the stadium we found out that Scotland were one-nil ahead but just as we took our places on the terraces, Iran equalised. Our day of disaster seemed complete.

'At the end, the Scots supporters in the stand were throwing their scarves, abuse and everything else at the players as they left the field. We had to wait until the players left to show our displeasure, screaming abuse with some guys spitting and banging on the bus as it left. The players looked disinterested; Ally MacLeod looked ill. It was just as well we had been in the *Cabildo* – the jail – it had sobered us up and prevented us from getting too steamed up.

'We had the suspicion after that incident with the banner that the military police were keeping an eye on our partic-ular group; we thought we were being followed and there were definitely plain-clothes guys about, wherever we were going. There was an incident when we were crossing back north from Argentina, coming home, and they knew who we were. They knew the names and they made some refer-ence to, "You were the guys in Cordoba." So they had their eye on us.'

There had been occasional scuffles between Scottish and Peruvian fans outside the ground after the first match and during the game with Iran some Scottish supporters – thoughts of glory torpedoed by the equaliser – had even-tually snapped and lost patience with the Iranian fans. It seems the Iranian support had spent the match goading their opposite numbers, directing chants and shouts at the Scotland supporters, but with no suggestion of aggression. One Iranian, in particular, had been especially raucous in blowing on a noisy Persian horn in the direction of the Scottish section. As a batch of Scottish supporters advanced on the opposition fans they were immediately confronted by Argentinian security officials who ejected one fan from the ground and turned back the others, away from a confrontation.

The Scottish support had then turned on their own team and even the most hardened professionals in the squad were affected by that. Joe Harper, who remains upset by the events of that evening, says, 'What did hurt was the fact that just after half time the Scottish fans started getting restless and that's when all the shouting, all the stuff and rubbish was coming out from the fans, which was pretty hard to take. It was hard – I've no qualms about it.

'The Scottish support were out of line; they were definitely out of line. If they honestly thought we could have gone and won the World Cup . . . OK, they might have expected us to get through but if they had known the circumstances we were living under, if they had known all about that . . . They might have been in nice hotels in Cordoba; our conditions were terrible. We've got the best fans in the world but at that particular time about twenty fans, not every Scottish fan, made it bad. They certainly made their feelings felt and I was disgusted by them.'

It had been a stern-faced MacLeod who had strode swiftly towards the dressing rooms at the Chateau Carreras stadium after the 1-1 draw with Iran; glancing frequently, as he moved, with understandable nervousness, towards the front section of the stand that overlooked the entrance to the tunnel. There, a compressed collection of Scotland fans waved saltires, shook fists and yelled abuse at the manager, throwing replica shirts and scarves at him and flicking V-signs in his direction. After the match, matters deteriorated further. 'There was a gantry where the supporters walked from the stand and the supporters were just doing their nut, shouting at Ally, giving him terrible verbals,' recalls Hugh Allan.

John McKenzie, one of the Scots supporters who had travelled to the World Cup overland from the US through South America, suggests that he, and others who trod the overland route, had a different perspective on Scotland's World Cup efforts to that enjoyed by some of those who had flown to the tip of the Americas.

'If you've made the trip, you've made the trip for better or worse. If you're having a good time without the football, it's not that the football pales into insignificance but it doesn't become as important. If, though, you've flown in for a two-week holiday to see Scotland play three games and you've paid several thousand pounds to do that, then it's a bigger issue.

'But if you've hitch-hiked or travelled halfway round the world, overland, you've already had more experiences than you're ever going to have, doing anything else, and you're not that bothered; you become quite a tightly knit bunch – the people that have shared these experiences coming down.'

Having jettisoned his job as a quantity surveyor in Edinburgh, McKenzie, aged twenty-four in 1978, had travelled to South America with £820 in his pocket, a considerable sum of money, and had obtained match tickets easily from a shop in Cordoba. 'The welcome you got in Argentina was absolutely incredible,' he says. 'You could not walk down the street without being mobbed by people; it was absolutely astonishing. They'd just want to shake your hand, buy you a drink, take you to their house, get your autograph. It was unbelievable.

'I thought at first it must have been because they thought we were players, because we had strips on, but it wasn't. I think it was, being under the dictatorship, the junta, they were so glad to see visitors to their country and that linked in with their passion for football. It was like a pressure being released for them, I think, for a month or so.'

A more direct route to the tournament was taken by Jim Todd from Kilmarnock, one of a group of twenty-two Scotland supporters who had flown from Glasgow to London to Madrid to Buenos Aires. They were in Argentina from the opening ceremony to the final, as part of a package that cost £1,500, a gargantuan sum in 1978 when £5,000 was a good annual wage and £1,500 would be almost enough to buy a new car. 'One of the reasons I went was because Ally had said we would win the World Cup,' says Todd. 'If Ally said we were going to win it, then we were going to win it. I thought we had a good chance and so did half of Scotland.

'We were based in Buenos Aires and flew from there to Cordoba for the Scotland games; we were ten days there, then flew on to Mendoza. There were all these stories that you couldn't go here and couldn't go there because it was dangerous but that was rubbish.

'The locals were great, friendly people who couldn't do enough for the Scots – and they would show us away from the expensive places to the places the locals used, and where you could get an eight-course meal, with as much wine as you desired, for two pounds. Some of the fans, after that game with Iran, just wanted to come home but we were there for a month so we couldn't do anything.'

Todd was an unusually colourful member of the Tartan Army, bestriding the streets of Argentina that month in an all-tartan suit with a tartan rosette on each lapel and wearing a tartan bonnet. Some fans wore replica Scotland tops, though for most it was enough to wear a tartan scarf or hat. The days of the support adopting full national dress – including kilt, sporran and dirk – were still some way off.

News of the Willie Johnston drug episode had stunned Todd and all those other Scotland fans who had made the trip to Argentina. 'We heard about that two or three days after the Peru game,' says Todd. 'One of the local guys said, "You had a player sent home because of drugs." We said we had never heard about that. Then the guy got the paper and showed us and read it out to us. So that didn't help the fans. We just couldn't believe it.'

Weeks and months after the 1978 World Cup had drawn to its frenetic conclusion, Scottish fans would remain in Cordoba, lazing around as if on one monstrous, extended, open-ended summer holiday granted to them by the god of football. One very good reason for this was that a number of these alcohol-happy, scruffy individuals had cast a spell on a number of the local Argentinian women – innately beautiful and well-kempt – who, for some unfathomable reason, found the Scots irresistible.

The women in Argentina were 'stunning', says John McKenzie. 'At one stage,' he adds, 'I thought I might actually go and live in Argentina.' McKenzie had found himself a girlfriend called Tichi, who was from a wealthy family – her father was a lawyer – and who resided in a house with a swimming pool in a village called Villa Allende, twelve miles outside Cordoba.

A number of Scotland supporters would spend languorous days in the company of the local – and in the eyes of the Scots, exotic – women, enjoying life-expanding experiences such as travelling to the Cordoba Sierras or introducing the girls, most in their late teens or early twenties, to the musical delights of the more melodious seventies stars such as Paul Simon whose style was conducive to Latin American ears. Most fans, in Argentina for the fun as much as to shout and sing at the football, found such pastimes more than adequate compensation for the poor early results that weighed down Scotland's World Cup chances.

Argentina in 1978 was repressive in every way and particularly for women, who had been put firmly in their place by the junta. Divorce was banned and opportunities for women to work and be independent shrank as the dictatorship encouraged them to remain at home as housewives. Women were also just as vulnerable to joining those who "disappeared" as were men. This may explain why the chance of obtaining a passport out of the country via an attachment to a visiting foreigner may have been an attractive prospect.

One of the priciest drinking establishments in Cordoba, and therefore rarely frequented by the Scottish fans, had been Ally's Tartan Bar. It became even more unpopular once the results began to unravel. MacLeod himself, on disembarking from the aeroplane on the day the Scottish squad had arrived in Argentina, had spotted a fearsome-looking supporter – beard, mound of hair, tendency to roar wildly – hanging from an airport building window and waving a Lion Rampant in the general direction of the squad.

MacLeod had made it his first action in Argentina to wave at this man, encouraging the players around him to do likewise. The manager had then punched the air with a clenched fist to show solidarity with this individual. In the wake of Ally's reception from the supporters after Scotland's first two matches, that day and that feeling of unity with the fans must have seemed a millennium away to the manager.

13

Missing Links

There is usually no need for ballast when jetting off to the finals of a World Cup but that was Gordon McQueen's unusual status on board Scotland's British Caledonian flight to the 1978 tournament. Derek Johnstone, Scotland's footballer of the year in 1978, should also have been issued with an excess baggage tag in both directions – he would win the undistinguished honour of being the only fit Scottish outfield player not to feature in any of the matches in Argentina. McQueen could at least point to a serious injury as his reason for sitting out the action.

Johnstone, a vigorous twenty-four-year-old, paced the gardens of the Sierras Hotel like a wild beast airlifted to a zoo on a different continent, peering at visitors with eyes that pleaded silently to be set free from his misery. Like a bear pitched into a cage with a new and alien set of rocks, he looked uncomfortable in every spot he tried; whether it was sitting on a hotel bench with Graeme Souness giving him a consolatory pat on the shoulder as journalists asked why he had come all that way not to play; or perched in another corner of the grounds with a Lion Rampant wrapped around his bulky body and a multi-pointed, straw sombrero sitting on his head. Johnstone was the saddest sight in South America, loping only to bench or training ground rather than roaming his natural environment – the football field. This was a different man to the one who had regaled his squad mates with a series of jokes during the flight to Argentina.

Two other significant Scottish players, Danny McGrain and Andy Gray, had missed the transatlantic flight entirely. McGrain had been earning justified plaudits as the finest right-back in world football but a debilitating ankle injury had afflicted him for most of the 1977-78 season and had ruled him out of the World Cup finals. Gray, who in 1977 had achieved the rare feat of becoming both footballer of the year and young player of the year in England, also missed out on selection. On learning he would be absent from the squad, the man who was enjoying the high life as a striker at Aston Villa sat in a Birmingham wine bar fulminating furiously about Ally MacLeod's judgement. No wonder MacLeod had stated, on naming his final twenty-two, 'All I need now is a bullet-proof vest.'

The omission of Gray from the squad was to earn MacLeod considerable criticism. A battling striker, particularly useful in the air, aggressive and brave, Gray's progress in the game was fuelled by a well of ambition so deep that it would have attracted envious glances from a Texan oil baron. It was that thwarted ambition that made Gray's disappointment so bitter. MacLeod had opted to take four forwards to Argentina and Gray found chosen ahead of him Kenny Dalglish, Joe Jordan, Derek Johnstone and Joe Harper.

The inclusion of Harper – who had been one of MacLeod's first signings for Aberdeen in early 1976 – was the one used most often to berate MacLeod, for supposedly showing provincial favouritism in opting for the rugged little Pittodrie player and omitting Gray, the flying, blond-haired striker who had steered Villa close to taking

the English League title in 1977 and who had participated in their run to the quarter-finals of the UEFA Cup
in 1978. Significantly, Gray had missed that quarter-final,
against Barcelona, through injury; although only twenty-
two years old he was already a player whose fierce commitment made for a tendency to leap into challenges with
boneshaking brio – challenges from which he often
emerged with limbs bruised and battered. MacLeod was
unsure about Gray's fitness, and about his tendency to
incur injury, but that was not why he omitted him from
the Scotland squad.

Unlike Jordan and Dalglish, both Harper and Gray had
been absent from the Scotland team for lengthy periods:
Gray for eighteen months; Harper for two-and-a-half years.
Gray had not appeared for Scotland since being dismissed
for violent conduct during Scotland's opening World Cup
qualifier in Czechoslovakia in 1976. Harper had not been
involved with Scotland since 1975 when he was arraigned
as one of the 'Copenhagen Five', a moniker that would
have sat beautifully with a Scandinavian avant-garde jazz
quintet but had actually been applied to a fivesome who
had been banned for life by the SFA after a night of mayhem
in the Danish capital. The escapade ended in the early
hours of the morning with an inebriated Billy Bremner
throwing a drink over a Danish barmaid, and another
Scottish player – although not Harper – splayed across the
bonnet of a police car after removing his shoe and threat-
ening to assault a police officer. All five players – Bremner,
Willie Young, Pat McCluskey, Arthur Graham and Harper
– were originally banned for life but the bans on Graham
and Harper, which had been unjustified, had later been
rescinded.

'When it came down to the last three strikers who could
be chosen,' recalls Harper, 'really, it was between me, Ian

Wallace and Andy Gray and I'd had a magnificent period just about six weeks before he [MacLeod] was picking his final squad and was scoring goals for fun; everything I was hitting was going into the back of the net.

'I was determined I was going to get a lot of goals and make it hard for Ally but once I got picked and spoke to Ally in Argentina, he said he had always been going to include me. He said he had enough boys like Andy Gray, Joe Jordan and Derek Johnstone up front – big boys, target men – and he didn't think Ian Wallace was anywhere near as good a striker as I was so, although it was virtually the last selection, it was pretty clear cut in Ally's mind. I was the foil for Joe Jordan or Derek if Kenny got injured. Hence the reason why I got on against Iran.'

Even if it had been a case of choosing between Gray or Harper on individual merits, it seems that Ally would still have opted for the latter. 'He was very much a guy that had his own mind in terms of making decisions,' says John Hagart, Ally's assistant for the tournament. 'He wasn't a guy for talking a lot, saying, "What do you think?" He would say, "We're going to do this" and "We're going to do that."

'I can remember talking to him one day at Easter Road about Andy Gray. I didn't know Andy Gray but I said, "You've got to put Andy Gray in the pool." I can always remember he said to me, "John, there are twenty minutes to go in the third game, we're drawing and we need to win to qualify. Who would you want sitting on the bench that might get a goal?" He said, "Joe Harper. If it's Joe Harper or Andy Gray, who's going to get the goal?" I said, "Well, you could argue that it might be Joe Harper and you could argue that it might be Andy Gray."

'He said, "Well, Andy Gray will knock people about; Andy Gray will put his head where guys wouldn't go but

Joe'll get you the goal." Now there was an element of truth about that but I can remember saying to him, "Take the two of them, then." He said, "No, no, we can't take the two of them because Derek Johnstone's there as well."'

As a back-up for Dalglish, Harper fitted the bill. Both were compact, touch players who thrived on knock-downs from a heftier, taller striking partner. Gray might have had a better case to be included ahead of Johnstone, especially as the Rangers player, unlike the eager Gray, had appeared to be doing his utmost to slowly talk himself out of a place in the squad prior to the finals. Before the friendly match with Bulgaria in February 1978, MacLeod was surprised to discover Johnstone telling him that, because of his limitations, most particularly his lack of mobility, he would be happy to be switched to centre-back – something that he had also told the management at Rangers. Although in previous seasons Johnstone had filled in at centre-half for Rangers from time to time, this seemed an awfully strange request from a player who had spent the 1977-78 treble-winning season notching up dozens of goals and had been named Scotland's player of the year on that basis. Even Ally was unlikely to take a proven goalscorer to the World Cup finals for the purpose of trying him out in a brand new position in an international jersey. Johnstone's own doubts over centre-forward being his best position appear to have made up the mind of MacLeod to keep him in reserve.

Back in the UK, Nottingham Forest manager Brian Clough, when sitting on a television 'panel of experts', had railed against Johnstone as being 'fly' in his request to move to centre-back. Turning to Johan Cruyff, seated beside him, Clough eulogised about how he – Cruyff – had never shirked the demands of playing up front, which was a bit unfair on Johnstone; like comparing a pavement artist to Picasso.

Johnstone had gone some way towards rebutting his own words when, in the Home Internationals, he had scored the Scots' only goals in their three games: the first a superb header from Bruce Rioch's cross during the game with Northern Ireland was topped, on the following Wednesday against Wales, by an even better goal, on this occasion scored by timing his run to meet a cross from Archie Gemmill with a fine header that butted the back of the net before Dai Davies, in the Welsh goal, could even move.

Johnstone admits that it was 'very frustrating' to be taken to the World Cup and not see even a smidgen of action. The manager, he states, gave him no reason why he was not selected to play but, accepts Johnstone, that was MacLeod's prerogative. Scotland's top league goalscorer in 1978 would now rather try to forget about the Argentinian World Cup than remember it. His favourite pastime in Argentina, he recalls, was sitting on the patio throwing pebbles at ants; a waste of talent from any angle.

The harshest fate of all fell to Gordon McQueen, the centre-back. McQueen had been good enough to be included in the 1974 World Cup squad, aged only twenty-one; he had also been indispensable during the qualifying matches for the 1978 finals and would have been a certain starter until suffering what would prove to be the cruellest blow of his career a fortnight before the tournament. McQueen had had to be nursed gently on board the departing aircraft for Argentina to protect a knee that he had injured after colliding with a goalpost in the Home International against Wales in mid-May. Initially, it did not seem too severe an injury but the knee ballooned overnight and McQueen had been having eight hours of physiotherapy per day at Manchester City prior to leaving for Argentina. He thought, on arriving in South America, that he could possibly play against Peru. Others knew differently.

'Gordon McQueen should never have gone to Argentina and I felt that at the time and said so privately,' says Hugh Allan, the physiotherapist who attended to the player at the World Cup. 'He had a medial ligament strain of the knee and it was what we would call in the trade "a good going one". Now I had never known that to recover in less than six weeks but the orthopaedic consultant whom he was referred to by the SFA said that he reckoned that he would be okay.

'Ally had to take the consultant's opinion because he would have been in trouble with the SFA if he had over-ruled that. So, sadly, Gordon was a waste of space, as it so happened, because although we treated him on a daily basis, he didn't kick a ball for us.'

MacLeod regarded McQueen – with his split-second timing in the tackle and ability in the air – as one of the best centre-halves that Scotland have ever had but, again, after things began going wrong on the field, the manager was castigated for taking a player who had little chance of participating in the finals. As Allan points out, though, once the orthopaedic surgeon had given his opinion that McQueen might make some of the games, MacLeod had little option but to take the player.

'You always think that you could make a difference to the team, because you're an eternal optimist,' says McQueen. 'The various managers of Peru, Iran and Holland were concerned about the aerial threat of Joe Jordan and Gordon McQueen and I thought that I and Joe could have taken advantage of that.

'In hindsight, I shouldn't have gone but you're clinging on in hope and I was desperate to play. Hughie Allan was working away and giving me treatment day after day to get the swelling down, but with an injury such as that one it is just a matter of giving it time to heal. I thought initially that there was an outside chance of playing if we reached the second stage but after a few days I knew I wouldn't have been fit even if we had got through. It's hard to describe how hard that hit me.

'I had been sent off in a semi-final of the European Cup in 1975 and had missed the final that year so I was desperate to feature at the World Cup. Still, today, I think back regularly to that disappointment at the '78 World Cup.'

The height and authority of the often underrated McQueen was badly missed by the Scots. 'Gordon was quite a solid guy to have in your team,' says Alan Rough. 'That was a problem, the way the defence was chopped about and changed. It's always better if you've got a solid four guys that play all the time; they all know each other better.'

An equally huge loss for the squad was that of Danny McGrain. Ally MacLeod regarded McGrain's absence from the Scottish side as more damaging than the loss of Johan Cruyff for Holland, and this was one occasion on which Ally was not exaggerating. McGrain himself states that several people have suggested he might have made the difference to Scotland's efforts in Argentina but he is not sure that one man could have had such a major influence on a team.

He is being unduly but naturally modest. It is difficult to imagine McGrain, then twenty-eight and at the peak of his powers, failing to shore up at least some of the flaws in the Scottish defence. The three goals from Peru arrived from the Peruvian left, Danny's natural beat, as did the Iranian strike. McGrain would have exerted a more powerful presence in that part of the pitch than did Stuart Kennedy, a fine player for Aberdeen but one unlucky to be pitched into serious international football for the first time at the 1978 World Cup.

It is impossible to judge how much Gray might have added. He was inexperienced, with only four caps prior to that tournament, and would appear only sporadically for Scotland over the remainder of his career, scoring only four goals in sixteen further appearances, two of those goals coming against Canada in a close-season friendly in 1983. Such a record tends to refute the cases of those who championed his cause so long and so loud in the summer of 1978. If Harper was selected on the basis of being similar in style to Dalglish, it might have made more sense for MacLeod to take Gray ahead of Derek Johnstone – as a like-for-like replacement for Jordan – but Ally had no choice but to include the Rangers man. Any prospect of omitting Derek Johnstone would have led to immediate uproar in Scotland.

If the cases for Gray and Johnstone remain unproven, the dual loss of Gordon McQueen and Danny McGrain really tore a hole in the Scotland team; the composure and authority that they could offer the defence was noticeable by its absence. McQueen's injury had occurred when he smacked his knee off the sharp-edged, 'square' posts at Hampden Park. Those posts would in time be replaced by rounded ones, but the man they had damaged and his doughty Scotland team mate McGrain were irreplaceable. Had they been available for action, Scotland might have been doing more than fighting for their World Cup lives as they prepared to face Holland in their third and final group match.

14

Glory Day

The players had little time for their manager as they sat in their secluded hotel in the foothills of the Andes above Mendoza prior to the final group game. The glowing reputation of the man in charge of team selection, which had caused him to be appointed in the first place, now counted for little in the heat of a World Cup, and the national press were barely speaking to him.

Arguments frequently broke out and the mood in the camp was one of simmering discontent. The bonus dispute that had disfigured the build-up to the World Cup was still rumbling on, unresolved. The nation's sparkiest players were parked at home, on the other side of the Atlantic, and the less than impressive performances against Peru and Iran had done little to lift the confidence and improve the togetherness of the squad that was there.

Gloom had descended on the camp, and it wasn't helped by the players being locked in tight by Argentinian security. Thoughts of winning the World Cup were now pushed to the back of everyone's minds and the players were united in desiring one thing above any other: a quick return home from sweltering South America to the cool climes of northern Europe. This was the state of affairs with the national team of Holland as they prepared for their final match of the opening phase of the 1978 World Cup, a match in which Scotland were to be their opponents.

It was difficult to dislike the Dutch in the seventies. They had burst in on the 1974 World Cup in magnificent style; bubbling over with youthful enthusiasm, beads around their necks, the traditional badged-blazer beloved of football squads ditched in favour of trendy, casual gear. Long-haired children of the sixties, their imaginative, unconstrained football embodied all of the better, more liberating aspects of the decade in which they had been honing their skills in preparation for a spectacular assault on the world stage. They played football with a joie de vivre, imagination and artfulness that took them all the way to the 1974 final, where, facing West Germany in Munich, the Dutch took the lead in the opening minute but failed to capitalise on that advantage and lost 2-1.

Their 'total football' was appealing in its purity of purpose; it demanded that every player ought to have consummate control of the ball, regardless of whether they were defender, midfielder or attacker, and embodying the democratic freedom of expression that they brought to the game of football. 'The ball is round to go round' as the Dutch phrase has it.

Style, more than anything else, appeared to matter to the Dutch. They had suffered defeat in that 1974 final but had won the hearts and minds of football followers world wide for the manner in which they had conducted themselves. As Johan Cruyff, their captain, stated, the Dutch had lost the 1974 final but had won a victory by displaying a form of football that, even today, brings joy to all who remember it.

'People talk of total football as if it is a system,' said Arie Haan, a key player for the Dutch in both the 1974 and '78 tournaments, 'something to replace 4-2-4 or 4-3-3. It is not a system. As it is at any moment, so you play. That is how we understand it. Not one or two players make a situation but five or six. The best is that with every situation all eleven players are involved, but this is difficult. In many teams maybe only two or three play and the rest are looking. In the Holland team, when you are sixty metres from the ball you are playing.'

The Dutch were now coached by Ernst Happel, a fifty-two-year-old Austrian drenched in experience of guiding teams through international and club matches of the highest quality. Jan Zwartkruis, who had led Holland through the qualifiers, was not felt to be enough of a heavyweight to undertake the same task at the finals and had been demoted to assistant. Happel had been manager of the Bruges side that had lost 1-0 to Liverpool in the European Cup final one month previously and at Bruges was the highest paid manager in European football on a salary of £80,000 a year, almost six times higher than Ally MacLeod's stipend from the SFA. Happel was now being paid £60,000 by the Dutch Football Association for the six-week duration of the 1978 World Cup campaign.

As part of his CV as a top-class coach, Happel claimed to have invented the sweeper position while a player at Rapid Vienna and he had a good record against Scottish sides. As an outstanding international with Austria, for whom he won fifty-four caps, he had played in the side that defeated Scotland 1-0 in the 1954 finals, and it was Happel who had coached Feyenoord of Rotterdam to victory against Celtic in the 1970 European Cup final – the first time any Dutch side had won a major trophy in European competition.

That strong Feyenoord association had initially caused some of the Ajax players in the 1978 squad to have a lack of respect for Happel and there was still an uneasy tension among the Dutch players as they prepared for the match with the Scots. But Happel's wealth of experience underlined the weighty task that lay ahead of Scotland in attempting to beat the Dutch. Even so, it might have encouraged the Scots, had they known about it, that the distance that had developed between Happel and his squad members – especially his younger players – had resulted in Zwartkruis taking over the pre-match instructions and talks with individual players.

The Dutch side to face Scotland in Mendoza's San Martin stadium on 11 June 1978 showed only three changes from the one that had contested the World Cup final four years previously but those changes were deeply significant. Haan, who had played in the matches with Iran and Peru, did not start against Scotland and two other absentees from the team had not travelled to Argentina at all; two men who would have strolled into the Dutch team but who had opted to remain at home.

Wim van Hanegem, their skilled midfielder, had withdrawn from the squad only on the night prior to the Dutch flying out to Argentina. After a one-and-a-half-hour meeting with Happel, Van Hanegem had told the manager he was withdrawing because he was unhappy about the way the team's World Cup-related earnings were to be distributed among the players. Van Hanegem had wanted all earnings to be distributed equally among the squad but, instead, the arrangements in place assigned the bigger names in the Dutch squad a greater share than their lesser-known colleagues. This demand by Van Hanegem was despite the fact that he was one of the biggest names in the Dutch squad and potentially one of the major beneficiaries of the scheme. It was a major bonus for Scotland: Happel had previously told Van Hanegem that he would be kept aside during the first two matches before being brought into action against the Scots – the match that Happel had always believed would decide the section.

An even more significant absentee for Holland was Johan Cruyff, the orchestrator of the team in 1974, creator of total football, the man with the long loping stride who could delicately push and pull a game of football in exactly the direction he chose; the greatest footballer ever to have swished around a football pitch. Cruyff would moan, gesticulate, shrug through a match, like some highly strung and temperamental artiste – a persona that he would live up to with goals scored in sumptuous style. He did not just put the ball in the back of the net; he delivered it there with a flourish, sweeping across penalty boxes with the grace of a ballet dancer and improvising with enormous intelligence, wit and control.

Total football may have been a great democratic footballing principle but it still needed the galvanising presence of Cruyff to provide it with the leadership and drive that really made it work. He would be missing in Argentina, following a decision he had taken shortly after lighting up the world at the 1974 finals. Two months out of his life preparing for and playing in the 1978 World Cup would, he said, be 'too much' for him.

Participation in the 1974 tournament had denied Cruyff a proper family holiday and he had subsequently become irritable; he had, he calculated, been away from home on seventy-eight out of 120 days between August and November 1974 and had enjoyed only fourteen free days in that time. 'I have to live so intensively now that I can't participate in the 1978 World Cup in Argentina,' he stated at the end of 1974, as he explained his decision to remove himself from what was, for him, the only stage that could do full justice to his talents.

Without Cruyff, Holland were not exactly only another team but much of the frisson, the excitement he had brought to them, even as recently as when leading them through the qualifying matches for the 1978 tournament, had gone. The opening two matches of the World Cup had been the Dutch team's first competitive fixtures for a decade without Cruyff so it was little wonder that in those meetings with Iran and Peru they had looked like a team feeling their way, slowly, towards a new era, finding a way of coping without the man who had made so much possible for them.

Scotland, too, were in a fragile state of mind. Following the devastating draw with Iran it had been assumed that, having floundered with two dreadful results in their opening two games, they were on their way out of the World Cup. But one little piece of luck had worked in the Scots' favour. On the same Wednesday that Scotland drew 1-1 with Iran, Holland had drawn 0-0 with Peru. This put the Scots two points behind Holland and meant they could still catch, and overtake, the Dutch on goal difference. Had the Dutch defeated the Peruvians, Scotland would have been relying on Iran to win or draw against Peru.

Now the Scots' fate was in their own hands – although they had to defeat the Dutch by three clear goals to over-turn the goal difference in their favour. It looked close to an impossibility based on Scotland's form in their previous two matches but it provided the players with a sharply focused target at which to aim. That had been of little consolation as spirits had plummeted in the immediate aftermath of the match with Iran. 'Everybody was looking over their shoulder,' says John Hagart, 'and wondering what was going to happen next. Ally went into a wee bit of a shell. Everybody was going about with doom and gloom faces, there was whispering here and there.'

Mutterings and mumblings were beginning to rumble among the players; some remained annoyed about the bonus arrangements; some were dissatisfied with the team selection against Iran, most notably the omission of Souness; some just wanted to get home and away from the fragmenting disaster area that Scotland's World Cup campaign had become. It didn't help that more than one player with a big-name English club had never rated Ally. With Scotland, as with Aberdeen, he would introduce unusual elements into training, such as a player making a misplaced pass having to hop around for the next minute or two. That type of fun had not gone down well at all with some who felt it beneath their status as highly paid professionals in England's top division and now that Ally's methods had yielded a lack of success at the World Cup, their contempt for him had grown.

'You could sense that there was a wee bit of an under-current among the players,' says John Hagart, 'but it wasn't something that was completely out in the open; whether some of them spoke to Ally I would never know; certainly none of them spoke to me and I'm quite sure that would be because they would be thinking I was on Ally's side of the fence; the management side. On the day after the match with Iran, Ally said to me to do what I wanted with the players. We just stayed in the grounds of the hotel and I can remember giving them a real, stiffish running session. One or two of them were moaning but I wasn't bothering about that. I can remember doing it with the thought that it was just to try and blow some of the cobwebs away and get their lungs going and their breath going and getting them thinking about getting their breath back instead of thinking about what had gone wrong. One or two were complaining that they had played two games, had another one to go and that this was like pre-season.'

The squad moved on to the San Francisco Hotel, fifteen miles outside Mendoza, venue for their third game, and the accommodation there was much more to their liking than that which they had found in Alta Gracia. On moving into the new hotel, MacLeod retired to his room and locked himself away from the world and its cup. Ernie Walker, the SFA secretary, noted the gradual withdrawal of the manager from interaction with his players but points out that SFA people did not interfere with how teams were run nor relationships between coaches and players – they would observe but would not intervene.

'We were all very conscious,' says Walker, 'that there wasn't leadership coming, at that particular time, from the coach, by his non-appearance when the whole thing started going badly. He wasn't seen to be around. He was no more the chirpy lad. We were conscious of the fact that he didn't seem to have a tight grip on the players. The atmosphere became depressing and pointless. I had a feeling that I was very much left as the figure to defend Scotland, to front things that I shouldn't necessarily have been fronting. I was always very friendly with Ally. You could not be unfriendly with Ally; he was a jovial kind of guy. He wasn't much of a drinker but he loved company and laughter and carrying on. He'd clown around a lot but when it didn't work out for him over there, I think he felt very sorry for himself in that regard.'

Sandy Jardine suggests that the effect on the squad of the result against Iran 'was a wee bit depressing. We had been built up to deliver something for Scotland and when it didn't materialise it looked as though we were going to come home with our tails between our legs. We got a huge amount of criticism from the press and the supporters so when a thing like that happens it's not the nicest thing in the world. If '74 was the best of times, '78 was the worst of times.' The transformation of Ally MacLeod from extrovert to introvert had an overall effect in dampening the group atmosphere; the manager was an altogether more subdued figure in the approach to the match with Holland.

There would, though, soon be some reason for optimism. On behalf of the players, Scotland captain Bruce Rioch had a crucial meeting with the now reclusive Ally MacLeod – a meeting that was to send Scotland's 1978 World Cup effort veering in a new and better direction. 'I can remember going in and having a talk with him in his room,' says Rioch. 'We talked about Holland and their strengths and how solid they were with the additional players in midfield.

'I discussed with him that if we went with a flat 4-4-2 we might not be able to control the match and that Souness was important to the team. You give your manager your opinion and then leave it to him to select the team.

'He went with the decision that we wanted, with a solid four at the back, a diamond in the middle with Souness at the base of the diamond and myself at the point of the diamond, and we did well on that particular day because it was a massive game. We knew we had to win the game by three clear goals and we were absolutely focused.

'We all knew how good a player Graeme was and what he could produce for us. Everybody knew this was the final throw of the dice. We didn't want to get overwhelmed by them in the middle of the park so you go head to head with the opposition in their diamond and win your individual battles.

'The thing about Holland that was different from the other games was that we knew all about them. I knew Ruud Krol and Arie Haan and Wim Suurbier, Wim Jansen and the Van der Kerkhofs. We knew what we were coming up against and we had a very competitive midfield in every way.'

That meeting between Rioch and MacLeod saw a subtle but significant shift in relations between manager and players. Rioch, decent and dignified, conducted the meeting with clever diplomacy and is keen to point out that he left the decision to the manager, but it is clear that Ally would have been foolhardy to reject the players' wishes and impose on them an alternative set of tactics and team selection of his own. Had he done so, the ingredients were in place for MacLeod to fall victim to a mutiny. The manager's acceptance of the players' wishes did him a lot of good; they would now be on his side.

The style of management employed by Ally at Ayr and Aberdeen had him firmly as the boss and the players at those clubs had followed his instructions to the letter as he transformed them, pied-piper like, from losers to winners. His all-encompassing enthusiasm had brought those clubs successes so there had been little argument with his methods. Matters were slightly different at international level where all of the players with whom he was dealing regarded themselves as successes already in that they were playing international football, especially when Scotland could draw on players from all of Britain's top clubs. In that situation, politics came into the equation to a much greater degree.

Some members of the Scotland squad would have felt they had already achieved more in the game than had their manager and would have expected to have been consulted by him; but that was not Ally's style. He had not previously used older, more experienced players, such as Rioch and others, to his best advantage. It's not that a manager should become friends with such players; more that he should keep them onside and make them feel that their stature is being acknowledged and that they are being consulted. If he does so, then, when times are tough, those players can act as a bulwark against dissent, using their influence to keep a squad together. Ally's lack of experience in European football – he had never taken a club into European competition – may have counted against him when dealing with big-name players who had been there and done that. It might have led them to think, 'Just who is this guy?'

The pressure had taken a severe toll on Ally after the anti-climax provided by the opening two fixtures. Hugh Allan noticed that his face was drawn and John Hagart observed more severe signs of stress. 'You used to be getting off the bus, walking to training, in Argentina,' recalls John Hagart, 'and Ally used to think out loud. Or we'd be sitting having a meal and he would say something like, "Ha ha, they're out to get you, Ally, but you've not cracked yet." And you would look and he would not be talking to anybody; he'd be addressing himself.'

The Scotland-Holland encounter was a significant match in the tournament, as demonstrated by General Videla's presence among the 35,000 who were inside Mendoza's 50,000-capacity San Martin stadium. Finesse would be needed if the Scots were to get the better of the Dutch: the Dutch may have efficiently brought in bulldozers to build a football pitch at their isolated hotel near Mendoza but their style of football was not based on bulldozing the opposition. They would kill a team while bestowing kindness on the watching supporters – passing the opposition to death, lulling them, mesmerising them, until it was time to speed things up and deposit the ball swiftly in the net. Scotland knew they would need to do something similar to live with the Dutch, who, using their positive-minded 3-4-3 system, were confident of finding a host of chances falling their way, through Scotland having to attack. The prospect of defeat did not even show up on the Dutch radar: they had not lost an international match for two years.

The Scottish team that lined up showed three changes from the opening match with Peru, but those changes would prove satisfyingly significant. The team against Holland was: Alan Rough, Stuart Kennedy, Tom Forsyth, Martin Buchan, Willie Donachie, Graeme Souness, Bruce Rioch, Archie Gemmill, Asa Hartford, Kenny Dalglish, Joe Jordan.

Souness was into everything from the start, bursting into tackles with fierce force and popping passes around, and after five opening minutes in which Scotland had buzzed around busily, he took the ball for a walk up the right wing then smoothed a cross into the Dutch penalty area, where Rioch, on the edge of the six-yard box, beat the Dutch goalkeeper Jan Jongbloed with his header but saw the ball smack back off the face of the bar; clear early evidence of the effectiveness of the Scots' new system.

Tom Forsyth, toe-poking the ball from fifteen yards, had the ball in the Dutch net, off a post, but was given offside when he clearly was not. Kenny Dalglish looked hugely unlucky to have a 'goal' disallowed – Wim Rijsbergen, the Dutch defender, had fallen over as he challenged Dalglish, who had chipped the ball over Jongbloed. It didn't look much like a foul but Erich Linemayr, the Austrian referee, called it that way. Two minutes later Dalglish, barely discouraged, sent a shot spinning just wide of the post, but within seconds the Dutch had responded through Rob Rensenbrink whisking the ball past Rough's post from twenty yards.

The match, apart from one or two flourishes on the part of the Dutch, appeared to be moving securely in the Scots' direction when, in thirty-five minutes, Souness, sensing Willy van der Kerkhof on his shoulder, pushed a safe looking pass back into the path of Stuart Kennedy, in the right-back position. The full-back was too slow to prevent

Van der Kerkhof advancing to clip the ball away from the Scottish defender and move it on Johnny Rep. Rep, under the weight of a retrieving tackle from Kennedy, crashed to the turf, leading the erratic Linemayr to point to the penalty spot. 'I didn't think that one was a penalty,' says Rough, who got a close-up of the incident as it unfolded in front of him. 'I thought Stuart Kennedy tackled him, got in and got the ball.'

Gemmill was yellow-carded for lifting the ball from the penalty spot and throwing it away before Rensenbrink swept it low into the corner of the net for the one thousandth goal in the World Cup finals. 'I usually played in the right-forward position,' says penalty-provider Rep, 'but now I played centre-forward, because Johan Cruyff wasn't part of the team.

'The Dutch team was optimistic about the end result of the match. We were confident of winning and the first team to score in the match was Holland: I dare to admit now, that after half-an-hour I committed a *schwalbe* [a show – a dive]. This action caused a penalty kick from which Rob Rensenbrink scored to make it 1-0. So far everything had gone according to our wishes.'

In Cordoba, Peru, simultaneously, went 2-0 up on Iran through a Cubillas penalty. Victory for Peru was going to put them out of sight as group winners. The walls seemed to be closing in on Scotland, especially as the Dutch were now clearly seeking a second goal to capitalise on their advantage – their defenders were frequently pushed up almost to the halfway line and they were launching into attack at every opportunity.

There were forty-two seconds remaining of the statutory opening forty-five minutes when Willie Donachie's cross was headed clear of the Dutch goal by the limping Rijsbergen – who had taken a knock earlier in the half –

to Souness, on the left, outside the Dutch penalty area. Rijsbergen, man-marking Dalglish, had followed the Scot everywhere on the field since kick-off but the Dutch centre-back was now too incapacitated to get back into position as Souness, falling backwards, swiftly spotted a run from Jordan and dug out a left-footed cross that the striker nodded down and across goal. Dalglish was there and, taking advantage of his freedom from Rijsbergen, steadied himself carefully, allowed the ball one bounce, then volleyed perfectly past Jongbloed and high into the Dutch net for a wonderfully crafted goal. Even before the game could resume with the Dutch kick-off, the injured Rijsbergen had been replaced by Piet Wildschut. One break had gone Scotland's way.

Scotland had, in fine style, made the most of the final minute of the first half and they did the same with the opening minute of the second period. Rioch's header found Souness easing into the six-yard box and the midfielder had no sooner made contact with the ball than a robust challenge by Willy van der Kerkhof sent him tumbling off at an angle and into a somersault. Linemayr was again quick to provide a penalty and Archie Gemmill planted a low, purposeful, left-footed shot in the corner of the Dutch net to put Scotland 2-1 ahead.

Souness continued to veer productively all over the field and one cross from him allowed Dalglish a disguised header that went excitingly close to the target. That was a rare sighting of goal for the Scots even though they remained very much alive in the match as it reached the mid-point of the second half. They were still plugging away when, in sixty-eight minutes, they headed towards dreamland.

Kennedy played a long ball down the right flank for Dalglish, who was surrounded, within seconds, by three Dutchmen – Jan Poortvliet, Ruud Krol and Wim Jansen who confronted him like a gang of muggers up an alleyway. Dalglish wound his way round Poortvliet but Krol's sliding tackle knocked the ball away from Dalglish as far as Gemmill, twenty-five yards out from goal and close to the corner of the Dutch penalty area, on the right. Jansen was quick to lunge at Gemmill with his right leg but the Scot used his left foot to smuggle the ball past the Dutch midfielder, who narrowly failed to connect.

Jansen may not have succeeded in winning the ball but he did appear to have forced Gemmill, in evading the challenge, to angle himself away from goal – Gemmill was now facing the centre of the field and a pass to a team mate looked the safest and most straightforward option as seven Dutch defenders milled around on the edge of their own penalty area. Krol now advanced to try to force Gemmill backwards and further away from goal but a swift, ninety-degree twist realigned Gemmill towards the target and he cleverly dinked the ball under one of Krol's long, outstretched legs, then under his other one, leaving the Dutch sweeper and captain sprawled on the turf.

Gemmill then nudged the ball round Poortvliet and unlocked a swathe of space for himself as Dutch defenders tumbled into one another or looked on in shock. Only Jongbloed – his twin kneepads making him look like a handball goalkeeper – now blocked Gemmill's path to goal. But the Scot was at an acute angle to the target. If he had any doubt as to whether to shoot or pull the ball back, his mind was made up for him when Jongbloed advanced a few steps then, as goalkeepers crazily tend to do, went to ground, full length, inviting Gemmill to scoop the ball over his body and into the net. Archie Gemmill did not decline the invitation.

This was the type of intricate goal, swerving in and out of players, that Gemmill must have scored on multiple occasions as a boy in the back streets of his native Paisley. And now here he was, acting it out for real on the biggest stage of all; a goal of instinct and imagination. In terms of knitted together teamwork and cool calculation the goal by Dalglish earlier in the match and the one scored by Jordan against Peru were both technically superior. But Gemmill's goal, for which the only use of the team was as a decoy as Archie habitually went his own way, was celebrated for its sheer individuality and because, for the first time in '78, Scotland were on the cusp of fulfilling their promise.

Gemmill was a man in whom every beat of the heart seemed to reverberate with suppressed anger as he grimaced, his face set hard as rock, through each ninety-minute segment of his life. As an England player, Bobby Robson was once described as having played 'with a smile on his face'; Archie played with a scowl on his face. He epitomised, in his wiry five-feet-five-inch frame, the diminutive Scot who, unwilling to wait and see who is going to try and trample on him next will, instead, assume that with everyone waiting to play him as a mug it is his imperative to get his retaliation in first. Archie Gemmill was no pop influenced, style merchant of the seventies: the thinning hair, wizened features and bristlingly aggressive approach by which he had long been recognised had remained unchanged throughout the ten years which saw him go from amateur football in Glasgow's tough Drumchapel area to the highest strata of the European and international game.

That goal against Holland would thrust on to Gemmill the type of fame as a Scottish international footballer that had eluded him comprehensively up until that point. To many Scots the tough little midfield player was, in comparison to many of his team mates, something of an unknown quantity, partly because he had spent only one season in Scottish club football – with St Mirren in the sixties – and also because he had never really had a run of regular appearances in the national team. The match with Holland would be his twenty-ninth appearance in an international career that stretched back, erratically, to his debut against Belgium in the spring of 1971. Many of those appearances had come in friendlies, or competitive fixtures that had been rendered 'meaningless' by other results. Many of his caps had come to him as a substitute and he had not been in the squad for the 1974 World Cup, despite having then been in his prime as a player.

One year prior to the 1978 World Cup, he had even hovered on the verge of being eliminated from Ally MacLeod's plans altogether. Gemmill had been reluctant to go on the three-game tour of South America if, as MacLeod told him was possible, he might not feature in the matches. It was, Gemmill had suggested to MacLeod, a long way to go just to sit on the bench. The manager had exerted his authority by telling the player that if he missed that tour he would be left out entirely of the World Cup qualifying matches in late 1977. Gemmill had accepted the suggestion and had gone to Argentina, Brazil and Chile and featured in all three games.

Now, one year later, one goal had provided him with lasting fame in an international career during which he had usually seen the spotlight seek out anyone else but him. If anyone owed Scotland a goal it was Gemmill, after his errors contributed to the Scots conceding the goal against Iran and one of those against Peru. For this little burrower of a player, his celebration of the goal was entirely in character. As the ball landed in the Dutch net Gemmill, grim-faced as a miner emerging after twelve hours down a pit, jogged away from goal, fist clenched defiantly towards the crowd, then all the way back to the halfway line without once allowing his features to break out even into a half-smile – despite his goal leaving Scotland just one goal and twenty-two minutes away from making it into the last eight of the 1978 World Cup. It could have been even better. If Linemayr had not been conned into giving the Dutch their penalty, Gemmill's goal would have had Scotland already sitting in a qualification spot as they entered the final stages of the match.

As it was, Scotland eased into the lead against Holland to find themselves balanced on the brink of a breakthrough that had seemed close to impossible just a couple of hours earlier. At this stage Gordon McQueen, sitting in the stand, injured and with no hope of participating in the tournament, experienced mixed feelings. 'The Iran game hadn't been a lot of fun. I watched it from the stand and it was horrible; not for the result but from the very fact that I wasn't playing and wasn't able to contribute. The Holland game was the worst of the lot because I knew deep down I still wasn't going to be fit for the second stage if we did get through.'

Within seconds of Gemmill's goal, Scotland came close to the type of self-destruction that is as characteristic of the national team as are inspirational goals such as Gemmill's. Martin Buchan fouled Jansen on the Dutch right and Jan Boskamp swung the free kick into the penalty area. Rep, Forsyth and Rough all went for the ball in the air, but it eluded them and arrived in the vicinity of Kennedy, facing his own goal, who headed the ball down and only a fraction past Rough's right-hand post.

'Then Johnny Rep sent another dagger through our heart,' says Bruce Rioch. Inspirational initiative had made Rep one of the great World Cup footballers of the seventies and with seventy-one minutes gone, he showed that there was still much more to his game than winning phantom penalties. A cameo of total football saw him make a great curving run back from the forward line into a midfield position where he picked up the ball from Krol, nudged it back to his captain, then swept past Rioch and Souness – neither of whom went with him – latched on to Krol's return pass and used the momentum built up by his run to shoot from thirty yards just as Ally McLeod was yelling encouragement from his dugout to 'shoot, shoot' – believing the Dutchman had no chance from that range.

Rep describes the moment that broke Scottish hearts. 'Nobody went to tackle me so I had a shot. You can never be absolutely sure of scoring with a shot like this, but I thought it was a good opportunity. I took the shot "the Brazilian way"; hitting the ball with three toes and then immediately just gently stroking the ball before it leaves you.'

Gemmill, just as Rep kicked the ball goalwards, had gone to close him down and the ball nicked off the Scot's boot and went slicing through the air in a fine arc. Rough got a touch to the ball; enough, he believed, to stop it, but when the goalkeeper looked round, the ball was nestling in his net.

'I thought that was a great strike,' says Rough. 'Everybody says it was forty yards or thirty-five yards out but it was only twenty-eight, thirty yards from goal. Again, I got a good hand to that and I couldn't believe it when I turned round and the ball was lying in the back of the net. I honestly couldn't believe it. I thought I'd done enough, got enough on it, to push it over the bar.

'The balls were much, much lighter than we were used to and they did move in the air. Watch the goals that were scored in that World Cup; past better goalkeepers than me, such as Dino Zoff. There were balls screaming in from all sorts of angles – and I'm not making that an excuse.

'I always asked the referee if I could get a hold of the ball before we went out and when I did that before the first game it bounced about thirty feet in the air because it was so light. I couldn't believe it. At home we were playing with the old, heavy, leather ball.'

That second strike for Holland, making it 3-2 to Scotland, proved to be crucial. 'After our second goal, there was no way the Scots could get back up to the level they had been at before,' said Ruud Krol after the match; the multilingual Dutch sweeper looking as casual as a young businessman after a Sunday afternoon game of squash.

Bruce Rioch remembers that there was little immediate satisfaction to be gained from Scotland's improved performance. 'The disappointment was enormous afterwards,' says Rioch. 'We had won but had gone out of the tournament.'

High above the pitch, in the commentary position for Scottish Television, Arthur Montford had been unsurprised with the way the match had developed in a manner more pleasing for Scotland than their previous two fixtures in that World Cup. 'The third game was totally predictable,' says Montford. 'The last thing I said before the game was that I would not be surprised if Scotland won – and that they would not lose. The Dutch had a great respect for Scotland. Happel said he expected a boomerang effect from the Scots and that it would be a hard game.

'Archie Gemmill said that great thing afterwards, "It wasn't about the goal; it was about pride." Remember, MacLeod knew Holland – how Rensenbrink played, and the Van der Kerkhofs would play – this, unlike Peru and Iran, was a European nation that he knew well. I can't remember Ally smiling from the first match until after the Holland game, and then it was a wry smile.'

Within minutes of the match concluding, theories had begun to be aired that the Dutch had deliberately lost the match; it was so typically Scottish to snatch defeatism from the jaws of victory. The suggestion was that, to avoid Brazil and Argentina in the next round, the Dutch had engineered the result from their match with Scotland so that they would finish second to Peru in group four. Happel had, indeed, said prior to the tournament that the Brazilians were the team he wanted to avoid – and anyone who had seen Argentina's opening three group games would have been rocked by the ferocity and fanaticism of the crowds of almost 80,000 who had backed the home side in each match.

It does, though, attribute almost supernatural powers of anticipation and control to the Dutch to suggest that they could let the scoreline against Scotland slip and slide as they pleased, especially against a team that they obviously rated, regardless of Scotland's form in their opening two matches. This was, after all, the Dutch side that, as Rep puts it, had 'forgotten to score the second goal' when 1-0 ahead of the Germans in the 1974 World Cup final. It seems unlikely that they would have run a similar risk against the Scots.

Rep himself quashes any thoughts of the Dutch playing for a manageable defeat as he casts his mind back over that match. 'It was partly true that we wanted to avoid Brazil,' he admits, 'but it was not something on which we calculated. The possibility relaxed us before the game but we didn't dare to adjust our tactics towards that aim. That would have been much too risky.

'Of the seven matches we played during the tournament, the one against Scotland was the hardest. It was a killer match. Scotland had nothing to lose and so they could play freely. We had gone 1-0 up but then the Scottish team started showing its soccer quality. They scored one-one, one-two and one-three – a very beautiful goal from Archie Gemmill, by the way. Scotland was now only one goal away from kicking Holland out of the tournament and that's exactly how we felt and thought.

'But then, Ruud Krol and I picked up the ball from our own half, built up an attack, and when I took a shot, the ball flew in the right upper corner. This demoralised the Scottish team and even though we lost the match with two-three, we stayed in the tournament, eventually to reach the final. And Scotland, though victorious over Holland, went home.'

Rep admits his goal was a little bit lucky and that when a player shoots from so far out he requires a lot of luck. He also absolves Rough of any blame for conceding the goal. 'I don't think he could have done any better than he did at that goal but Alan probably doesn't have many good memories about me. I met him three times; the first time was in a European Championship under-eighteen match in Scotland, when I scored against him in the semi-final by lobbing the ball over him to make it one-nil. The second time was the match on the high grass field of Mendoza. The third time was at the end of my career; I played with Feyenoord in Edinburgh and I was the only one that scored in that match. He did recognise and remember me then. Ha ha! When the ball hit the net for that goal, it was a liberation: we would play in the next round!'

The idea that Holland played for a defeat also tends to fall apart under the consideration that a draw would also have landed them second place in the group. In finishing second to Peru in group four they may have avoided Argentina and Brazil but they would now have to face an Italian side that was progressing sleekly through the tournament and that had, indeed, one day prior to the Holland-

Scotland match, defeated Argentina to top that group. West Germany, nemesis of the Dutch, were also now awaiting them in the second group stage; as were an Austrian side that had won a group containing Brazil and Spain.

The Dutch had hated living in Mendoza, venue for all three of their group games, where they had found the heat deeply oppressive. Following the match with Scotland, some Dutch players told their Scottish opponents that they were the lucky ones – to be going home.

The Dutch had possibly even thought that, with Scotland almost out of business, they could stroll through this game. It was so difficult to tell how committed the Dutch were in any match; always relaxed in possession, they could look as though they were meandering when they were actually probing and passing their way through a game. 'The Dutch attitude against Scotland that day was an arrogant one,' suggests Gordon McQueen. 'They thought they would win by just turning up.'

The suggestion that the Dutch wished to lose by a desirable margin is one that John Hagart sets aside. 'I don't think they wanted to lose but I can remember, late in the first half, thinking, "They think they don't need to do any more – that it's all over." We all know in football that if you take your foot off the gas it's sometimes hard to click back in again.

'Then we scored and scored again and you could see them look at each other and that's where I think they were good enough to get it back on track. I don't mean that in any disrespectful way to our players.'

The irrepressible MacLeod was at it again in the minutes after the match. 'If we'd played like that, there's no doubt we could have gone on and won the thing,' he said as he thought back ruefully to the two matches that had preceded the victory over Holland. It was puzzling to those back home and around the world that the Scots had won in such style against Holland but there was no real mystery about it. Scotland's success that day in Mendoza was encapsulated in the desire of the country's footballers to play off a tackle. Probing gently and smoothly isn't Scotland's style; there needs to be an element of competitiveness, of battle, before they get really interested.

In facing skilled opponents, such as the Dutch, whose talents need no introduction, the Scots realise the need to get in about them, win the ball and take the game to them. The game then develops into a battle – a battle to see who can display the most skill within the rules of the game – but a battle nevertheless, where it is seen as necessary to take the initiative from the start, where the ball is to be seized under pressure before it can be used constructively. The Dutch might enjoy thinking languidly on a football pitch; not so the Scots. Matches in which opponents sit back and allow the Scots to have the ball are less conducive to the Scottish style because the element of battle is missing for long stretches of encounters in which opponents say, through their actions and attitude, 'There's the ball, take it, we won't fight you for it too much. Go on, beat us.' In such circumstances, a mild depression bites at the Scottish footballer's psyche. The Scottish mentality is at its best when smacking into forceful challenges and counterattacking in high-tempo games with a lot of tackling going on, matches that resemble the way the game was learned on Scottish streets and youth-team pitches and the way it is played, to keep warm, on Saturday afternoons in sweeping rain and bone-numbing cold.

'I was elated, delighted. I thought, "That'll show them,"' says Faye MacLeod as she remembers watching the television pictures of that glorious evening in Mendoza flooding her front room in Ayr with gaudy colour and brightness. It had been an uplifting event with the Scots, like a collection of cornered alley cats, coming out fighting once they had nowhere else to turn. With their pride stripped bare, they had done all they could to regain it.

'Ally had faith in the squad of players that he took to Argentina,' states Joe Harper. 'He absolutely believed that he had a team that could win the World Cup; realistically, I wouldn't have said that. You're going to the other end of the world and you've got all the problems about staying there. It's very, very hard. Realistically, we could have got to the next phase and that's where the players let Ally down.

'In a one-off situation, you would have taken Scotland at that time against any team. It was a squad full of class. After the Peru game and the Iran game and before the Holland game, we were put down so much by our own press and by the English press that we had a meeting about it amongst ourselves and said, "Let's show these people what it's all about."

'We went out and beat Holland and deserved to beat Holland; it wasn't a fluke. It just proves that we were capable; if we had got to the final, like Holland, then, in a one-off game against Argentina, then maybe . . . but it was always going to be Argentina's cup that year. It would have been very hard for anybody to beat them.'

Sandy Jardine also looked on in some surprise at the standard of football being displayed by his fellow squad members against the Dutch. 'If Scotland had put in the same level of performance against Peru and Iran as against Holland, they would have progressed in the tournament, although I'm not saying we would have won it or anything like that.'

Mythology would, in later years, paint this as one of the

great Scottish victories but in the minutes immediately after the match that was not the feeling of those on the ground in Mendoza. 'You were disappointed, there's no doubt about it,' says John McKenzie, who had, along with his fellow supporters, been lurched through the emotions that evening inside the San Martin stadium.

'I know there was a lot made of the jeering and the stoning of the players' bus after the Iran game,' continues McKenzie, 'but there was also a lot of genuine anger after the Holland game because people realised we were out; even though we had played some lovely football and got a great result. There was anger that we were going home and that anger from the fans was directed at Ally MacLeod. He was this guy that had told us we were coming out to win the World Cup and here we were having had a disaster.

'I do remember stuff being thrown at the bus after the Holland game; scarves and things like that, not stones. People were spitting at the bus. We saw it while we were waiting for the crowd to clear. It didn't surprise me although we, as a group, were not involved in that. I thought that was a bit unfortunate, the way the fans took their frustration out on the bus after the Holland match; I didn't think that was right. You could understand it after the Iran game but the Holland game was something different.'

It must have been especially confusing for the Argentinian bus driver attached to the Scotland squad who had thought that Scotland only had to win their game – not by three goals – to go through and who had been running up and down hugging everyone in the Scottish party after the match.

It had been the first time at any World Cup finals that Scotland had defeated a nation of a higher standing in international football than Scotland themselves and Gemmill's goal would grow in magnitude down the years but it ultimately, at the time, produced a dull feeling of failure and confusion. It would have been easier, in a way, to accept elimination if Scotland had lost to the Dutch. That way, MacLeod's promises would have been perceived as entirely hollow. Now, the spirited manner in which victory had been achieved and elimination on goal difference once again embraced, opened up doubts as to whether Scotland really could have competed with the world's best once they had hit their stride.

Holland now moved into the Sierras Hotel in Alta Gracia for the second set of group games. The Scottish players had despised that accommodation during their fortnight there. Now it was the one place in the world they would have liked to be as they prepared to leave the most momentous World Cup the Scottish nation has ever experienced.

15

After Argentina

Football proved to be a matter of life or death for Ally MacLeod after the 1978 World Cup tournament. One year after he had held his head in his hands during the match with Iran, with his heart, soul and stomach plummeting to the base of the dugout, the cumulative effects of the Argentina experience, which had been chiselling away at him in the subsequent twelve months, did their best to deal him a fatal blow. On holiday with his family, MacLeod was brought to his knees by a ruptured ulcer that confronted this most light hearted of men with the seriously deadly prospect of mortality.

'Argentina aged him,' says Faye MacLeod. 'We were on a holiday in Ibiza the year after and he took a burst ulcer. He said he had brought up Coca-Cola but I knew it wasn't and we got a doctor, who said it was sunstroke. A second doctor said, "No, no," and wanted him to go to hospital. He couldn't walk.

'They said that if he hadn't been such a fit man it would have killed him. He'd lost two-thirds of his blood. They said it had been a build-up of the strain and the tension of all that had happened. That was the effect of the World Cup: he had obviously bottled it all up inside himself. He had to receive iron injections after that. He'd never previously been ill.'

MacLeod was not the only individual to suffer lingering

after-effects from the Argentina experience but the manager, who had lost two stones in weight during the tournament, would feel the consequences more severely than anyone else.

Following their elimination from the 1978 World Cup, there had been several swift, sudden and harsh reminders to the Scotland squad that they should no longer regard themselves as particularly privileged or welcome in Argentina now that they had nothing more to contribute to the tournament. On attempting to leave the country, the Scotland party found themselves fogbound in Mendoza and from there diverted to the obscurity of a military airport in Buenos Aires. An overnight stay in that jostling, bustling city was required prior to their departure for home and although the tournament's local organising committee in the Argentinian capital had booked certain hotels for those national teams that had been eliminated, they had not been too choosy in terms of whether these establishments were in the more salubrious parts of town. The Scots found themselves in a slum hotel up a shabby alleyway; a sharp reminder of their ejection from a starring role at the centre of the glittering whirl of the tournament to that of down-beat, backstreet losers.

The players stated that they would rather walk the streets and squares of the city all night than remain in such an establishment. Martin Buchan, an unusually cerebral foot-baller, whose hobbies included playing classical guitar and learning foreign languages, could speak Spanish and came to the rescue, quickly making a deal to have the team moved to a five star international hotel for their overnight stay. There, for the first time on their sojourn in Argentina, the players could pad around on plush carpets, enjoy cool, controlled air conditioning and wall-to-wall colour television and relax in the manner that they, as leading footballers, felt was just reward for their status. One SFA official remembers Archie Gemmill commenting, 'If we'd had this type of hotel from the start, we would have done a lot better . . .'

That upgrade did little to lift a generally sombre mood that had settled on the Scottish squad, as Joe Harper recalls: 'Ally took it all. I remember standing with a few of the boys, on the way back, and we said to him, "Don't worry, boss, it wasn't your fault." It was the players on the day that let us down; we, as players, all let ourselves down, to a certain extent.

'On the way back, when we were out of the competition, Roughie said, when we were coming back on the plane, "Remember I said we would die when we were on the bus into Alta Gracia and we were being choked by smoke? Well, I now wish we had . . ."'

There was a final flourish of zaniness on the SFA party's arrival at Glasgow airport on the late afternoon of Thursday 15 June. A coach was despatched to meet their plane as it sat on the tarmac – this was to be a way of bypassing any angry demonstrations by disgruntled supporters. It had, though, been overlooked that members of the party would have to get off the coach and go into the terminal to identify and collect their baggage. Even before they could do that, players found themselves on the end of serious abuse from airport workers.

'About five of us got back into Glasgow,' recalls Joe Harper, 'myself, Derek, Bobby Clark, Stuart Kennedy and Roughie; the rest of the players had disembarked elsewhere. We had people spitting on the bus, a welcoming committee with all the gear on, calling us everything under the sun. It was just pathetic.

'I'll be honest; had I been young enough to make the next World Cup, I would have thought very, very seriously about whether I would have gone or not, even though it will always be on my CV that I played in the World Cup, and I am proud about that and happy for my family.

'I came back, got off the plane, drove to Ardrossan and got the ferry over to Arran and it was the only place I could get peace. I had played thirteen-and-a-half minutes against Iran and some of the things that were being said to me, such as, "You're a wee bastard; you've let us down; you've done this and you've done that . . ." I actually had a good thirteen-and-a-half-minutes when I had come on but to be treated like that by your own fans when you had gone to the other end of the world . . . was absolutely abysmal.'

The elongated journey back to Scotland from Argentina was 'the worst trip home ever', according to Alan Rough. 'Generally, coming back from a trip, you'll have a few drinks, a laugh, a carry-on, but morale was very, very low and everybody was anticipating being met by a hostile media when we got back. It wasn't until we stopped at London that we found that everybody got off the plane apart from a few of us; me, Ally, Derek Johnstone, Joe Harper, Stuart Kennedy and a couple of others took the brunt rather than the twenty-two that went.

'I couldn't believe it when we got to Glasgow airport; the press were actually on the tarmac. I still can't fathom that out. They were about fifty yards from the stairs; a huge crowd of them. I don't think it helped matters much when Ally got out of the plane and waved to everybody. I think he thought it was a welcoming party and, here, it wasn't. Again, he was great; he was big enough to talk to them. He took most of it.

'The best thing was getting on that bus because it was really bad. Even the airport people were baying for blood. It was like a hanging mob the way they were screaming at us. It was pretty much fever pitch; pretty bad.'

Of Ally's return to Scotland, Faye MacLeod recalls, 'A friend ran me up to the airport in Glasgow and they took us into a separate room to wait for Ally to come out; I don't know whether they thought we were going to get lynched or what . . . We came home to our wee cul-de-sac and he didn't say much about the World Cup; not much at all.'

Sympathy for Ally was forthcoming, post-World Cup, not only from some of his players but also from another, unexpected quarter. One month after the match with Peru, Ally and Faye MacLeod were among a select group of invited guests who attended a private dinner party hosted by the Queen and the Duke of Edinburgh. At first, MacLeod, still reeling from the shock of the events of Argentina, had been disinclined to take up the invitation. He believed that they had been asked to a large-scale event at which their absence would go almost unnoticed. It was only at the last minute that he and Faye decided to zip over to the Palace of Holyroodhouse in Edinburgh, the venue for the event.

'He kept asking me if I wanted to go,' recalls Faye MacLeod. 'I was thinking it would be like the garden party but it wasn't. There were only about thirty of us at the one big table. He kept saying to me, "Can you imagine if we hadn't turned up? These two conspicuous folk absent." The Queen said how happy she was to see him smiling again and the Duke of Edinburgh came over and wanted to know all about it.'

Both royals mentioned having watched the match between Scotland and Iran. Ally took that as his cue to throw in a joke: 'With a bit of luck in the World Cup in Argentina, I might have been knighted. Instead, it looks as if I may be beheaded.' Four days later, Ally was to attend a meeting at the SFA headquarters at Park Gardens, Glasgow, at which it would be decided if he should remain as

Scotland manager. The MacLeods' regal Edinburgh engagement was on Monday 3 July 1978 and the following
morning at Park Gardens, Ernie Walker, unaware of Ally
and Faye MacLeod's attendance at Holyrood, sat Ally down
to impart what he believed would be some bad news to
the manager. There had, said Walker, been invitations sent
to the SFA for a royal garden party at Holyroodhouse on
the evening of Thursday 6 July. Walker then told Ally, 'I'm
sorry but you appear to be the only member of our official World Cup party who has not been invited.' Ally
responded, 'That's all right. Faye and I had dinner with
Her Majesty and the Duke of Edinburgh in the Palace last
night.' Walker, rocked back on his heels, did not know
whether or not Ally's imagination had gone into overdrive
yet again.

The final of the 1978 World Cup had taken place eight
days prior to the MacLeods' royal engagement. It had ended
with Holland losing 3-1 to Argentina after extra time in a
sour conclusion to a World Cup that had been patchy in
terms of overall quality. Argentina had, to put it neutrally,
found favour from referees throughout the tournament.
They had gone almost entirely unpunished by Antonio
Garrido, the Portuguese referee, after committing a series
of both niggly and severe fouls in defeating Hungary 2-1
in their opening match and had been awarded a penalty
for nothing by Jean Dubach, a Swiss referee, to win their
second game, against a fine French team, by 2-1. So it had
gone on, all the way to their last match of the second
stage, with Peru, who had lost to both Brazil and Poland
prior to meeting the Argentinians.

Argentina required a win by at least four goals to reach
the final and what they wanted they tended to get during
that tournament. Reports would later suggest that millions
of pounds worth of aid had been sent by the Argentinian

junta to the cash-starved Peruvian government to ensure that the home nation got the right result. A 6-0 Argentina victory put them in a final with Holland to which FIFA, on the casting vote of Artemio Franchi, an Italian, appointed Sergio Gonella, an Italian referee. This was a ludicrous decision: 98 per cent of Argentina's population was composed of descendants of emigrants from Italy and Spain. The result was a final in which Argentina were able to disregard, blatantly, the rules as and when they pleased and they won 3-1. The fanatical joy of the Argentinian people in that triumph was one that few who had watched closely the progress of their team could share. As the ticker tape cascaded from the stands in Buenos Aires and the crowds shouted 'Ar-gen-ti-na' over and over again, the Argentinian junta had their victory.

Back in Scotland, repair work was underway at the SFA, who had had a window smashed by louts at their Park Gardens offices after the Iran game. On Friday 7 July, the day after SFA members had been wining and dining in the grounds of Holyrood Palace, the damage done to the Scottish national team was scrutinised by the SFA's international committee.

Rumours of Ally MacLeod's demise as Scotland manager had been circulating for weeks. On the day after the Holland-Scotland game David Scott, a serious newspaper and, by then, television news reporter, had led the national one o'clock BBC television news with the story that Ally had resigned. 'I presume he was acting on information received,' says Rodger Baillie of Scott. 'He was a very experienced professional and not someone given to conjecture. He must have been told by someone that Ally had resigned. The feeling before the Holland game was that Ally was going to be sacked.' A leak from a senior source at the SFA had indicated as much.

MacLeod was asked to be at Park Gardens at half-past-two on that Friday, 7 July, but was, signally, kept waiting outside the meeting room for two hours before being taken in and given a grilling over the way in which he had conducted himself as manager before, during and after what Scotland had seen of the 1978 World Cup. The questions came thick and fast and MacLeod did all he could to attempt to deflect them deftly before being asked to leave the meeting but to remain close at hand. He was then summoned to return and told that there had been a motion to remove him as manager but that it had been defeated. The vote on the motion by the six-man committee had ended three-three before Tom Lauchlan, the committee chairman, had used his casting vote to save MacLeod's job.

That weekend, details of the motion to remove MacLeod and of the split vote were leaked to the press – a calculated action that left MacLeod fizzing at such duplicity and feeling that his position as Scotland manager was now, as he thought privately, 'well-nigh untenable'. The creation of such a sense of unease in the manager may have been exactly the intention of whichever Machiavellian individual had tipped off the press.

This was only the latest in a series of experiences which helped transform Ally from extrovert to temporary introvert. The man who had been so devil-may-care before the World Cup was now like one who has been knocked down by a juggernaut: before making any move he always looked very carefully to his left and to his right. He had, though, lost none of his determination and stubbornness and was set on not becoming a victim of what he thought to himself was a 'witch hunt' that had developed in the wake of the Argentinian escapade. The louder his critics called for his head, the more determined MacLeod became to refuse them satisfaction. Had they been less strident, he would have been more willing to walk away with some dignity intact and to make a return to club management.

It all meant that MacLeod was still Scotland manager in the autumn of 1978, even though he knew that his position had been undermined to a severely damaging degree. Nine days before Scotland played their first match after Argentina, a European Championship qualifying match against Austria in Vienna on 20 September 1978, MacLeod named his squad and then sidestepped the usual press conference to discuss it. He did so, he said, not out of malice or bitterness but because he felt he had been too accommodating to the press prior to Argentina and that it had not helped him.

Bruce Rioch was missing from the squad, as was Derek Johnstone, who was ruled out by MacLeod because the player had been granted his wish by Glasgow Rangers to be switched from centre-forward to centre-back. Bobby Clark, Joe Harper, Kenny Burns, John Robertson, Jim Blyth and Sandy Jardine were others who were omitted; some on the basis of age, Burns and Robertson because they had not performed as MacLeod had hoped they would in Argentina. Ally may have tinkered with the squad but his starting eleven was close to the one that had defeated Holland 111 days previously: the only two changes were Gordon McQueen, fit again, replacing Tom Forsyth in central defence and, significantly, Andy Gray taking the place of Rioch.

'By that time paranoia at the SFA had become so severe that Harkness was planning to ban everyone on the official charter flight from carrying duty free bags because people would assume there was drink in there,' says Rodger Baillie.

'Ally was ill at ease with the whole thing by then. The SFA were conscious that the press relations had just about broken down to zero so they held a cocktail party in Vienna for us and I remember when we were going in Ally was keeking round a corner. By this time he was paranoid – "What are they saying about me?" – and that was three months down the line. I think he was expecting the firing squad from the press any time.'

The inclusion of Gray against the Austrians ensured an enforced change of style for MacLeod's team, in tandem with his change in approach to the press. A three-pronged strike force in a 4-3-3 formation took the field in the Prater stadium, Vienna. Jordan and Gray, more usually central target men, played wide, with Dalglish operating in the centre of the attack. It did not work. Ally replaced Jordan with Arthur Graham, a more conventional wide player, after an hour, with Scotland 2-0 down. Another goal for the Austrians followed swiftly but in the closing stages Scotland fought hard and goals from McQueen and Gray made it a more respectable 3-2.

It had been a tough fixture with which to resume after Argentina: Austria had been one of the European finalists at the 1978 World Cup and had played well to reach the second stage. A better result might have convinced MacLeod he could still achieve things with Scotland but six days later, on 26 September 1978, Ally MacLeod resigned as Scotland manager to take up the offer of becoming manager of Ayr United. One week after leading Scotland into a European Championship qualifier in front of 70,000 revved up Austrians, MacLeod was back where he had begun as a manager, in the dugout at Somerset Park, Ayr, for an encounter between two sides sitting close to the foot of the Scottish First Division, Ayr United and Arbroath, in front of a smattering of dedicated supporters.

'He would have been sacked; I'm prepared to say that,' says Ernie Walker, the SFA secretary in 1978, confirming that if Ally had not jumped he would have been pushed. 'It could not have gone on. To be in the SFA in the aftermath of all this was extremely difficult. I felt personally as if I had to rebuild the place from the ashes, from the floor upwards.

'Everything becomes difficult. You lose the respect of the public, the media. Sponsorship became very difficult for a period. The morale of my staff had never been lower. As well as being at home crying, they were getting rocks through the window. So it was a question of trying to rebuild and we could not have gone on indefinitely with Ally. He'd lost the boardroom.'

MacLeod had not been sacked immediately because, suggests Walker, 'I think there might have been a feeling that it would have been a bit much to say, "And you're getting the sack. Everything's down to you; nothing to do with us." That didn't happen and I think it is probably correct that it didn't happen. He had had a bad enough time without everything being put on his shoulders. It was a relief to us and to him, I'm sure, when the parting was made.'

Blackburn Rovers had also offered Ally their manager's job in the autumn of 1978, but Rovers were by 1978 in the second strata of English football and facing a struggle against relegation and he decided to turn them down. At Ayr, Ally was, on the surface, and as far as his players could see, once again the same exciting extrovert. He would breeze into the dressing room at two o'clock on a match day, announce the team, then go through the team lines of Ayr's opponents, one by one. 'I've never heard of him,' he would say of the first name on the opposition team sheet. 'I've never heard of him either,' he would say of the next one and so on down the team before crumpling it up into a ball and throwing it into the wastepaper basket. 'You're playing a bunch of nobodies.'

He could also use the opposite of such a tactic. Prior to a cup tie with a top class Dundee United side, featuring David Narey and Paul Hegarty at centre-back, MacLeod strolled into the dressing room and said to his two strikers, Danny Masterton and Walker McCall, 'You've got no chance of doing anything against those two; no chance at all.' As bemused players looked on, Ally continued, 'So we'll not play anyone up front against them.' He then instructed Masterton and McCall to play wide, on the wings, away from Narey and Hegarty. Confusion broke out among his team at using such a tactic but they gradually saw the sense in Ally's seeming madness and Ayr managed a 1-1 draw against opponents a division higher than them.

'We zoomed up to the top of the division in the twelve or thirteen games after Ally's arrival,' says Robert Connor, then a teenage player with Ayr, 'because of the way Ally built players up. Then he left to go to Motherwell and Willie McLean, whose style was the opposite of Ally's, came in and we started to tumble back down the table.'

At Ayr Ally had asked for a pension scheme, found it refused to him, then discovered that the previous Ayr manager had had such a scheme. That, plus the offer of a higher salary at Motherwell, prompted Ally to move on. 'I was with him at Motherwell,' says John Hagart, 'but he was a different guy – a lot of the effervescence had gone out of him. I think it took him a long time to get over Argentina.

'There were days and spells when he was back to his old effervescent self but one felt that he was a wee bit more suspicious of people that he didn't really know; and with some of the ones that he thought he knew, he wasn't so sure that he knew them as well as he had thought. Before the World Cup, his disposition had been to think that everybody was a good guy. I don't mean that he was naïve;

I just mean that that was his disposition and that had changed after Argentina.'

A change may have come over Ally but some traces of his previous outlook on life, such as the ebullient desire to let the facts fit in once he had announced his view of the world, could not be scrubbed entirely from the make-up of the man. 'The chairman at Motherwell when we were both there was a guy called Bill Samuel,' remembers John Hagart, 'and he was a pretty wealthy guy in steel stockholdings and was a Motherwell man.

'On one occasion, he took Ally and I down to the Derby and we stayed in a beautiful hotel for a great two days. On the day of the Derby, after the racing was over and we had had a meal, we were in a marquee at night, Acker Bilk and his band were playing, there had been plenty of drink flowing, and Mr Samuel said, "John'll sing a song." So I got up, we were all half gassed, and sang a Scottish song.

'Of course, they were all saying, "If John can sing, Ally must be like Caruso." So they were asking Ally to get up but he said, "There's no way I'm singing." Five minutes later, Ally said to me, "Do you think he would let me play his clarinet?" And I said, "You can't play the clarinet." He said, "Aye, I can." So I said, "Oh, well go and ask him." He said, "No, no. You go and ask him." So I said to Acker Bilk, "Can Ally MacLeod play your clarinet?" So he said, "Yes, what does he want to play?" I said, "He says he'll just join in with whatever your next tune is."

'So Ally gets the clarinet and the band starts playing. Ally goes through all the actions but there's not a note comes out of the clarinet although the rest of the band is playing. Ally finishes and they're all going daft, clapping, because, to be honest with you, half of them are half gassed and he had mimed it beautifully.

'I was in hysterics, I'd had a few glasses of champagne, and he came up to me and he said, "How did it sound?" He was dead serious. I said, "Ally, you were absolutely brilliant." And he said, "Will I give them an encore?"'

The chance to put forward his side of the story of the 1978 World Cup was offered to Ally when he was commissioned to write an autobiography, weeks after his return from Argentina. John Mann from the *Scottish Daily Express* had been one of the most prominent Scottish sportswriters not to have travelled to Argentina for the World Cup and that lack of a connection with what Ally considered to have been the excesses of the press towards him in Argentina won Mann the work of ghosting the book on Ally's behalf. Mann had got to know him well during Ally's stint as club manager at Aberdeen and had liked him enormously.

'The *Express* used the good guy, bad guy approach,' says Mann. 'Ian Archer had been critical of Ally in Argentina and there was never any suggestion of Ian Archer being sent to see him; it was me, even though I was ninety miles north.' It proved a testing assignment for Mann. MacLeod was now a much more difficult man with whom to deal and he quickly lost enthusiasm and interest in the book project.

Journalists were not welcome in the MacLeod household; Ally and his wife Faye had made a pact, following the World Cup, that no journalist would again darken their door. Mann also discovered that people reacted with something close to disgust in that immediate World Cup period when hearing that Mann was working on a book with Ally MacLeod.

'It was sad that he turned out the way he did; sort of hang-dog,' says Mann. 'I remember, at the time I was writing this book, going to see him in that pub he had in

Kilmarnock and thinking, "What's he going to give behind the bar?" He wasn't a jolly "mein host" then. I could imagine football fans going into this pub to talk but I couldn't see him indulging in the happy banter that at one stage he had.

'I was quite sorry for him in the end because I don't think it was all his fault. Willie Johnston, for instance, definitely wasn't his fault. I think Ally thought that, apart from the results, the football had gone fairly well. He certainly was blaming people although he never criticised any of his players. He was never even very critical of Willie Johnston.

'As the book was being produced, he just became more and more withdrawn. He was very, very prickly and easily offended, which is not something I'd ever come across in him at Aberdeen at all. It wasn't so much a change in his character as in his attitude and not so much personally to me but there was a suspicion about him that there hadn't been at Aberdeen; there was a sense of him weighing words. To get the book finished I had to resort to cuttings and a lot of my own talks with him. After the book was produced, he was supposed to be in this bookshop or that bookshop to sign and I don't think he turned up for any of them.

'He had not been alone in building up Scotland's chances for the World Cup,' says Mann as he looks back on that strange period when he renewed acquaintance with the man he'd known so well at Aberdeen. 'Yet when it all went pear-shaped he seemed to be the only one that was found guilty. I've a feeling he believed that the SFA hierarchy also considered that it had been his fault. Tommy Younger was one to whom he was very antagonistic when he came back but he never went into detail on what Tommy Younger had done or said.'

Several paragraphs of Mann's original manuscript, in which MacLeod made comments that were considered defamatory to the SFA, never appeared in the book. MacLeod also had an idea for a dark and dramatic book jacket to shock the public that was jettisoned sharply by the publisher. On the jacket front he had wanted to use a picture, taken prior to the World Cup, of himself walking across the Hampden pitch, looking relaxed and happy in a light, oatmeal suit, wearing a super-sized smile and carrying a saltire; on the back of the book, MacLeod had wanted a saltire, again, but with a dagger stuck in the middle of it and blood running down it.

Ally failed in his stated ambition of taking Motherwell into the Premier Division but in the 1981-82 season, after Ally's departure, Davie Hay, who had stepped up from being his assistant to Motherwell manager, took the team Ally had helped to construct into the top tier. A return to Ayr beckoned for Ally and, during his third period as the club's manager, he won them promotion to the First Division in 1988. He also managed Airdrieonians and concluded his career as a manager at Queen of the South in the early nineties. Much to the surprise of the Dumfries side's supporters, in April 1992 Ally played in a Queen of the South reserve match against St Mirren at Love Street. By then aged sixty-one this, not surprisingly, made him the oldest player ever to have played for the club. Not only that, but he made a notable contribution to the game by scoring with a penalty kick and was given a standing ovation as he walked from the field after the final whistle. All this almost half a century after he had made his debut as an eager teenager for Third Lanark.

'What annoys me is that Argentina was two weeks in a football career that lasted for nearly forty-five years – only two weeks out of it all – and yet that's what people talk about out of it all,' says Faye MacLeod.

'It hurts a little bit when you see the bad press that Ally gets for Argentina because I don't think he deserved it,' says Willie Miller. 'He gave the nation a belief that something was possible and I don't think he should be pilloried for giving anybody that belief. He has left a lasting memory and while it did go wrong in Argentina, these things can happen and I think that Scotland as a nation is much better prepared to handle these types of events now.

'I don't think the infrastructure was particularly good round about him to give him the support required when things weren't going well. You could say there was a little bit of naïvety about him there but I think he should be applauded for what he achieved in the build-up to that World Cup and players have got to take their responsibility too.

'I don't think tactics was his strongpoint but I don't think necessarily that that should be something which he should be slated for. Having worked with other great managers, I think they've all got different shortcomings and different strengths. Ally was an enthusiast – he generated excitement; Jock Stein was a man-manager type of coach; Alex Ferguson was a bit more tactical but definitely shrewder in how he manipulated things and events; Jim McLean was outstanding with tactics and on the training field but he maybe didn't handle the press or people particularly well. So I don't really think that should be a particularly big negative with Ally because he had other strengths, and he wasn't devoid of tactics and awareness – it would be wrong to suggest that.

'As a nation, we lift expectations and then we let the nation down. That's what our team does, whether the manager is Ally MacLeod, Jock Stein, Alex Ferguson; that's what we've done. They take that responsibility and I as a player take that responsibility too, because the plain fact is that we don't qualify for the latter stages of World Cups.

'Ally's no different from anybody else, in that respect, and the players that played for him are no different from anybody else because, so far, we haven't achieved that. If you compare him with the greats who have managed the Scottish national team, then, when you boil it down, he has done no worse and he has done no better than them.'

The man who got closest to Ally during his Argentinian adventure, John Hagart, comments, 'He put the team together, he gave the team a structure but he left them to get on with it because his theory was that they were good players. Even in hindsight, you can't even look back and say, "That was right" or "That was wrong." You could say, "Well, it wasn't right because we didn't qualify for the second stage." Maybe it wasn't just that that was wrong; there was this factor, there was that factor or the next factor.

'When we did get back I can remember thinking, "I wish he'd used me more. I could have been a bigger help to him." Then I thought that maybe I had been out of my depth a wee bit there because you do question yourself and the part that you played or didn't play or tried to play, but I always came back a wee bit to thinking that at the end of the day Ally was a one-off. That helped me through my darker moments when I was questioning whether I had been good enough to be in Argentina with the Scotland World Cup squad.'

Ally had believed, before travelling to Argentina, that the World Cup would 'change our lives and deeply affect the future of football here in these islands'. That assertion had, at the time, been a positive one that went with Ally's vision of Scotland finally branding itself as a new member of that thin sliver of elite World Cup nations – in a similar manner to the way in which the Dutch had established themselves in 1974. That did not happen but Ally was still correct – the 1978 World Cup did change Scottish football for ever. A massive downscaling of attitude and ambition would follow; it was like seeing bankrupted aristocrats forced by circumstance to move into a suburban semi-detached and get used to new, narrower, more mundane horizons.

The new realism that began to bite at the national team after 1978 is best exemplified in Ally MacLeod being the last young, up-and-coming club manager to be appointed Scotland manager; or for that matter, the last such rising manager to envision taking the Scotland job as an attractive prospect. Caution, conservatism and low ambition in the three decades after Argentina have become the hallmarks of the national team.

The Argentinian World Cup was not a profitable one on the field of play for Scotland but it was a triumph in terms of it filling the coffers of the SFA. The association made £219,315 out of the tournament and it became imperative in the SFA's thinking that, to maintain profitability, Scotland should qualify for every World Cup. That was the premier task in the succeeding two decades for all of MacLeod's successors: Jock Stein, Andy Roxburgh and Craig Brown. All talked down Scotland's chances at the finals in contrast to the way in which Ally had talked them up but the result proved the same: Scotland dropped out of the World Cup after the opening, group, stage in 1982, '86, '90 and '98. Scotland barely broke even in football terms but reaching the finals in itself was hugely profitable: by 1990, the sum earned by the SFA from the tournament had become a tidy two million pounds.

The people at the top of the SFA were often portrayed in the tabloid press as unfeeling ogres but this public image was at variance with their private desire to see Scotland win and win well on the field of play. Ernie Walker, SFA secretary for thirteen years from July 1977, and most of those around him were fervent football fans in tandem with being able administrators, but their principal task was to run the SFA with efficiency.

'There was this illusion that the SFA was a very wealthy organisation,' says Walker. 'In the first year after I was in the job the auditors came to me and told me that if we didn't qualify for the 1978 World Cup, they couldn't guarantee the staff's salaries for the following year. Qualification was very, very important in terms of the Association's finances. So I was determined that we would not be in that position again because you cannot run a business or an institution on whether or not some boy will score or will not score from a penalty. So I made it my number one responsibility to build up the funds and leave them in a sound financial position, which I did.'

After Argentina, the desire not to see the hopes of the nation fuelled by hyper-inflated promises stifled much of the fun that would normally be associated with achieving a place at a World Cup finals tournament. Once the over-riding ambition of Scotland reaching the finals had been achieved, much of the zest seemed to disappear from each enterprise, in contrast to the fervour-filled months before Argentina. As MacLeod himself put it in 1986, prior to the finals in Mexico, 'We've qualified but you wouldn't know there was a World Cup on . . .'

The feeling was that, after Argentina, Scotland had better not try, ever again, to overreach itself and that quashed the very self-belief, ambition and drive that any team requires if it is to progress at a World Cup. Super-confident sportspeople who express self-belief can at times sound hopelessly deluded but such self-belief is often a necessity to enter into the correct frame of mind for competition. Ally MacLeod's words, excessive at times, were a variation on this theme. After '78 Scotland's humble view of itself turned it into a nation that made up the numbers at each tournament, took its cut of the proceeds and then went home almost as part of a self-fulfilling prophecy.

'My target from the SFA was to get us to the World Cup,' says Andy Roxburgh, who led Scotland to the 1990 tournament. 'It was just simply about being practical; trying to be modest about what we were doing. Ally was just trying to get everybody to think big and had an enormous amount of talent available to him. We had to take into account the context we were working in.'

MacLeod's successor, Jock Stein, created the template for keeping everything low key. 'Jock had a great humility about him,' recalls Roxburgh. '"Everything we do," he would say, "will be because of our actions, not what we say."' Stein also commented at the 1982 tournament, 'Scotland winning the World Cup isn't even imaginable.'

Andy Roxburgh was, in complete contrast to Stein, a figure almost completely unknown to the public when given charge of the Scottish national team in July 1986. Pointedly, Roxburgh was given the title of national coach, rather than team manager. Almost a decade after Ally had bowled into position with Scotland there seemed to be a surge towards anonymity, rubber-stamped by Stein, for the man in charge of the national team. Roxburgh was frequently panned by the media for his low-key approach but it had been Stein himself who had identified in Roxburgh the necessary qualities for leadership of the national team. 'Sitting in the back of a car with Jock on the way to Florence in the summer of 1985,' remembers

Roxburgh, 'he said, "Have you ever thought of taking my job?" I said to him, "I'm not trying to take your job." He said, "No, no, I know that. I'm just saying that maybe you should think about it."'

The quelling of expectation that began after Argentina has gone on for far too long. It was acceptable to take it from the great Stein at the 1982 World Cup – when it seemed likely that he might be using it to disguise a clever, hidden strategy. By the time of the Craig Brown era, in the nineties, it seemed too easy for the manager to use humility as a crutch on which to lean and to disguise an overall lack of enterprise and fire. Brown would only have had to suggest that Scotland's followers should not get too carried away with themselves for those listening to make a lightning mental back-flip to the events of Argentina. The weight of history took the weight off the manager.

As Brown's Scotland prepared to play Brazil in the 1998 World Cup in France, two decades after Ally MacLeod had swept like a storm into Argentina, the quizzical headline in the French sports paper *L'Equipe* on the opening day, read, 'So just who are these Scots?' The search for anonymity had reached fruition and Scotland duly struggled to obtain just one point from a possible nine at that tournament prior to slipping quietly off home. That was no improvement on the World Cup in Argentina.

With his memories of Argentina, Joe Harper was bamboozled at seeing how subsequent Scottish World Cup sides managed to secure a safe landing thanks to the padding afforded them by a lack of build-up or expectation – something that would have been anathema to Ally MacLeod. 'We went to the other side of the world in terrible conditions,' says Harper. 'Years later, they went to France in 1998 – which is just across the channel – had the best of hotels, best of food, best of conditions, got beaten by Brazil, drew with Norway, Morocco humped them, and they came back heroes; fans were out to greet them and wave to them. I couldn't understand it.'

Comparing today's Scotland players to those of 1978, one member of the party that travelled to Argentina asserts that the '78 guys look like 'Goliaths'. That still did not prevent the SFA attempting to cut several of them down to size on their return from South America. Don Masson had expressed the sentiment in his newspaper article that he would wish never to play for Scotland again so the SFA, as if striving to blend the most obdurate characteristics of a particularly uncooperative branch of the civil service and a provincial bowling club, stated that he should be 'accommodated in his desire'. A similar pronouncement was made on Macari, who had used the press to pass adverse comment on the organisation of the World Cup trip by the SFA. Macari was not banned from playing for Scotland but the SFA, again in prize, catty mode, suggested that the manager 'should give serious consideration to the advisability of subjecting the player again to these arrangements, which he professes to find unsatisfactory'.

Macari and Masson would never play for Scotland again, while the ban on Johnston that had been promised by the SFA in Argentina was ratified. Never before or since have there been so many Scottish team casualties in the wake of a World Cup. There was even a rift inside the SFA as to who ought to take responsibility. Ernie Walker comments, 'I remember when we came back, the president saying to the media, "I have demanded that the secretary produce a report explaining it all." It was as if he hadn't been there. There's always a willingness to stand back and wash hands of it when you're losing.'

On the question of responsibility, Sandy Jardine says, 'Everybody that went to Argentina could look at themselves in the mirror and say that they didn't do themselves justice and that includes everybody that was on that plane, from players to SFA officials, management, everybody. A lot of things that were supposed to be put in place weren't put in place and the team didn't play to form.'

The international careers of Jim Blyth, Bobby Clark, Tom Forsyth, Joe Harper and Bruce Rioch ended with the Argentinian World Cup. Some, such as Sandy Jardine, Stuart Kennedy, Derek Johnstone, Martin Buchan and Willie Donachie lingered on for a few more games before being discarded by Stein.

'It taught me a great deal,' says Bruce Rioch. 'I came away from that World Cup able to reflect on what I should do in management. It emphasised to me the need for preparation, organisation, focus, and hotels, and making sure everybody knew what they were playing for.'

After all the furore over bonuses, preceding and during the tournament, there was no requirement for the SFA to make any sizeable payments to the players. The few – such as Alan Rough, Joe Jordan and Kenny Dalglish – who had participated in all three matches, would receive £600 for their escapades in Argentina: appearance money of one hundred pounds per match and a bonus of one hundred pounds per point.

'I do remember Willie Harkness holding a press conference for the Sunday papers, in Cordoba,' remembers Rodger Baillie, 'and admitting that they had made mistakes with the bonus and that the bonus thing should have been sorted out totally before.'

In the wake of the team's failure to progress in Argentina it showed considerable character on Margo MacDonald's part that she was one of the few to wish Ally MacLeod and the squad a safe journey home; something that set her apart from those who tend only to hitch a lift when the bandwagon is freewheeling downhill. 'After the severe disappointments of the campaign, people do believe that it fed back into the politics,' says MacDonald, 'that it helped to depress the confidence and optimism in Scotland that had been noticeable before '78.

'The World Cup didn't stand alone – all sorts of other things surrounded the mood in Scotland, but arguably Scotland's defeat had the same sort of negative effect on the Scottish national political movement as winning the World Cup had a very positive effect on how people felt about themselves in England. People sort of lost a lot of faith in Scottishness and their own abilities. Football is woven through the Scottish psyche.'

As a sop to the agitation for devolved government and self-determination in Scotland that had spanned the seventies, the Labour Government had organised a referendum on Scottish devolution in early 1979, but with the rider that 40 per cent of the electorate had to vote in favour of devolution for it to be allowed. The 'Yes' side won but garnered only 32 per cent of the vote to 30 per cent against and the 40 per cent rule that had been set in place was used to ditch devolution. Within months, the SNP in Westminster would use its muscle to help vote out the Labour Government. But the SNP lost nine seats in parliament at the subsequent General Election and the Margaret Thatcher era ensured that independence was further away than ever.

'It would have made a great deal of difference if Scotland had done well in Argentina,' says MacDonald. 'It might have been enough to obtain 40 per cent of the vote. I think Ally was seen as a nationalist. If they'd won it [the World Cup], if they had done what England had done, that would have done it because that would have meant we were just as good as England.

'You wouldn't have sounded ridiculous then because you could have said, "Look, if you can do it in football, why can't you do it in this, that or the next thing?" That's because, at that time, football, absolutely, definitely, was at the heart of Scotland.'

As the seventies drew to its conclusion, the possibility of Scotland achieving independence seemed as tattered and battered as the national team's prospects of making an impact on a future World Cup. Politics and football remained entangled but now in failure rather than in triumph.

Back in Ayr, in retirement, Ally MacLeod had moved home to Bruce Crescent, named after the architect of Scottish victory at the Battle of Bannockburn, and could gaze across the Atlantic seafront to ponder what might have been in far away Argentina. 'Folk in the town would say, "Oh Ally, I wish you were back,"' says Faye MacLeod, remembering the reaction he would get from fans as Scotland made their unspectacular progress through the subsequent two decades. 'They'd say, "We would have some fun; we would have some laughter again."'

Ally would also turn his attention to the grassy enclosure outside his home to allow his eyes to alight upon St John's Tower, the only remaining relic of the church in which Robert the Bruce had attended a meeting of the Scottish Parliament in 1315, after the Battle of Bannockburn. A saltire flies from the top of the tower.

'Ally used to look at the flag of Scotland,' says Faye MacLeod, 'and say, "I wonder if they'll lower that for me."' And they did,' she adds as she recalls a mark of respect for Ally's passing in early 2004. 'They lowered all the flags in Ayr, which, I thought, was very nice.'

It was always difficult for Scotland supporters to avoid reminders of the Argentina World Cup. Those travelling by train to Malaga – the venue for two Scotland matches at the Spanish World Cup in 1982 – had to pass through the town of Cordoba with all the reminders that that name held of the matches with Peru and Iran. The Dutchman whose shot had finally finished off Scotland in 1978, Johnny Rep, was also present again that June of 1982, hovering on the sidelines, like a spectre of Mendoza, in the sweltering heat of the Benito Villamarin stadium in Seville one Friday evening to observe the Scots in their next attempt to make even a slight dent on the World Cup.

'I was at the next world championship, in 1982,' says Rep. 'The Dutch team hadn't qualified because of a 0-2 defeat against France, and I visited the Scotland-Brazil match. I was standing in a section with Scottish fans when something special took place. After a few minutes in the play, all the Scottish fans were looking at me instead of the match for a moment. One of them had recognised me and shouted the historic words, "He's the fucker that killed Scotland!" Yes I am, thank you.'

He certainly is. Scotland had been the smallest nation to compete at the 1978 World Cup and after it, it seemed to have shrunk even smaller. Never again would anyone so much as even dare to breathe that Scotland might win a World Cup.

Index

Aberdeen FC 11-14, 17–20, 39, 61-2, 100-1, 212, 227, 230
Adidas (company) 74
advertising campaigns 67–73
agents 173–4
Airdrieonians FC 264
Alianza Lima 97
Allan, Hugh 21–2, 49, 60, 92–3, 141, 164, 206, 217–18, 231
Allan, Willie 46, 156
Alta Gracia 90–1; see also Sierras Hotel
Anfield 35–6
anti-English sentiments 66–7, 198–9
Aramburu, Juan Carlos 86
Archer, Ian 177–8, 262
Argentina (country and state regime) 54–5, 85–7, 93–7, 114, 144–5, 209, 254–5
Argentinian national team 29–30, 54, 143, 196, 240–1, 245, 254–5
Argentinian women 208–9
Aston Villa FC 212–13
Atkinson, Ron 137, 141
Auld, Bertie 174
Austria 54, 196, 223, 242, 257–8
Ayr United FC 8–12, 16, 23, 39, 81, 172, 183, 230, 258, 260, 264

Baillie, Rodger 179–85, 255, 257, 272
Baxter, Jim 47–8
Bayern Munich 111
BBC see British Broadcasting Corporation
Beat the Clock 64–5
Beattie, Andy 44, 46
Beckenbauer, Franz 54
Bilk, Acker 261
Blackburn Rovers FC 9–10, 64–7, 259
Blackley, John 71
Blue Peter 70
Blyth, Jim 57, 130, 257, 272

bonus payments to players 73–7, 127, 153–5, 192, 221, 226, 272
bookmakers' odds 53–4, 152, 168
Boskamp, Jan 238
Brazil 18, 29–30, 41–2, 50–1, 54, 111, 196, 240–1
Bremner, Billy 48–51, 151, 185–6, 213
British Broadcasting Corporation (BBC) 70, 190–5, 255
Brown, Craig 267, 270
Buchan, Martin 36, 53, 91, 107–9, 116, 119, 121, 157, 160, 164, 232, 238, 250, 272
Bulgaria 152
Burley, George 52
Burns, Kenny 52–3, 61, 102, 107, 109, 115–21, 157, 160–4, 257
Burns, Robert 80
Busby, Matt 46

Calderon, Marcos 113, 120
Cameron, Alex 180–1, 195
Cameron, Andy 3, 63–4, 68, 70, 132, 168
La Cantella (restaurant) 90
Cavan, Harry 113, 134–5
Celtic FC 14, 17–18, 47–8, 165, 171, 223
Charles, Prince of Wales 1–2
Chateau Carreras stadium 96, 114, 205–6
Chile 28–31, 39
Chumpitaz, Hector 98, 112, 119, 120, 121, 125
Chrysler cars 70–2, 167–8
Clark, Bobby 15, 29–30, 74, 251, 257, 272
Clark, Tom 18
Clough, Brian 215
Clydebank FC 31
Coleman, David 172–3

commercial ventures 71–4, 156
Connor, Robert 260
Cooper, Davie 31
'Copenhagen Five' 213
Coppell, Steve 57
Cordoba Jockey Club 181, 184
Coutinho, Claudio 196
Coyle, Johnny 47
Cropley, Alex 142
crowds for Scottish matches 32–6, 47,
    56–8; see also supporters
Cruyff, Johan 43, 54, 215, 222–6
Cuba 151
Cubillas, Teofilo 99–100, 112, 115–17,
    121–6, 143, 233
Cueto, Cesare 115, 118, 121–2
Cyprus 150
Czechoslovakia 32–5, 39, 199–200

Daily Record 182, 184, 195
Dalglish, Kenny 17, 26, 28, 34, 37,
    52–3, 60, 74, 106–7, 110–11,
    113–19, 129–30, 143–4, 155–6,
    160–5, 172, 178, 212–15, 219,
    232–6, 258, 272
Danaifar, Iraj 164–5
Davies, Dai 36–7, 216
Derby County FC 105
devolution 273
Diaz, Toribio 117–18
disciplinary issues 22, 48, 113, 182–3
Docherty, Tommy 105, 108–9, 174
Donachie, Willie 57, 105, 108, 154,
    157, 160, 164, 190, 232–3, 272
Donald, Peter 136
drugs testing 129–34, 138–9, 143–5, 203
drunkenness 185–9, 200–3
Duarte, Jaime 98, 121–2
Dubach, Jean 254
Dunblane Hydro 58, 69–72
Dundee United FC 260
Dunn, Clive 64
Dutch national team 42–3, 54, 152,
    196, 221–6, 229–33, 240–4, 247,
    267, 275

Edinburgh, Duke of 253
English national team 25–7, 47, 50, 58,
    80, 151, 192; see also anti-English
    sentiments
L'Equipe 270
Eriksson, Ulf 120
Eskandarian, Andaranik 163–4
European Cup 47, 53, 106, 110, 158,
    218, 223
European Cup-Winners' Cup 142

European Nations Cup 5
Eusebio 151
Evans, Bobby 45
Evans, Ian 17
Everton FC 174

FA Cup 9–10
Faraki, Hossein 162, 164
Fédération Internationale de Football
    Association (FIFA) 43–4, 98, 113,
    129, 131, 134, 138–9, 144–5, 255
fencamfamin 129–30
Ferguson, Alex 11, 16, 100–1, 265
Ferguson, Taylor 170
Feyenoord 223, 242
FIFA see Fédération Internationale de
    Football Association
Fitzsimmons, John 96, 132–4, 140, 147
Flavell, Bobby 10
Football Association 43, 198–9; see also
    FA Cup
football management at club and inter-
    national level 104, 230
Football Writers' Association 191
Forsyth, Bruce 64–5
Forsyth, Tom 53, 72–3, 107, 109, 117,
    119, 132, 164, 232, 238, 257, 272
France 54, 152, 254, 270
Franchi, Artemio 255

Garrido, Antonio 254
Gemmell, Tommy 47
Gemmill, Archie 52–3, 61, 105–6, 110,
    121–3, 144, 157, 160, 164, 216,
    232–42, 246, 251
Germany see West Germany
Ghasempour, Ibrahim 164
Gillespie, Pat 92
Glasgow Press Club 183
Glasgow Rangers FC 9, 11, 13, 44, 47–8,
    53, 62, 106, 141–2, 169, 215, 257
Gleneagles hotel 106–7
goalkeepers 175–6
Gonella, Sergio 255
Good, Hughie 20
El Gráfico 186, 188
Graham, Arthur 71, 142, 213, 258
Gray, Andy 212–15, 219, 257–8
Gray, Eddie 48
Grimshaw, Rankin 18
Guevara, Che 90–1

Haan, Arie 222, 224, 229
Hagart, John 3, 20–1, 58, 100–1,
    133–4, 158–61, 180, 195, 214–15,
    226–7, 231, 243, 260–2, 266

hairstyles 169–71
Hamilton by-election 83–4
Hampden Park 2, 9, 26, 32–3, 47, 57, 74, 199–201, 219, 264
Hansen, Alan 52
Happel, Ernst 196, 223–4, 241, 243
Harkness, Willie 30, 153, 257, 272
Harper, Joe 23, 56, 60, 73, 76, 92, 95, 99, 102–4, 125, 145–7, 165, 187–9, 205, 212–15, 219, 245, 251–2, 257, 270, 272
Harris, Rolf 64
Hartford, Asa 34, 107, 110, 115–21, 154, 160, 162, 169, 232
Havelange, Joao 54
Hay, Davie 264
Hegarty, Paul 260
Heineken (company) 73
Hejazi, Nasser 162–3
Henderson, Willie 47–8, 137
Hibernian FC 10, 65
Hill, Benny 64
Hill, Jimmy 198
Holland see Dutch national team
    Scotland v Holland (1978 World Cup) 149, 161, 196, 219–24, 229–47
Howell, Denis 130
Hughes, Emlyn 26
Hull City FC 174
Hungary 54
Hutchison, Tommy 142

Ipswich Town FC 52
Iran 94, 99, 226, 233
    Scotland v Iran (1978 World Cup) 148–53, 159–68, 175, 204, 214, 218–21, 226, 228, 238, 245–6
Italy 43, 54, 151, 242

Jansen, Wim 229, 234–5, 238
Jardine, Sandy 34, 50, 51, 53, 72, 74, 77, 95, 107, 126, 140, 157, 160, 164–7, 182, 228, 245, 257, 271–2
Jean-Joseph, Ernst 134
Jensen, Birger 53
JJB Sports 67
Johnston, Willie 26, 29–36, 66, 76, 92, 95, 103, 107–10, 116–19, 126, 129–49, 153, 182, 184, 203, 208, 263, 271
Johnstone, Bobby 45
Johnstone, Derek 53, 56–7, 60, 61, 72, 106, 169–70, 211–16, 219, 251–2, 257, 272
Johnstone, Jimmy 47, 50, 185
Jones, Dave 36–7

Jongbloed, Jan 232–5
Jordan, Joe 33–7, 53, 56, 60, 73, 105–7, 110–11, 115–22, 154, 160, 163, 212–19, 232–6, 258, 272
journalistic practices 177–8, 183–96
Juventus 107

Keegan, Kevin 170
Kennedy, Stuart 107–9, 119–23, 157, 186–7, 218, 232–4, 238, 251–2, 272
Killer, Daniel 29
kit, supply of 155–7
kit worn by fans 189–90
Krol, Ruud 229, 234–5, 239–42

Ladbrokes 53
La Rosa, Guillermo 117–20
Lauchlan, Tom 18, 153, 256
Lauder, Harry 80
Law, Denis 48, 50
Leeds United FC 48, 53, 172
Linemayr, Erich 232–4, 238
Liverpool FC 52, 105–6, 110, 158
Luque, Leopoldo 143
Luxembourg 150

Macari, Lou 29, 53, 73–6, 91, 99–106, 111, 121–3, 154–60, 181, 192, 271
McCall, Walker 260
McCluskey, Pat 213
MacDonald, Margo 81–5, 272–4
McDonald, Trevor 130–1, 185
McGovern, John 52
McGrain, Danny 34, 105–8, 170, 212, 218–19
McIlvenny, Eddie 151
Mackay, Dave 48
McKenzie, John 193, 202–8, 246
McKinnon, Donnie 22
McLean, George 11
McLean, Jim 100, 265
McLean, Willie 260
MacLeod, Ally 1–6, 9
    appearance 6–7
    personality 7–8, 14, 20–3, 61, 138, 197, 256, 260–4
    sense of humour 22–3, 228, 261–2
    as a national serviceman 8
    as a pub landlord 8
    as an all-round sportsman 16
    home life 21–2, 193–5
    playing career 9–10, 66, 259, 264
    as a club manager 7–17, 20, 30, 39, 172, 183, 212, 230, 259–60, 263
    appointment as Scotland team manager 18–24, 27–8, 65–6

early days as Scotland manager
30–1, 37–9, 105
managerial style with Scotland
team 59–62, 74–7, 124–5,
228–31, 237, 266–7
relations with the media 8, 12–15,
19, 124, 127, 131, 148, 161, 167,
175, 178–89, 194, 221, 257
confidence about 1978 World Cup
53–62, 98–9, 126–7, 132, 160–1,
179–81, 207, 247, 265–6, 269
in Argentina 95–111, 117–18,
121–6, 132, 140, 153–4, 157–66,
209–10, 213–19, 238–40
return from Argentina 252–3
reaction to World Cup failure 204,
226–9, 243–5, 251, 256
criticisms of 66–7, 205–6, 212,
226–7, 246
retention of Scotland team
managership 255–9
resignation from Scotland team
managership 258
personal notes kept by 31, 157, 172
radio and television appearances
64–7
promotional work 66–8, 71–2
showmanship 81–2
ruptured ulcer 249
autobiography 262–4
retirement and death 274
MacLeod, Andrew 193
MacLeod, David 22
MacLeod, Faye 7–8, 11–12, 19, 22–3,
37, 62, 64–8, 81, 138, 166, 194,
244–5, 249, 253, 262, 264–5, 274
MacLeod, Gail 138
McMenemy, Lawrie 137
McNeill, Billy 101
McQueen, Gordon 4, 25–6, 33–4, 53, 57,
72, 93, 103–9, 154–5, 166, 189–90,
211, 216–19, 238, 243, 257–8
Manchester City FC 174
Manchester United FC 53, 76, 105,
108–11
Mann, John 12–13, 262–4
Mason, Jimmy 20
Masson, Don 29, 33–8, 74, 102,
105–10, 115–22, 125–6, 130,
138–40, 157, 271
Masterton, Danny 260
Menotti, Cesar Luis 196
Mexico 55, 152, 168, 188–9
Middlesbrough FC 53, 151, 174
Miller, Willie 14–16, 19–20, 61–2,
265–6

Mohajerani, Heshmet 152
Montford, Arthur 8, 29–30, 38, 99,
123, 138, 160, 166–7, 177, 180–1,
191, 240
morale 126–7, 129, 146, 190, 195–6,
241, 252, 259
Motherwell FC 260–1, 264
Muller, Gerd 54
Muñante, Juan José 97, 121–2
Murdoch, Bobby 48
musical entertainment 63–4, 68–70,
168, 209

Narey, David 260
nationalism, Scottish 79, 82–3, 201–2,
273
Nationwide 137
Neeskens, Johan 43
Neill, Terry 174
Newcastle United FC 174
News of the World 139–40
Ninian Park 35
North Korea 151
North Sea oil 82–3
Nottingham Forest FC 52–3, 105, 157

Oblitas, Juan Carlos 115–19, 122
O'Hare, John 52
Ormond, Willie 17, 21–2, 28, 31, 50,
141–2

Partick Thistle FC 169–74
Parvin, Ali 161–2
Pele 41
Pernia, Vicente 29
Peru 97–9, 111–22, 226, 233, 254
Scotland v Peru (1978 World Cup)
103–4, 107–9, 113–31, 142, 148–9,
158, 165, 173, 218, 221, 245
Pinochet, Augusto 28
Poland 54, 102, 151–2
Polaroid (company) 72–3
politics and politicisation 79–87, 272–4
Poortvliet, Jan 234–5
Port Brae Bar 141
Portugal 151
promotional appearances 66–8, 71–2,
156

The Queen 253
Queen of the South FC 264
Quiroga, Ramon 113–21

Radio Clyde 66–7
radio coverage of football 45
Rangers see Glasgow Rangers FC

Reactivan 129–34, 138–40, 145
refereeing decisions 37, 113, 120, 254
referendum 273
Reid, Tam 45–6
Rensenbrink, Rob 232–3, 240
Rep, Johnny 233, 238–42, 275
Rijsbergen, Wim 232–4
Rimet, Jules 43
Rimmer, Roger 132–3
Rioch, Bruce 33, 61, 70, 74, 91–2,
    103–10, 115–22, 125–7, 153–7,
    164–7, 190, 216, 228–34, 239, 240,
    257, 272
Robertson, Archie 47
Robertson, George 85
Robertson, John 52–3, 102, 160, 162,
    257
Robins, Tessa 70
Robson, Bobby 236
Rough, Alan 30, 36, 70–1, 92, 95, 107,
    109, 117–18, 121–3, 160, 164–6,
    169–76, 182, 218, 232–3, 238–9,
    242, 251–2, 272
Roxburgh, Andy 4, 19, 89–90, 127, 267,
    269–70
Rust, Jim 11–12

St Mirren FC 9, 236
Samuel, Bill 261
San Francisco Hotel 227
San Martin stadium 231
Santiago 28–30
Schoen, Helmut 5–6, 34, 196
Scotsport 180
Scott, David 255
Scott, Sir Walter 80
Scottish Daily Express 192–3, 262
Scottish Football Association (SFA) 3,
    8, 17–19, 37, 43–8, 59, 65–7, 74–5,
    89, 132–42, 146–7, 153–7, 182,
    186, 190–1, 194–5, 202–3, 213,
    217, 227–8, 251–9, 263–4, 267–9,
    271–2
Scottish footballers with English clubs
    52–3
Scottish footballing mentality 244
Scottish identity and culture 80–1, 273
Scottish League Cup 13–14, 171
Scottish National Party (SNP) 79–85,
    273
Scottish Premier Division 3–4, 14
Sierras Hotel, Alta Gracia 90–6, 101–2,
    127, 130–1, 135, 140, 145, 161,
    179–82, 187, 190, 192, 211, 221, 247
Simon, Paul 209
Sotil, Hugo 112, 120

Souness, Graeme 52–3, 105–6, 125,
    157–9, 166, 169, 211, 227, 229,
    232–4, 239
Spain 54
sponsorship deals 50, 156–7, 259
Sporting Cristal 97
Steele, Jimmy 21, 104
Stein, Jock 14, 17–20, 48, 100, 137,
    265–70
Stewart, David 172
Stewart, Jim 30–1
Stewart, Rod 68–70, 89–90, 127, 132
Stirling University 202
Strum, Michael 170
supporters, behaviour of 189–93,
    197–210, 228, 246, 252; see also
    crowds
Suurbier, Wim 229
Sweden 54, 151

tax-free payments to players 75
team selection 56, 60, 104–11, 125–6,
    157–60, 212–16, 221, 226, 229–30,
    257
television coverage of football 3, 8,
    41–2, 45–50, 114, 130–1, 137–8,
    166, 184, 191, 195
Templeton, Henry 16
Thatcher, Margaret 84, 273
Third Lanark FC 9–10, 20
Todd, Jim 207–8
Top of the Pops 63–4
Toshack, John 36
'total football' 42–3, 222–5, 238
Tottenham Hotspur FC 48
Tramp (London nightclub) 69
Tunisia 152

UEFA Cup 141, 147
Umbro (company) 71, 155–7
Union of European Football
    Associations (UEFA) 35; see also
    UEFA Cup
United States 150–1
Uruguay 44, 46

Valcareggi, Ferruccio 151
Van der Kerkhof, Willy 229, 232–3,
    234, 240
Van Hanegem, Wim 54, 224
Vancouver Whitecaps 147
Velasquez, José 114
Videla, Jorge 85–7, 231

Walker, Dawson 46–7
Walker, Ernie 18–19, 59–60, 75, 93–4,

132–40, 153–7, 178, 194–5, 200–2,
228, 254, 258–9, 268, 271
Wallace, Ian 213–14
Wallace, Jock 62
Wark, John 52
Welsh national team 17, 35–7, 152
West Bromwich Albion FC 76, 132–3,
137, 140–2, 147
West Germany 5, 43, 54, 102, 196, 242
Whelan, David 67
Wigan Athletic FC 67
Wildschut, Piet 234
Wilson, Alex 84
Wilson, Bill 186–7, 190, 193–6
World Cup
status of 41–2
1938 tournament 151
1950 tournament 44
1954 tournament 44–6, 223
1958 tournament 46–7
1962 tournament 48
1966 tournament 48
1970 tournament 41–2, 79, 99, 111
1974 tournament 5, 42–3, 48–51,
54, 107, 150–2, 201, 216, 222,
224, 228, 241, 267
1978 tournament
anticipation of 43, 53–62
qualifying matches 17, 32–5,
38–9, 51–2, 104, 125, 178,
200, 213, 216, 225, 237
draw for 98–9, 178, 205
team send-off 1–4, 200–1

team selection 56, 60, 106–11,
125–6, 157–60, 212–16, 221,
226–30
Scotland's first match, against
Peru 103–4, 107–9, 113–31,
142, 148–9, 158, 165, 173,
218, 221, 245
Scotland's second match, against
Iran 148–53, 159–68, 175,
204, 214, 218–21, 226, 228,
238, 245–6
Scotland's third match, against
Holland 149, 161, 196,
219–24, 229–47
misbehaviour by players 185–91
Scotland team's return from 250–3
final stages of 254–5, 258
aftermath of 197–8, 249–50,
266–73
official song (Ole Ola) 69–70
1982 tournament 267–71, 275
1986 tournament 267–9
1990 tournament 267
1998 tournament 267, 270
Wurtz, Robert 36

Young, Willie 213
Younger, Tommy 47, 153, 155, 263
Yugoslavia 50–1, 151–2

Zaire 51, 150
Zoff, Dino 240
Zwartkruis, Jan 223–4